The Routledge Introduction to American Renaissance Literature

Examining the most frequently taught works by key writers of the American Renaissance, including Poe, Emerson, Fuller, Douglass, Hawthorne, Melville, Thoreau, Jacobs, Stowe, Whitman, and Dickinson, this engaging and accessible book offers the crucial historical, social, and political contexts in which they must be studied. Larry J. Reynolds usefully groups authors together for more lively and fruitful discussion and engages with current as well as historical theoretical debates on the area. The book includes essential biographical and historical information to situate and contextualize the literature, and incorporates major relevant criticism into each chapter. Recommended readings for further study, along with a list of works cited, conclude each chapter.

Larry J. Reynolds is University Distinguished Professor at Texas A&M University. He is a leading scholar of the American Renaissance and has abundant experience teaching and writing for undergraduate audiences.

Routledge Introductions to American Literature

Series Editors: D. Quentin Miller and Wendy Martin

Routledge Introductions to American Literature provide critical introductions to the most important topics in American Literature, outlining the key literary, historical, cultural, and intellectual contexts. Providing students with an analysis of the most up-to-date trends and debates in the area, they also highlight exciting new directions within the field and open the way for further study.

Volumes examine the ways in which both canonical and lesser known writers from diverse class and cultural backgrounds have shaped American literary traditions, addressing key contemporary and theoretical debates, and giving attention to a range of voices and experiences as a vital part of American life. These comprehensive volumes offer readable, cohesive narratives of the development of American Literature and provide ideal introductions for students.

The Routledge Introduction to African American Literature
D. Quentin Miller

The Routledge Introduction to American Modernism
Linda Wagner-Martin

The Routledge Introduction to American Women Writers
Wendy Martin and Sharone Williams

The Routledge Introduction to American War Literature
Jennifer Haytock

The Routledge Introduction to American Postmodernism
Linda Wagner-Martin

The Routledge Introduction to Native American Literature
Drew Lopenzina

The Routledge Introduction to American Renaissance Literature
Larry J. Reynolds

For more information on this series, please visit: https://www.routledge.com/Routledge-Introductions-to-American-Literature/book-series/ITAL

The Routledge Introduction to American Renaissance Literature

Larry J. Reynolds

LONDON AND NEW YORK

First published 2022
by Routledge
2 Park Square, Milton Park, Abingdon, Oxon OX14 4RN

and by Routledge
605 Third Avenue, New York, NY 10158

Routledge is an imprint of the Taylor & Francis Group, an informa business

© 2022 Larry J. Reynolds

The right of Larry J. Reynolds to be identified as author of this work has been asserted by them in accordance with sections 77 and 78 of the Copyright, Designs and Patents Act 1988.

All rights reserved. No part of this book may be reprinted or reproduced or utilised in any form or by any electronic, mechanical, or other means, now known or hereafter invented, including photocopying and recording, or in any information storage or retrieval system, without permission in writing from the publishers.

Trademark notice: Product or corporate names may be trademarks or registered trademarks, and are used only for identification and explanation without intent to infringe.

British Library Cataloguing-in-Publication Data
A catalogue record for this book is available from the British Library

Library of Congress Cataloging-in-Publication Data
A catalog record has been requested for this book

ISBN: 978-1-138-80654-2 (hbk)
ISBN: 978-1-138-80655-9 (pbk)
ISBN: 978-1-315-75162-7 (ebk)

DOI: 10.4324/9781315751627

Typeset in Bembo
by Taylor & Francis Books

Contents

	Acknowledgements	vi
	Preface	vii
1	Longfellow, Poe, and American literary emergence	1
2	Emerson, Thoreau, and transcendentalism	30
3	Fuller, Fern, and women's rights	65
4	Hawthorne, Melville, and suffering humanity	95
5	Douglass, Stowe, Jacobs, and anti-slavery	127
6	Whitman, Dickinson, and the Civil War	157
	Index	193

Acknowledgements

I wish to thank Leslie Eckel at Suffolk University for recommending me as prospective author of this book, and I am grateful to editors D. Quentin Miller and Wendy Martin for inviting me to contribute to their Routledge Introduction to American Literature series. I benefited from the input of the six anonymous scholars who read the proposal for this book, and I have incorporated as many of their suggestions as I could into the final version, knowing full well that the term and topic "American Renaissance" remain heavily contested in the academic community.

Because this *Introduction* is designed to appeal to students, tutors, and non-specialists, I enlisted the help of two Texas A&M University undergraduate students, Lily Jameson and Emily Robertson, as readers of drafts of my chapters, and I am grateful to them for helping me work toward a level of clarity and interest suitable for the book's audience. My daughter, Charlotte Reynolds, also an Aggie, gave me helpful feedback. As I began the project, Robert S. Levine of the University of Maryland gave me invaluable advice about canon formation, and Maurice S. Lee of Boston University generously shared with me his C19 Conference paper "The End of the End of the Canon?" and his PowerPoint that accompanied it. Brigitte Bailey, at the University of New Hampshire, read the chapter on Margaret Fuller and Fanny Fern for me, and I thank her for her expert critique. My colleagues Joe Golsan, David McWhirter, Anne Morey, Claudia Nelson, and Mary Ann O'Farrell have provided needed friendship and support for years, and, although my department head, Maura Ives, does not know it, her calm and thoughtful leadership, during the horrible year 2020, gave me the opportunity and inspiration to complete this book. Finally, as always, my greatest debt is to my wife Susan Egenolf, who took precious time away from her own scholarship to help me make this book far better than it would otherwise have been.

Preface

Since the beginning of the twentieth century, the American Renaissance has been recognized as a moment in the mid-nineteenth century when writers in the United States created a body of literary works distinguished by their originality, their aesthetic achievement, and their cultural impact. The works that literary critics and historians have singled out for praise within this moment have never been a fixed canon, but, rather, an evolving group determined by prevailing tastes and standards. F. O. Matthiessen's classic study *American Renaissance: Art and Expression in the Age of Emerson and Whitman* (1941) made one of the strongest cases for an outpouring of exceptional works during 1850–1855 by a select group of male authors, namely, Ralph Waldo Emerson, Henry David Thoreau, Herman Melville, Nathaniel Hawthorne, and Walt Whitman. Beginning in the 1970s and continuing into the present, critics and scholars have challenged the exclusivity of Matthiessen's canon and made persuasive arguments for the inclusion of major writings by women, ethnic minorities, and popular authors. Matthiessen's time frame has also been expanded to the years 1830–1870, and his formalist critical methods have been superseded by more capacious ones featuring social and political issues, as well as aesthetic ones.

The major American literature anthologies have responded to and often influenced the diversification and expansion of the American Renaissance canon, as issues of race, class, gender, and nation have come to the fore. At the end of the twentieth century and the beginning of the twenty-first, transatlantic, transnational, and hemispheric studies generated even larger contexts for understanding the major literature of the period. These alternative approaches and contexts have not displaced the idea of an American Renaissance, which has shown remarkable staying power. As Samuel Otter has pointed out, the focus of Matthiessen's *American Renaissance* has proven "generative, providing a model for explaining United States literary traditions that has been taken up—not replaced but revised and expanded—by later scholars and by editors of literature anthologies (234). As Robert S. Levine has also shown, the diversification of the canon has led to new understandings of the more traditional authors within it. Matthiessen's Hawthorne, for example, "is different from the Hawthorne read in relation to African American and women writers of the same period" (138).

While academics continue to debate the nature, scope, and justice of the term "American Renaissance," course catalogues and class syllabi indicate a tentative consensus regarding the major authors and texts currently grouped under that heading. The works most frequently taught in college courses are Edgar Allan Poe's poems and tales, Ralph Waldo Emerson's early essays, Margaret Fuller's *Woman in the Nineteenth Century* (1845), Frederick Douglass's *Narrative of the Life* (1845), Nathaniel Hawthorne's *The Scarlet Letter* (1850), Herman Melville's *Moby-Dick* (1851), Harriet Beecher Stowe's *Uncle Tom's Cabin* (1852), Henry David Thoreau's *Walden* (1854), Walt Whitman's *Leaves of Grass* (1855), Harriet Jacobs's *Incidents in the Life of a Slave Girl* (1861), and Emily Dickinson's poetry. Some individual instructors choose to teach other, shorter works by these authors (such as Fuller's "The Great Lawsuit," Hawthorne's short stories, and Melville's novellas *Benito Cereno* and *Billy Budd*) and a few supplement their courses with lesser known works such as Henry Wadsworth Longfellow's poems, Fanny Fern's newspaper columns, and her novel *Ruth Hall* (1855).

The Routledge Introduction to American Renaissance Literature seeks to provide undergraduates and non-specialist readers with a clear, reliable introduction to this rich, diverse, and evolving set of authors and texts, which, it should be noted, comprise only a select portion of nineteenth-century American literature.

The six chapters that follow are roughly chronological in order and will focus on those authors, texts, and issues that now enjoy prominence in current university curricula. Each chapter foregrounds important biographical and cultural information and highlights some of the most significant, engaging, and relevant aspects of the authors' works. Within chapters, authors are situated side by side when possible to reveal both their similarities and differences, especially with regard to decisive issues of the day. The major relevant criticism is incorporated into each chapter, and issues that remain unanswered or controversial regarding the authors and their works will be pointed out. Each chapter ends with a short list of recommended further readings and a list of works cited.

References

Avallone, Charlene. "What American Renaissance? The Gendered Genealogy of a Critical Discourse." *PMLA* 112, no. 5 (1997): 1102–1120.

Bercovitch, Sacvan and Myra Jehlen, Eds. *Ideology and Classic American Literature*. Cambridge, UK: Cambridge University Press, 1986.

Jay, Gregory S. *American Literature and the Culture Wars*. Ithaca, NY: Cornell University Press, 1997.

Lee, Maurice S. "Introduction: A Survey of Survey Courses." *J19: The Journal of Nineteenth-Century Americanists* 4 (Spring 2016): 125–130.

Levine, Robert S. "The Canon and the Survey: An Anthologist's Perspective." *J19: The Journal of Nineteenth-Century Americanists* 4 (Spring 2016): 135–140.

Mallios, Peter. "On Foreign Grounds: Toward an Alternative US Literary History, Archive, Methodology." *American Literary History* 29 (Summer 2017): 352–373.

Matthiessen, F. O. *The American Renaissance: Art and Expression in the Age of Emerson and Whitman*. New York: Oxford University Press, 1941.

Morrison, Toni. *Playing in the Dark: Whiteness and the Literary Imagination.* Cambridge, MA: Harvard University Press, 1992.

Otter, Samuel. "American Renaissance and Us." *J19: The Journal of Nineteenth-Century Americanists*, 3 (Fall 2015): 228–235.

Von Frank, Albert J. and Jana L. Argersinger, Eds. *ESQ: A Journal of the American Renaissance.* Special Issue: Reexamining the American Renaissance, vol. 49, no. 1–3 (2003).

1 Longfellow, Poe, and American literary emergence

American writers who came of age in the early 1830s faced numerous challenges to becoming professional authors, even though the new nation was growing and prospering. The United States population surged during 1810–1850, from seven million to over twenty-three million, as the country experienced a new market economy, industrialization, massive immigration, and expanding territory. An increase in schools and libraries contributed to rising literacy rates, and thanks to technological advances in publishing, such as the fast cylinder press and machines for rapidly producing paper, cheap periodicals and books became readily available to the growing reading public. At the beginning of the century, printing shops in small towns produced books by local writers for local distribution, but by the 1820s, peddlers with book wagons "travelled by poor roads and unreliable rivers" to reach the country market (Charvat 35–36). As the nation grew, and transportation improved, large-scale publishers in the cities of New York and Philadelphia were able to print and distribute books widely at a profit. Exceptionally talented American writers, however, struggled to earn much compensation for their work.

British writers, such as Sir Walter Scott and George Gordon Lord Byron, became best-sellers in the United States, after achieving success with the British reading public; however, they received no royalties in the United States, because their books were pirated. The absence of an international copyright law worked against serious American authors as well, for it was far more profitable for booksellers to reprint cheap editions of successful foreign works, than to take chances on unproven native writers, to whom they would have to pay royalties. Some American authors took the risk of self-publishing, paying printing and distribution costs and hoping that sales of their books would yield profits. For James Fenimore Cooper (1789–1851) and Washington Irving (1783–1859), this method paid off. Cooper's career began with his historical romance *The Spy* (1821), which featured American characters and settings but borrowed its methods from Scott's historical romances. It enjoyed modest success. Cooper's *The Pioneers* (1823), the first of his Leatherstocking novels, sold well, and thereafter a leading Philadelphia publisher, Carey, Lee & Carey, brought out his works.

Irving, who moved to Europe in 1815, where he stayed for seventeen years, was able to circumvent the lack of international copyright by obtaining British

DOI: 10.4324/9781315751627-1

and American copyrights for his books at the same time. He thus became the first American author able to support himself by his writing. He enjoyed initial success with *The Sketch Book* (1820), which included the tales "Rip Van Winkle" and "The Legend of Sleepy Hollow," adapted from European folk tales, and he followed up with best-selling histories, including *The Life and Voyages of Christopher Columbus* (1828) and *The Conquest of Granada* (1829). Henry Wadsworth Longfellow, advised by Irving when he visited him in Spain, wisely purchased the plates of his books, which allowed him to control some reprints and achieve sizable royalties. He even came to approve of some British pirating of his works, as Katie McGettigan has shown, because it increased his "prestige on both sides of the Atlantic, and most importantly championed Longfellow's cosmopolitan vision for American letters" (728).

Other American writers did not fare so well, especially with self-publishing. Thoreau, for example, who was encouraged by Emerson to try it, ended up having to collect the unsold copies of his *A Week on the Concord and Merrimack Rivers* (1849) from his printer/bookseller James Munroe, and famously joked, "I have now a library of nearly nine hundred volumes, over seven hundred of which I wrote myself" (*Journal* 5: 460). Poe, too, began his career with self-published volumes of poetry, but when they sold poorly, he turned to work as an editor and reviewer for various periodicals. He also placed his poems and tales in literary magazines to supplement his small income. In 1845, he lamented,

> The want of an international copy-right law renders it impossible for our men of genius to obtain remuneration for their labors. Now since, as a body men of genius are proverbially poor, the want of the international law represses their efforts altogether. Our sole writers, in consequence, are from the class of dilettanti.
>
> (qtd. Moss 166)

Obviously, such a lament was phrased in such a way as to offend his more financially secure fellow writers. It also ignored the American bias against authorial possessiveness. As Meredith L. McGill has shown, "*Personal* private ownership and control over printed texts was unacceptable in a culture that regarded the free circulation of texts as the sign and guarantor of liberty" (48).

In addition to the lack of an international copyright law (not established until 1891), American authors faced the task of writing in English, the dominant language in the United States, and thus to invite comparison with Britain's finest authors, past and present. Writing in English also meant struggling with an aristocratic value system prevalent throughout the British empire. That is, a system based not on virtue and talent, but rather, on birth and breeding, rank and caste, which was being promulgated by the romances of Sir Walter Scott, the plays of William Shakespeare, and other forms of political persuasion.

Although Henry Wadsworth Longfellow (1807–1882) and Edgar Allan Poe (1809–1849) aligned themselves with the dominant British tradition, they contributed to the exceptional body of national literature that emerged in the

United States at mid-century. Longfellow has seldom been mentioned as a contributor to the American Renaissance, but in the last several decades his reputation has undergone a reconsideration, based in part on his international impact and his reconceptualization of what it meant to be a popular literary figure. Poe, too, now stands as the equal to more celebrated figures of the American Renaissance, due to his impact on international modernism and his contributions to popular literature, aesthetic theory, and new literary genres, especially the short story and detective fiction. Although born just two years apart, the two writers had strikingly different personalities and careers. Longfellow, quiet and genial, achieved fame and fortune in his lifetime, while Poe, impetuous and combative, died impoverished and vilified.

You are probably familiar with the writings of Poe, especially his poem "The Raven" (1845), which begins,

> Once upon a midnight dreary, while I pondered, weak and weary,
> Over many a quaint and curious volume of forgotten lore—
> While I nodded, nearly napping, suddenly there came a tapping,
> As of some one gently rapping, rapping at my chamber door.
> "'Tis some visitor," I muttered, "tapping at my chamber door—
> Only this and nothing more."
>
> (*Portable* 422)

You may also have heard of Longfellow, or at least of the opening of one of his poems:

> Listen, my children, and you shall hear
> Of the midnight ride of Paul Revere,
> On the eighteenth of April, in Seventy-five;
> Hardly a man is now alive
> Who remembers that famous day and year.
>
> (*Poems* 362)

Longfellow's poems were once recited aloud by schoolchildren across the country, and in some schools, they still are. Longfellow, along with other popular poets, such as John Greenleaf Whittier (1807–1892) and James Russell Lowell (1819–1891), were known for many years as "schoolroom poets." Poe, however, was never among this group. He lacked conventionality and respectability. He made a number of enemies by his savage reviews of other writers, especially Longfellow. In fact, he was known as the "Tomahawk Man," and, though fellow authors appreciated his genius, a number found him personally obnoxious.

Despite Poe's attacks on Longfellow, the two shared many attributes that distinguished their creative works, including impressive erudition, heightened aesthetic sensibility, masterful command of imagery and atmosphere, and an affinity for melancholy subjects. They chose in their poems to focus on lost loves, dreams, and fantasies, as opposed to every-day realities. Their main divergence was in matters of genre and tone. That is, Longfellow excelled in narrative poetry with historical themes, and his poems tend to be uplifting, even as they focus on death and dying. Poe wrote short poems, called lyrics, which express intense feelings, usually of hopelessness. His "The City in the Sea," for example, features Death personified, looking down upon a lifeless world; "The Haunted Palace" (a poem he placed within his story "Ligeia") describes a play at which a crawling blood-red thing appears, and at the end we learn "the play is the tragedy, Man / And its hero, the Conqueror Worm." And, of course, there is "The Raven," with its haunting refrain "Nevermore."

Sentiment and craft

In many respects, Longfellow, inspired and encouraged by Irving, became America's first professional poet, though his rise to literary fame and financial independence did not occur rapidly or without serious challenges, some of the most severe coming at the hands of Poe, who seems to have been envious of Longfellow's success and attacked him relentlessly. Unlike Poe, Longfellow enjoyed a life of privilege. He was the second of eight children born into a well-established and prosperous family residing in Portland, Maine. His paternal grandfather was a state senator and his father a lawyer and graduate of Harvard. His maternal grandfather was a Revolutionary War general and Congressional representative from Maine. Young Henry during his boyhood found Portland a congenial place. In the poem "My Lost Youth" (1858), he recalls the pleasant streets, the shining sea, the ships, the woods, his friends and "early loves." He ends by writing "with joy that is almost pain":

> My heart goes back to wander there,
> And among the dreams of the days that were,
>   I find my lost youth again.
>   And the strange and beautiful song.
>   The groves repeating it still:
>   "A boy's will is the wind's will,
> And the thoughts of youth are long, long thoughts."
>   (*Poems* 340)

The poem captures the nostalgia and melancholy infusing most of Longfellow's poetry, and readers responded appreciatively to his evocation of such sentiments. Longfellow's personality was apparently as calm and soothing as his poetry. He had a deep baritone voice and was quiet, reserved, and charming in person.

Longfellow attended Portland Academy, and at age fifteen, he enrolled at Bowdoin College, a small rural school in Brunswick, Maine, with limited academic standing at the time, but promising students. His class of thirty-eight included Nathaniel Hawthorne and a future president of the United States, Franklin Pierce. Longfellow published a few poems while in college and studied the work of established poets. At age sixteen he wrote his mother that he was reading the eighteenth-century English poet Thomas Gray and admired the obscurity of his work. His mother replied,

> Obscurity is favorable to the sublime, you think. It may be so, but I am much better pleased with those pieces that touch the feelings and improve the heart than with those that excite the imagination only and raise perhaps an indistinct admiration. That is, an admiration of we know not exactly what.
> (qtd. Thompson 37)

His mother's comments go far to explain why Longfellow worked earnestly to make his poetry accessible to readers of all ages, especially with those poems evoking sadness and longing. In "The Day Is Done" (1846), he lauds poems that "have power to quiet / The restless pulse of care, / And come like the benediction/ That follows after prayer" (*Poems* 49). Such interests and preferences were later cited against him by anti-Victorian modernists, who disdained maudlin sentiments.

While a student at Bowdoin, Longfellow excelled as a scholar. Although his father wished for him to become a lawyer, the boy chose literature as his main field of interest. In a letter home during his senior year, he wrote,

> I will not disguise it in the least… the fact is, I most eagerly aspire after future eminence in literature, my whole soul burns most ardently after it, and every earthly thought centres in it… . I am almost confident in believing, that if I can ever rise in the world it must be by the exercise of my talents in the wide field of literature.
> (qtd. Thompson 57–58)

In his commencement speech, titled "Our Native Writers," he called for a national literature, and observed the inability of American authors to "throw off our literary allegiance to Old England." He explained that "the fault is not writers but the modes of thinking… . aversion to everything that is not practical, operative, and thorough-going." He called for patronage of native writers and claimed to see signs that "a generous spirit has gone abroad in our land, which shall liberalize and enlighten" (qtd. Higginson 31–33). He identified American scenery as one means to distinguish this national literature, a point that was informed by Irving's Hudson River Valley landscapes and Cooper's similar ones of upper New York State.

Years later, in his novel *Kavanagh* (1849), however, Longfellow satirizes the notion that impressive scenery leads to literary genius. He has an exuberant editor named Hathaway engage the skeptical protagonist Churchill:

> "I think, Mr. Churchill," said he, "that we want a national literature commensurate with our mountains and rivers,—commensurate with Niagara, and the Alleghanies, and the Great Lakes!"

"Oh!"
"We want a national epic that shall correspond to the size of the country ..."
"Ah!"
"We want a national drama in which scope enough shall be given to our gigantic ideas, and to the unparalleled activity and progress of our people!"
"Of course."
"In a word, we want a national literature altogether shaggy and unshorn, that shall shake the earth, like a herd of buffaloes thundering over the prairies!"

(*Poems* 754–755)

Although the speech drips with irony, it echoes rhetoric by Longfellow's friend Ralph Waldo Emerson and a host of other contemporaries, who were calling for a literature as magnificent as Niagara Falls.

Following the War of 1812, there were insistent and frequent calls for the development of a national literature, able to establish the United States' cultural independence from England, commensurate with the country's political independence. Not only the American landscape, but also colonial history, democratic themes, and native character types were all suggested as materials for achieving this distinctiveness. Longfellow was one of many young authors who took the call seriously, but he insisted that America's national literature should also have universality, and he argued against praising unworthy books by American authors. As a result, Longfellow's Americanness, or lack thereof, has long been a point of contention among his admirers and detractors. He was particularly critical of the dominant utilitarian spirit in the new United States, and urged support of poetry and the fine arts, which are, he declared, "the instruction as well as the amusement of mankind. They will not till our lands, nor freight our ships, nor fill our granaries and our coffers; but they will enrich the heart, freight the understanding, and make up the garnered fullness of the mind." As he explained, "True greatness is the greatness of the mind;—the true glory of a nation is moral and intellectual preeminence" ("Review" 61). This was a minority view in Longfellow's time and remains so today.

After Longfellow's graduation in 1825 at age eighteen, he was offered a position as Professor of Modern Languages by the college. His father paid for a European tour that allowed the young man to acquire the expertise in languages he needed to accept the offer. He spent three years abroad (1826–1829) and became fluent in French, Spanish, and Italian. After his return from Europe, he labored over a travel book titled *Outre-Mer: A Pilgrimage Beyond the Sea* (1835), modeled on Irving's *Sketch Book* and on Lord Byron's *Childe Harold's Pilgrimage*, yet lacking their vitality. During his six years as a professor at Bowdoin (1829–1835), he published a few poems but devoted most of his energies to teaching introductory language courses and publishing scholarly articles, textbooks, and translations. Like many would-be authors, he resented that his teaching kept him from doing the creative writing he loved.

In 1831, he married a childhood friend Mary Storer Potter, and in 1834 he landed a job at Harvard, as Smith Professor of Modern Languages and Belles Lettres. The college required him to take another year abroad to improve his skills in Germanic languages. The trip, which he took with his wife, involved travel to Scandinavia, where he studied the myths and ballads of the region. In October 1835, while the couple were in Holland, Mary, who was about six months pregnant, suffered a miscarriage. As she slowly recovered some strength, they made their way to Rotterdam, Germany, but there she became weaker and died at age twenty-two. Longfellow blamed himself for taking her on the trip in her pregnant condition and was tormented by memory of the fateful night in their hotel room when he struggled alone to relieve her distress and deal with the gruesome realities of the miscarriage.

Longfellow, when tragedy struck, often turned to work and travel. Despite the optimistic nature of his writings, he periodically suffered from bouts of loneliness, lethargy, and depression. After his wife's death, he remained in Europe, studying. On a summer vacation in Switzerland, he met and joined for a time a family of wealthy Americans. They included an accomplished young woman named Frances "Fanny" Appleton, with whom he fell in love. The feeling was not mutual at first, and he ended up courting her for seven years. His book *Hyperion* (1839) was a semi-autobiographical romance that included a veiled account of his unrequited love. Fanny did not appreciate the attention, and when a friend asked to dedicate his poems to her, she replied that she had already been brought before the public in that way and had been "entirely disgusted with the honor" (qtd. Thompson 335).

Fanny's feelings for Longfellow eventually altered, and she agreed to marry him in 1843. As a wedding present, her father, Nathan Appleton, a wealthy New England industrialist, bought the couple Craigie House, a mansion in Cambridge, where Longfellow had been renting rooms. During their eighteen years of marriage, they had four surviving children, and several of Longfellow's poems describe the pleasures of family life. "The Children's Hour," from *Tales of a Wayside Inn* (1863), became a favorite of readers as it tells of the playfulness of his three young daughters, who surprise him in his study with hugs and kisses, until he captures them:

> I have you fast in my fortress,
>   And will not let you depart,
> But put you down into the dungeon
>   In the round-tower of my heart.
>
> And there will I keep you forever,
>   Yes, forever and a day,
> Till the walls shall crumble to ruin,
>   And moulder in dust away!
>   (*Poems* 348)

His daughters were no longer young when he wrote the poem, so the experience indeed stayed with him, apparently.

Longfellow's early poems appeared in three volumes: *Voices of the Night* (1839), *Ballads and Other Poems* (1841), and *Poems on Slavery* (1842). The first, made up mostly of translations, contains his most famous poem, "A Psalm of Life," which has the memorable conclusion "Let us, then, be up and doing, / With a heart for any fate; / Still achieving, still pursuing, / Learn to labor and to wait" (4). Since Longfellow suffered from bouts of lethargy, the poem contains advice for himself as well as his readers. The metaphors in the poem undercut the message a bit, though, for the "footprints in the sands" left by us to inspire a future shipwrecked sailor, seem more likely to have been washed away before such a sighting.

His second volume contains the more accomplished popular ballads "The Skeleton in Armor," "The Wreck of the Hesperus," and "The Village Blacksmith." The first draws upon Longfellow's studies of medieval Nordic culture during his second trip abroad in 1835–1836. In Denmark he visited the Museum of Northern Antiquities and there saw Viking artifacts that made their way into his rousing ballad about a wild Viking warrior who kidnaps a Norwegian maiden, escapes the pursuit of her father, lives with her until she dies, and then takes his own life. As a skeleton, he appears to the poet demanding his tale be told, though, to tell the truth, it does not reflect well upon him. "The Wreck of the Hesperus" likewise features an arrogant man of the sea, the captain of the *Hesperus*, who refuses to put into port during a freezing blizzard, and causes the death of his young daughter, his crew, and himself, as his ship is dashed on the rocks at Norman's Woe reef, near Gloucester, Massachusetts. Longfellow's galloping rhythm and dramatic imagery make the poem an exciting read:

> And fast through the midnight dark and drear,
>   Through the whistling sleet and snow,
> Like a sheeted ghost, the vessel swept
>   Tow'rds the reef of Norman's Woe.
>   (*Poems* 14)

As for "The Village Blacksmith," it, too, rings with vivid imagery and sentiment evoked by the death of an innocent woman. The blacksmith

> ... goes on Sunday to the church,
> And sits among his boys;
> He hears the parson pray and preach,
>   He hears his daughter's voice,
> Singing in the village choir,
>   And it makes his heart rejoice.
>
> It sounds to him like her mother's voice
>   Singing in Paradise!
> He needs must think of her once more,
>   How in the grave she lies;

And with his hard, rough hand he wipes
  A tear out of his eyes.
                    (*Poems* 16)

Despite Longfellow's privileged background, he often expressed, like Whitman, ardent sympathy toward the common man.

Longfellow's *Poems on Slavery* contains his contribution to the contemporary anti-slavery movement. With the poem "The Slave Singing at Midnight," he evokes sympathy for slaves, while "The Warning," imagines the destruction to follow if the slaves are not freed. The last stanza, based on the biblical story of Samson in Judges 13–16, warns,

There is a poor, blind Samson in this land,
  Shorn of his strength and bound in bonds of steel,
Who may, in some grim revel, raise his hand,
  And shake the pillars of this Commonweal,
Till the vast Temple of our liberties
A shapeless mass of wreck and rubbish lies.
                    (*Poems* 28)

Longfellow was not an abolitionist, as his friends Whittier and Lowell were, for he found them too extreme in their demands for immediate emancipation. Yet, he was deeply sympathetic toward the anti-slavery cause, and favored compensated emancipation, that is, reimbursing slave owners for the loss of their "property." Great Britain, as part of its Abolition of Slavery Act of 1833, had given its West Indian planters twenty million pounds in compensation, but the freed slaves received no compensation, just the opportunity to keep working as "apprentices." In the United States, with its four million slaves, such a policy was viewed as impractical.

Some commentators have speculated that Longfellow's failure to join the abolitionists was influenced by his father-in-law's investments in the textile mills of New England, which depended upon cheap southern cotton, which in turn depended on slave labor. This criticism, however, seems unfair, for Longfellow publicly critiqued mill life. In his poem "The Ropewalk" (1854), he recalls the dehumanization of workers in a mill like that he visited as a youth in Portland. The poem begins, "In that building, long and low, / With its windows all a-row, / Like the port-holes of a hulk, / Human spiders spin and spin" (*Poems* 340). These "human spiders" are mill girls, some of the thousands of young single women who worked twelve to fourteen hours a day in New England factories for a few dollars a week plus room and board. Despite his reserve, Longfellow cared about those suffering from oppressive social conditions. As one scholar has recently pointed out, "a closer inspection of the available evidence—including the account books listing his donations to fugitive slaves and black churches—shows that very little else about the image of the aloof Longfellow is actually correct" (Irmscher 4).

Although Longfellow was the most popular American poet of the nineteenth century, he did not gain respect from some of his peers. He was criticized for having depended on books rather than actual experience for the sources of his writings. The nineteenth-century writer Margaret Fuller, for one, declared,

> He has no style of his own growing out of his own experiences and observations of nature. Nature with him, whether human or external, is always seen through the windows of literature. There are in his poems sweet and tender passages descriptive of his personal feelings, but very few showing him as an observer, at first hand, of the passions within, or of the landscape without.
>
> (Fuller, *Critic* 288)

Viewed from the outside, Longfellow did seem rather dull, and after the death of his second wife, when he stopped going to meetings of the Saturday Club (an elite social group of writers and editors in Boston), Nathaniel Hawthorne informed a British friend,

> The dinner-table has lost much of its charm since poor Longfellow has ceased to be there, for though he was not brilliant, and never said anything that seemed particularly worth hearing, he was so genial that every guest felt his heart the lighter and the warmer for him.
>
> (*CE* 18: 421–422)

Emerson called him "a trivial, to make my meaning plainer, say, a vulgar poet," and for Whitman he was "the poet of melody, courtesy, deference," who lacked "racy nativity and special originality" (qtd. D. Reynolds 318). When Queen Victoria met Longfellow in 1868, her apparent putdown was more subtle, for she told him all her servants read him.

Poe's attacks

The harshest criticism of Longfellow in his lifetime came from Poe, beginning in 1840. At that time Poe was working in Philadelphia as an assistant editor of *Burton's Gentleman's Magazine,* and finding one of Longfellow's early poems similar to one of Alfred Lord Tennyson's, he charged Longfellow with a plagiarism

> too palpable to be mistaken, and which belongs to the most barbarous class of literary robbery: that class in which, while the words of the wronged author are avoided, his most intangible, and therefore his least defensible and least reclaimable property is purloined.
>
> (qtd. Moss 138)

Longfellow did not reply in print, but he tried to defend himself to friends by saying he had not read Tennyson; however, he owned the volume in which the poem appeared and had praised it to a friend. When another friend insisted that Longfellow had not imitated Tennyson, Poe replied, "Mr. Poe does not say that Professor Longfellow's poem is 'imitated' from Tennyson. He calls it a bare-faced and barbarous plagiarism" (qtd. Moss 142).

Ironically, Poe, himself, plagiarized from other authors, as scholars have discovered, but near the end of his life, he made a case for the innocence involved in an eminent poet's borrowing:

> the poetic sentiment (even without reference to the poetic power) implies a peculiarly, perhaps abnormally keen appreciation of the beautiful, with a longing for its assimilation, or absorption, into poetic identity. What the poet intensely admires, becomes thus, in very fact, although only partially, a portion of his own intellect ... all literary history demonstrates that, for the most frequent and palpable plagiarisms, we must search the works of the most eminent poets.
>
> (qtd. Moss 180)

It should perhaps go without saying that this is not an argument a college student of today should attempt.

Poe also charged Longfellow with "the heresy of the didactic," that is, violating the beauty of a poem by foisting an explicit moral upon it. One of Poe's aesthetic ideas, expressed in his well-known essay "The Poetic Principle," was that truth was best conveyed through prose, whereas poetry should focus on "that *Beauty* which is the atmosphere and the real essence of the poem" (*Portable* 562). One version of this is the idea of "art for art's sake." In other words, there is a need for the true artist to focus upon aesthetics, not upon advancing some social, political, or religious cause. Most contemporary artists now agree with Poe on this, though some accept the notion that everyone has an ideology (that is, a system of values and beliefs) that cannot help but inform their artistic expression. Of course, Poe did not reject the notion that poetry can convey truth, but he objected to its being featured in a work, as for example, at the end of Longfellow's famous poem "The Village Blacksmith," where he writes, "Thanks, thanks to thee, my worthy friend, / For the lesson thou hast taught! / Thus at the flaming forge of life / Our fortunes must be wrought; / Thus on its sounding anvil shaped / Each burning deed and thought" (16). Longfellow, unlike Poe, believed that poetry should "give us a correct moral impression" (Moss 149–150), which is why he wrote as he did, stressing lessons to be learned. In this sense, he was a true native of New England, which produced the majority of teachers in the nineteenth century, many of them migrating into the Middle West.

Despite the attacks on his character, Longfellow, when approached by Poe in 1841 for a contribution to *Graham's Magazine*, which Poe was then editing, declined the invitation, but added "all that I have read from your pen has inspired me with a high idea of your power; and I think you are destined to stand among the first romance-writers of the country, if such be your aim" (qtd.

Moss 143). Despite Longfellow's politeness, Poe's obsession with him became almost pathological, and he kept denigrating him, year after year. In 1845, following the success of "The Raven," Poe publicly compared Longfellow to Hawthorne, identifying Nathaniel Hawthorne as a genius struggling with poverty, and Longfellow as a wealthy Harvard professor, who had a host of toadies praising his writings. In 1846, Poe published his famous essay "Philosophy of Composition," explaining how he came to write "The Raven," and insisting that "If any literary work is too long to be read at one sitting, we must be content to dispense with the immensely important effect derivable from unity of impression" (*Portable* 545). Therefore, he decided the proper length for "The Raven" should be about one hundred lines (it is a hundred and eight). Longfellow, if he read the essay, must have shook his head, for he was in the process of publishing a book-length poem of some 1,250 lines, *Evangeline* (1847), which sold well and made him famous. It marked the beginning of his transition from Harvard professor to professional author. As Poe's life moved toward its tragic end in 1849, Longfellow's fame and fortune soared, as he taught the American reading public the joys of reading narrative poetry.

Evangeline (1847)

Longfellow's *Evangeline* tells a moving story of loss and perseverance, featuring a young woman, Evangeline, who is separated from her bridegroom, Gabriel, on their wedding day during the 1755 British expulsion of the French-speaking Acadians from their home in Acadie (present-day Nova Scotia). France and Great Britain were at war on the North American continent at the time, and the Acadians refused the British demand to take up arms against France and renounce their Catholic faith. As Longfellow describes the Acadian colony in Part I, it becomes a pastoral ideal, featuring lovely farms and homes, genial neighbors, and rural simplicity. All is changed as the colonists are marched to ships by British soldiers (actually New England militia). The Acadians suffer separation from families and loved ones and must watch the burning of their village:

> There disorder prevailed, and the tumult and stir of embarking.
> Busily plied the freighted boats; and in the confusion
> Wives were torn from their husbands, and mothers, too late, saw their children
> Left on the land, extending their arms, with wildest entreaties.
>
> (*Poems* 81)

The colonists are taken to various sites in North America, where some prosper but many do not. In Part II of the poem, Evangeline wanders for years in search of Gabriel, west to the Mississippi River, then south to Louisiana, then West into Native American territory, and finally to a Quaker almshouse in Philadelphia, where she finds him on his deathbed. She whispers his name and

Vainly he strove to whisper her name, for the accents unuttered
Died on his lips, and their motion revealed what his tongue would have spoken.
Vainly he strove to rise; and Evangeline, kneeling beside him,
Kissed his dying lips, and laid his head on her bosom,
Sweet was the light of his eyes; but it suddenly sank into darkness,
As when a lamp is blown out by a gust of wind at a casement.

(*Poems* 114)

Despite this sad conclusion and the persistent disappointments that mark the stages of Evangeline's journey, Longfellow's soothing tone and hypnotic unrhymed hexameters relieve the gloom that frames the tale, which begins and ends with the wail of "the forest primeval" and the answering "deep-voiced neighboring ocean."

Evangeline became immensely popular, selling almost 36,000 copies within ten years of its publication. Remembrance of an idyllic rural past permeates the poem, and adds a pleasurable balm to those readers struggling with difficulties in their own lives. Contemporary social developments also contributed to its appeal, especially the unsettling dispersion of young rural New Englanders during the early nineteenth-century as industrialization, urbanization, and westward expansion drew them away from the struggling farms of their native region. The poem also silently alludes to the recent forced removal of Native Americans from their homes in the Southeastern United States, not to mention the mass dispersion of peoples from Africa throughout the Americas as a result of the slave trade.

Longfellow took a keen interest in the plight of African-Americans and did his best to assist them. As historian Jill Lepore has pointed out, "month by month, year after year, in dozens and dozens of carefully recorded entries, Longfellow noted sums of money given to black newspapers, black schools, black churches, and, especially, to fugitive slaves." Despite his sympathy for dispossessed and oppressed peoples, Longfellow, like almost all white citizens of the United States in the nineteenth-century, subscribed to the prevalent racialism of his age, put in motion by Jefferson's stated suspicion in his *Notes on the State of Virginia* (1785), that nature, not circumstance, was responsible for the distinctive hierarchy of races on the American continent, and that the white race was innately superior "in the endowments both of body and mind" to blacks and Indians. His suspicion was taken up in the 1840s and "proven" by a series of pseudoscientists including Josiah Nott, a Southern race scientist, whose best-selling *Types of Mankind* (1855) described and ranked the so-called races and argued that the "inferior races" (i.e., all but the "Caucasian" group) were destined to become extinct, or, as Emerson put it, to "serve & be sold & terminated" (*JMN* 2: 48). Emerson in his "Ode, Inscribed to W. H. Channing," explains, "The over-god / Who marries Right to Might, / Who peoples, unpeoples,— / He who exterminates / Races by stronger races, / Black by white faces,— / Knows to bring honey / Out of the lion" (*Collected Poems* 63–64). In other words, some races may disappear, but it is all to the good and part of god's plan. (The honey/lion reference is to the carcass of a lion Samson killed, in which a swarm of bees made honey that Samson later discovered and ate.)

Sympathetic racialism

With the same racial fatalism, Longfellow, in his poem "The Jewish Cemetery at Newport" (1854), written after visiting Newport, Rhode Island, and viewing the gravesites in the neglected cemetery, meditates upon the disappearance of the colony of Jews who once lived in the town:

> But ah! What once has been shall be no more!
>   The groaning earth in travail and in pain
> Brings forth its races, but does not restore,
>   And the dead nations never rise again.
>   (*Poems* 337)

Despite this racialism, Longfellow throughout the poem, extends respect and sympathy toward the Jewish people and all they have endured. In fact, his lines contain a passion unusual for him:

> How came they here? What burst of Christian hate,
>   What persecution, merciless and blind,
> Drove o'er the sea—that desert desolate—
>   These Ishmaels and Hagars of mankind?
>
> They lived in narrow streets and lanes obscure,
>   Ghetto and Judenstrass, in mirk and mire;
> Taught in the school of patience to endure
>   The life of anguish and the death of fire... .
>
> Pride and humiliation hand in hand
>   Walked with them through the world wher'er they went;
> Trampled and beaten were they as the sand,
>   And yet unshaken as the continent.
>   (*Poems* 336–337)

As Longfellow's biographer Charles C. Calhoun has pointed out,

> Amid the crude boosterism and often vicious nativism of antebellum America, the poem stands out as a small beacon of sympathy for the oppressed and the maligned, a celebration of a vanished "race" for whom few others gave a thought.
>   (200)

A similar combination of respect, sympathy, and racialist assumptions informs Longfellow's second long narrative poem *The Song of Hiawatha* (1855), told in accentual folk meter. This work exceeded the popularity of *Evangeline,* selling 30,000 copies in six months, and eventually being translated into twelve languages during Longfellow's lifetime. Although Longfellow researched contemporary studies of the Indian nations, he idealized Hiawatha and presented Indian culture as fated to disappear in the face of civilized "progress." Thus, the poem has been dismissed by modern academics as a racist fantasy that contributed to the displacement of Native American people during the nineteenth century. What can be said on Longfellow's behalf is that out of sympathy for Native Americans, he tried and failed to understand his subject from the perspective of a more progressive future. Also, as Lawrence Buell has pointed out,

> *Hiawatha* was a one-time experiment for him, not to be taken as the quintessence of his muse but as one among other occasional attempts to extend his treatment of American life beyond the regional and cultural boundaries he knew best.
>
> (xxix)

A growing number of academics today are beginning to praise Longfellow for the diversity of his metrical skills, his command of atmosphere and tone, his willingness to write with clarity and simplicity, and for giving his American readers a sense of community, one attached to the old world as well as the new. His famous poem "Paul Revere's Ride," collected in *Tales of a Wayside Inn* (1863), first appeared in the *Atlantic Monthly* in 1860, a year before the Civil War began, and it contributed to a spirit of nationalism that would support the Union cause. Jill Lepore has also shown its relation to the abolitionist movement, especially through its emphasis on liberty. She points out that it is a poem about waking the sleeping and the dead, especially those "entombed in slavery, an image that was, at the time, a common conceit: Douglass called his escape 'a resurrection from the dark and pestiferous tomb of slavery'" (Lepore quoting *Autobiographies* 286). The final lines of the poem are particularly martial and stirring:

> So through the night rode Paul Revere;
> And so through the night went his cry of alarm
> To every Middlesex village and farm,—
> A cry of defiance, and not of fear,
> A voice in the darkness, a knock at the door,
> And a word that shall echo forevermore!
> For, borne on the night-wind of the Past,
> Through all our history, to the last,
> In the hour of darkness and peril and need,
> The people will waken and listen to hear
> The hurrying hoof-beats of that steed,
> And the midnight message of Paul Revere.
>
> (*Poems* 365)

At the same time Longfellow supported the Union war effort and the anti-slavery cause, he remained a pacifist. His earlier poem "Arsenal at Springfield" (1845) shows the intensity of his aversion to war:

> Were half the power, that fills the world with terror,
>   Were half the wealth bestowed on camps and courts,
> Given to redeem the human mind from error,
>   There were no need of arsenals or forts:
>
> The warrior's name would be a name abhorred!
>   And every nation, that should lift again
> Its hand against a brother, on its forehead
>   Would wear for evermore the curse of Cain!
>
> *(Poems* 34)

Personal losses

During his career, Longfellow wrote eighty-two sonnets, and two of his last are personal and moving. He wrote "The Cross of Snow" on the eighteenth anniversary of the day his wife Fanny burned to death in a fire in their home. Apparently, their young daughter Annie had been playing with a box of matches beside Fanny, who was cutting the hair of another daughter Edith. One of the matches fell on the floor beneath Fanny's thin summer dress, and when she or Annie stepped on it, it flared and caught the dress on fire. In flames she ran into Longfellow's study for help, and he tried to put out the fire with a rug and then by hugging her, suffering severe burns on his face and hands in the process. Taken to her bedroom, Fanny died the next day. The couple had been married eighteen years. "The Cross of Snow," published after Longfellow's death, ends with the following lines:

> There is a mountain in the distant West
>   That, sun-defying, in its deep ravines
>   Displays a cross of snow upon its side.
> Such is the cross I wear upon my breast
>   These eighteen years, through all the changing scenes
>   And seasons, changeless since the day she died.
>
> *(Poems* 671)

A second late poem, written following the death of Nathaniel Hawthorne, is also quite original and moving. It focuses on the details surrounding his friend's funeral, but like his poem about his wife, and Whitman's poems about Lincoln, the subject remains unnamed. Longfellow had known Hawthorne in college, wrote a positive review of *Twice-Told Tales* (1837), and received from him the idea for the poem *Evangeline*. The two writers shared the same pacifism and conservatism.

Poe's early struggles

As Longfellow suspected, Poe's hostility toward him grew out of circumstances in his life that had hurt him, emotionally and materially. Beginning in early childhood, Poe suffered a series of wrenching disappointments that seem to have dominated his life. He was the second of three children born to a struggling young actress, Elizabeth Arnold Poe, and her husband, David Poe, Jr., an unstable mediocre actor who drank too much. David deserted Elizabeth and the children when Poe was two years old, his brother William Henry four, and his sister Rosalie just a baby. The following year Poe witnessed his mother's lingering death from tuberculosis at age twenty-four. Three different families took the children in, and Poe grew up in the home of his foster parents, John and Frances Allan, who never adopted him, though he thought and hoped they would. Although Poe felt much affection for Frances, she suffered from poor health and found it difficult to be an attentive mother, while her husband, John Allan, a hard-working Richmond merchant, provided Poe with a good education, but was tight-fisted with his money and moralistic about Poe's behavior, which was often willful and extravagant.

The Allans and their foster son moved to London in 1815 in an effort to help Allan's mercantile business. Poe attended several boarding schools in London and Stoke Newington, which he later used as the setting for his story about a mysterious double "William Wilson" (1839). Though Poe excelled academically at school, especially in Latin, he was restless and unhappy. In 1820, Allan and his family returned to Richmond, where Poe attended school. Despite his slight build, he was an excellent swimmer, runner, and boxer. As a young teenager, he fell in love with Mrs. Jane Stanard, the thirty-year-old mother of a classmate. At about age sixteen, he proposed to a fifteen-year-old girl, Sarah Elmira Royster, who accepted, but her father interceded and put an end to the relationship. Subsequently, Poe became a high-spirited and mischievous teenager and quarreled with his foster father, who accused him of lacking respect and gratitude.

Allan, who inherited a fortune in 1825, paid for Poe's first year at the University of Virginia, which he entered at age seventeen, but according to Poe's letters, Allan failed to give him adequate funds to maintain himself in a respectable fashion. Thomas Jefferson, the designer of the new university, invited groups of students to dinner on Sundays, so Poe may have met him. The student body, mostly sons of wealthy planters and merchants, tended to be wild and violent. Assaults, drunkenness, gambling, cockfighting, and dueling were commonplace on the beautiful new campus. In 1840 a professor was murdered while trying to stop a student riot. It has also recently come to light that some students violently abused the male and female slaves who worked on campus for the students, making their fires, blacking their boots, and cleaning their rooms. Although Poe excelled in his studies, he lost thousands of dollars through gambling (in an attempt to win money to keep up appearances, he said), and Allan at first refused to pay his debts. After Poe begged him, Allan went to Charlottesville, settled most of the debts, and withdrew Poe from the school.

Humiliated and resentful, Poe quarreled with Allan, left home, and traveled to Boston, where he took odd jobs and worked on his poetry, publishing anonymously a little booklet of forty pages titled *Tamerlane and Other Poems* (1827), "by a Bostonian." It went unnoticed and now is a rare book, with only twelve copies still known to exist. In 1827 Poe also enlisted in the army as a private using the name Edgar A. Perry. He served at Fort Independence in Boston Harbor, Fort Moultrie in South Carolina, and Fortress Monroe in Virginia. In 1829 he was promoted to the rank of Sergeant Major and published a second book, *Al Aaraaf, Tamerlane and Minor Poems* (1829), a small volume of seventy-one pages, which includes his well-known poem "To Science," which laments the destruction of Romance by Science's "dull realities."

Frances Allan died in February 1829 at age 44, which led to a temporary reconciliation between Poe and Allan, who agreed to support Poe's plans to enter West Point. Poe gained admission in the spring of 1830, and while he exceled in French and mathematics, he again ran up debts that Allan refused to pay. Without the means to stay in the military, Poe got out of his five-year commitment by drinking, skipping classes, and ignoring duty calls. Before he left the Academy, more than half of the 232 cadets subscribed to Poe's book titled merely *Poems* (1831) dedicated "To the U.S. Corps of Cadets." It contains what are now some of his most frequently anthologized poems, including "To Helen," "Israfel," and "The Doomed City," (later "The City in the Sea").

"To Helen" was a tribute to Jane Stanard, who died from mental illness at age thirty-one. This older woman had given the motherless Poe the attention and affection he apparently could not find elsewhere, and in the months after her death, he visited her grave often. The poem is famous for its restrained manner and classical imagery, especially its allusions to Helen of Troy, the goddess Psyche, and the voyage of Ulysses. Under the inspiration of the poem's Helen, the speaker journeys "home / To the glory that was Greece, / And the grandeur that was Rome" (*Portable* 409).

Poe's poem "Israfel" refers, as its epigraph states, to the Koran, which mentions the angel Israfel, whose heart-strings are a lute, and "has the sweetest voice of all God's creatures." Poe's poem conveys the idea that passion, whether grief or joy, hate or love, is the essence of poetry, which an earth-bound poet can only dream of creating:

> If I could dwell
> Where Israfel
>   Hath dwelt, and he where I,
> He might not sing so wildly well
>   A mortal melody,
> While a bolder note than this might swell
>   From my lyre within the sky.
>   (*Portable* 413)

In the fall of 1830, the fifty-one-year-old John Allan married his second wife, Louisa Gabriella Patterson, the thirty-one-year-old daughter of a prominent New York lawyer. Allan also sent a letter to Poe indicating he wished no further communication with him. Among other grievances, Allan had heard that Poe had spread a rumor that Allan "was not often sober." After leaving West Point, Poe drifted and apparently experienced considerable grief and despair. In early 1831, he went to Baltimore to live with his aunt Mrs. Maria Clemm ("Muddy") and her eight-year-old daughter Virginia ("Sissy"). In 1833, Poe wrote a desperate letter to Allan, pleading for help:

> If you will only consider in what a situation I am placed you will surely pity me—without friends, without any means, consequently of obtaining employment, I am perishing—absolutely perishing for want of aid. And yet I am not idle—not addicted to any vice—nor have I committed any offence against society which would render me deserving of so hard a fate. For God's sake pity me, and save me from destruction.
> (*Letters* 1: 49–50)

Allan did not answer. He had fathered three children with his second wife and was quite ill. He died eleven months later and left Poe nothing from his estate, valued at $750,000 (equivalent to more than $21,000,000 today).

While coping with disappointment and severe poverty, Poe started writing short stories, one of which "Ms Found in a Bottle" won a $50 first prize offered by the *Baltimore Saturday Visitor*. Impressed by Poe, one of the editors, the southern author John Pendleton Kennedy, recommended him as an assistant editor of a new magazine the *Southern Literary Messenger*, published by Thomas Willis White in Richmond. During his seventeen months on the *Messenger*, Poe published tales and poems, wrote reviews and gained notoriety as a take-no-prisoners critic. He also increased the journal's circulation, though perhaps not as much as he claimed. Let go by White in 1836 for being "rather dissipated" and unreliable, Poe fled to Baltimore where he privately wed his thirteen-year-old cousin Virginia, and during the next fourteen years of his life, he moved from one editorship to another, always in financial difficulty, always having drinking problems, and always on the verge of disaster.

In 1837 Poe, his wife, and aunt (now mother-in-law) moved to New York City, where he completed his one and only novel, *The Narrative of Arthur Gordon Pym*, which began as a serial publication in the *Southern Literary Messenger* and was published as a book in 1838, the year Poe and his family moved to Philadelphia. While completing *Pym*, Poe was unemployed, and he, Muddy, and Sissy were practically starving. A visitor to their home reported they were existing on bread and molasses for weeks at a time. Surprisingly, at this desperate time in his life, Poe also wrote some of his finest tales, including "Ligeia," "The Fall of the House of Usher," and "William Wilson," which he would collect in *Tales of the Grotesque and Arabesque* (1839). Neither *Pym* nor the *Tales* sold well.

Pym (1838)

Pym is a strange and wonderful account of the adventures of a young stowaway, Pym, who endures a series of incredibly terrifying moments, each followed by an improbable means of escape or rescue. In the course of his "Narrative," Pym faces shipwreck, incarceration in the hold of a ship, starvation and thirst, an attack by a ravenous dog, a gun fight with mutineers, a hurricane, another shipwreck, more starvation and thirst, cannibalism, dismemberment of a mate, sharks, a massacre by black natives, and a fall off a cliff face. Finally, he and his shipmate Dirk Peters, in a canoe with a dead black native, are pulled into a cataract at the South Pole where a chasm opens before them and a giant human figure arises in their path with skin "the perfect whiteness of the snow" (*Pym* 175). There the novel mysteriously and abruptly ends, perhaps because Poe had exhausted available knowledge about the South Pole. In a note by an "editor," the reader is told that Pym, after returning from the South Seas and writing about his adventures, suffered a "sudden and distressing" accidental death and that the remaining chapters of his narrative have been lost.

As should be apparent, *Pym* is a riveting read. In fact, British poet W. H. Auden has called it "one of the finest adventure stories ever told" (vii). Poe, however, called it "a very silly book," and in many ways it is. From beginning to end, it is a hoax, of course, though the introductory note by "A. G. Pym" swears to its authenticity. In a number of chapters, Poe includes pages of materials "borrowed" (i.e., plagiarized, word for word) from other travel books. This "borrowing" adds authenticity to the account, making the hoax more convincing. It also provided enough padding for Poe to fill two volumes as his publishers required. The strengths of the novel are the same as those of Poe's tales—precise realistic detail, skillful creation of suspense and terror, a fast-moving plot, and a rich trove of sense impressions. The weaknesses include absurd hyperboles, which may be intended as ironic. For example, after his first shipwreck, Pym hears a scream and declares,

> "Never while I live shall I forget the intense agony of terror I experienced at that moment. My hair stood erect on my head—I felt the blood congealing in my veins—my heart ceased utterly to beat, and ... I tumbled headlong and insensible upon the body of my fallen companion".
>
> (*Pym* 8)

Similarly, late in the novel, as Pym and Dirk Peters escape in a canoe from the tribe of Tsalal Island natives, Pym declares, "In truth, from every thing I could see of these wretches, they appeared to be the most wicked, hypocritical, vindictive, bloodthirsty, and altogether fiendish race of men upon the face of the globe" (*Pym* 169).

In the same hyperbolic vein, Poe includes moments that are so gross they strike the reader as laughable. One suspects that Poe himself found them so. For example, a few days after Pym and three shipwrecked companions, dying of thirst and hunger, encounter a vessel with some thirty bodies putrefying on the deck of a nearby ship, a huge seagull gorging on one of the bodies, rises up and flies over them, dropping a morsel of "clotted and liver-like substance" on their deck. Pym declares, "May God forgive me, but now, for the first time, there flashed through my mind a thought, a thought which I will not mention, and I felt myself making a step towards the ensanguined spot" (*Pym* 82). On second thought, he picks it up and throws it into the sea, to the reader's relief. The moment foreshadows what happens several days later, as their thirst and hunger have become extreme. Pym and his three companions draw lots and cannibalize the body of the loser, a sailor named Parker. Several days later, Pym remembers where he put an axe that allows the three remaining survivors to break into a storeroom for provisions, and at that moment, the reader cannot help but think of poor Parker, who surely would have appreciated Pym's having had a better memory.

Despite Poe's comment about *Pym*'s silliness, critics have taken it very seriously and offered a number of interpretations about it. Some have drawn upon Freud to argue that Pym's journey toward the South pole with its warm milky sea and mysterious figure behind a veil represents a dreamlike return to the womb, to the body of the mother. The novel has also been interpreted as showing the intellectual and spiritual growth of a young man coming to maturity through confrontations with natural and human obstacles. J. Gerald Kennedy has argued that for all its gory sensationalism, *Pym* raises provocative questions of epistemology and metaphysics, that is, questions about how do we know and what lies beyond our physical existence. For Kennedy, *Pym* "enacts the metaphysical crisis of modernity itself: the longing for faith before the great, silent void of nonbeing" (*The Narrative* 13).

The emphasis on race in the novel has evoked a number of arguments about Poe's own views of black people and slavery. At one level, the portrayal of a murderous black cook on the *Grampus*, and the demonic behavior of the black warriors on the island of Tsalal can be seen as revealing Poe's own latent fear of black people and slave rebellion. On the other hand, given the fact that Pym and his shipmates on the brig *Jane Guy* are tricked by the natives, it can be argued that Poe may be critiquing white assumptions of racial superiority. As Kennedy has observed, "in puzzling yet unmistakable ways, Poe works against the grain of his own racial prejudices, producing a novel that both enforces and subverts conventional white attitudes about race" ("'Trust No Man'" 243–244). Poe's short stories "The Gold Bug," "Hop-Frog," and "Murders in the Rue Morgue" have also received thorough study with regard to Poe's racial attitudes, yet they remain puzzling. Poe appears to have been quite racist, yet at times he identified with oppressed black people and dramatized their rage at the cruelties of slavery.

Major tales

As is well known, Poe's fiction borrowed from the popular Gothic tradition, especially as it featured primary sensations and the means of arousing them, including dark confined spaces, mirrors, portraits, tapestries, dim lighting, physical decay, degeneration, mental instability, bordering on madness, plus characters addicted to opium or alcohol. Yet, as Kenneth Silverman has pointed out, Poe did not merely imitate the popular Gothic tales.

> He enriched their texture, managing to preserve the narrative drive of some central action while embroidering the whole with philosophical speculation and lore that deepen the mood of dire awe, and with sense details that lend the improbable events a feeling of reality.
>
> (112–113)

Poe's tales are also distinguished by his poetic effects, that is, his skillful use of sound, rhythm, repetition, and imagery.

"Ligeia," "The Fall of the House of Usher," and "William Wilson" stand out as the most accomplished tales in *Tales of the Grotesque and Arabesque*. "Ligeia" begins with an epigraph announcing the theme about the power of the will and its capacity to triumph over death. The narrator claims to have known the perfect woman, Ligeia, the love of his life, yet he cannot remember specifics about their past, which immediately raises questions about her reality:

> I cannot, for my soul, remember how, when, or even precisely where, I first became acquainted with the lady Ligeia. Long years have since elapsed, and my memory is feeble through much suffering. Or perhaps, I cannot *now* bring these points to mind, because, in truth the character of my beloved, her rare learning, her singular yet placid cast of beauty, and the thrilling and enthralling eloquence of her low musical language, made their way into my heart by paces so steadily and stealthily progressive that they have been unnoticed and unknown.
>
> (*Portable* 111)

What he does recall is her appearance, especially her dark hair and penetrating eyes, and her belief in the power of the will. After her death, he seeks out and marries the lovely fair-haired Lady Rowena Trevanion, but soon comes to detest her for not being Ligeia. "I loathed her with a hatred more belonging to demon than to man" (*Portable* 120). When Rowena becomes ill, ruby drops appear out of mid-air and she passes away, presumably dead; however, in a final scene she seems to return to life as Ligeia. Whether the event is real, supernatural, or a result of the narrator's vivid imagination remains unclear as the tale ends. Poe's friend and critic Philip Pendleton Cooke objected to the conclusion calling it impossible, and Poe replied "you are right—all right—throughout … I should have intimated that the *will* did not perfect its intention—there should have been a relapse—a final one—and Ligeia … should be at length entombed as Rowena—the bodily alterations having gradually faded away" (*Portable* 462–463). Many readers find the indeterminant ending fascinating, leaving open the possibility that the narrator murders his actual wife to possess a fantasy.

Poe told James Russell Lowell that "The Fall of the House of Usher" was one of his finest productions, and it is a classic of its genre, demonstrating the "unity of effect" Poe insisted a tale should have. From the very first paragraph to the final sentence, the story surges toward dramatic annihilation, of the mansion, the Ushers, the family line, and reason itself. The first sentence represents one of the finest examples of foreshadowing in American fiction:

> During the whole of a dull, dark, and soundless day in the autumn of the year, when the clouds hung oppressively low in the heavens, I had been passing alone, on horseback, through a singularly dreary tract of country; and at length found myself, as the shades of the evening drew on, within view of the melancholy House of Usher.
>
> (*Portable* 126)

The narrator goes on to explain that he is visiting an ill schoolboy friend, Roderick Usher, who has summoned him to the mansion, which is in the same state as Roderick—unstable, gloomy, and on the verge of collapse. One cause of Roderick's distress, it appears, is the mysterious illness of his twin sister, Madelaine, who apparently dies soon after the narrator's arrival. He and Roderick place her in a coffin, which they take to an underground vault. Seven or eight days pass, and when a fierce cyclone storm awakens the narrator in the night, he and Roderick wait it out together, as the narrator reads from the *"Mad Trist"* of Sir Launcelot Canning (a fictitious medieval romance), which describes sounds that coincide with others coming from within the house itself.

Finally, Roderick identifies the sounds, which he has heard for days, as made by his sister struggling out of her coffin and the underground vault. "We have put her living in the tomb!" he declares, and in response to the implicit question, why did he not rescue her when he first knew she was still alive, he declares, "I *dared* not speak!" which raises more questions than it answers. At the end, the doors to the room blow open and Madelaine falls "heavily inward upon the person of her brother, and in her violent and now final death-agonies, bears him to the floor a corpse" (*Portable* 143). Immediately, the narrator flees the house, and turns to see it falling into the tarn before it. Multiple causes have been offered for the "falls" in the tale, including the toxic atmosphere surrounding the mansion, the anguish of the Ushers' social isolation, the inbreeding within the Usher family, brother-sister incest, sexual repression, and general moral decay. Poe's poem "The Haunted Palace" works well within the tale, most readers agree, for it emphasizes the contrast between the past and the present, order and chaos, yet Poe's use of the *Mad Trist* has been critiqued by some as unnecessary flummery.

As for "William Wilson," that intricate tale explores the problem of dealing with one's conscience, as its epigraph suggests: "What say of it? What say of CONSCIENCE grim, / That spectre in my path?" (*Portable* 168), attributed to Chamberlayne's *Pharronida*, but probably invented by Poe. The narrator, calling himself William Wilson, has lived a life of "unspeakable misery, and unpardonable crime," which he attributes to his own "evil propensities" and to the "constitutional infirmities" of his family line. He recalls that at his boarding schools, later at Oxford, and finally during subsequent travels on the continent, he found himself thwarted in his vices by a figure bearing his own name and having his same age, height, features, and dress. This "perfect imitation" speaks in a low whisper and confronts him whenever he engages in various forms of immorality. In the climactic scene, at a party during the Carnival in Rome, narrator Wilson, drunk on wine, stabs a figure he believes is the other Wilson, but finds himself looking into a mirror at his own image, pale and dabbled in blood, while a voice declares, "*You have conquered, and I yield. Yet, hence forward art thou also dead—dead to the World, to Heaven, and to Hope! ... thou hast murdered thyself*" (*Portable* 186). This use of a doppelganger, or exact double, was not original with Poe; however, he endows the device with believable psychological realism, showing the suicidal self-hatred that can accompany a life at odds with one's principles.

Sensation and satire

As one of the first American writers to focus on forms of mental derangement, Poe anticipated a number of mental illnesses elucidated by modern psychology. For this reason, his work, and his own life, have seemed to invite psychological analyses by literary critics and biographers. Nevertheless, it is important to keep in mind that Poe was first and foremost an ambitious, hard-working magazinist, and the focus on gruesome effects in his tales owes more to the literary marketplace at the time than to Poe's own morbid obsessions. As Poe struggled to make a living as a writer, he paid close attention to what was popular. His early horrific story "Berenice" (1835), for example, features a monomaniacal narrator who becomes obsessed by the teeth of his emaciated cousin, Berenice. When she is mistakenly buried alive after suffering an epileptic seizure, the narrator in a dreamlike state digs up her body and extracts her teeth, leaving a "shrill and piercing shriek of a female voice," ringing in his ears and a box with "thirty-two small, white, and ivory-looking substances" (*Portable* 104), sitting on a table beside him. When queried by the publisher of the *Southern Literary Messenger* about the poor taste of this tale, Poe responded, "Your opinion of it is very just," but he added, "The history of all Magazines shows plainly that those which have attained celebrity were indebted for it to articles *similar in nature—to Berenice* ... To be appreciated you must be *read*" (*Letters* 57, 58).

There has been much critical discussion and debate surrounding Poe's sensational tales. Are they serious fictions or parodies? Of course, it is possible Poe himself did not know, for despite their gruesomeness, they obviously display much art and craft. Poe directed self-mockery at his Gothic effects in two witty pieces titled "How to write a Blackwood's article," and "A Predicament," both first published in 1838 as "The Psyche Zenobia" and "The Scythe of Time," before being retitled and collected in *Tales of the Grotesque and Arabesque* (1840). The narrator in both tales, Suky Snobs, is an earnest would-be author, who seeks advice from a *Blackwood's Magazine* editor about writing for his magazine, known for its bloodcurdling tales. He tells her she must get herself into a fix, a predicament, and then report all the sensations she feels, the more unusual and frightening the better.

In "A Predicament," Suky narrates her adventure of climbing up into a clock tower with her slave Caesar and her little dog Diana. Standing on Caesar's back, she looks out on the town through an opening in the face of the clock, but the minute hand catches on her neck, and slowly cuts off her head while she reports her feelings about it. When her eye and then her head fall to the ground, she remains the calm observer:

> I will candidly confess that my feelings were now of the most singular—nay, of the most mysterious, the most perplexing and incomprehensible character. My senses were here and there at one and the same moment. With my head I imagined, at one time, that I, the head, was the real Signora Psyche Zenobia—at another I felt convinced that myself, the body, was the proper identity. To clear my ideas on this topic I felt in my pocket for my snuff-box, but, upon getting it, and endeavoring to apply a pinch of its grateful contents in the ordinary manner, I became immediately aware of my peculiar deficiency, and threw the box at once down to my head. It took a pinch with great satisfaction, and smiled me an acknowledgement in return. Shortly afterward it made me a speech, which I could hear but indistinctly without ears. I gathered enough, however, to know that it was astonished at my wishing to remain alive under such circumstances.
>
> (*Selected* 189)

Obviously, Suky's tale parodies Poe's own narrative techniques in his serious tales of terror. A number of Poe's less well-known works, including his hoaxes, burlesques, and pranks are similar attempts at humor.

Innovation and celebrity

When Poe moved with his small family to Philadelphia in 1838, most of his income resulted from his efforts as an editor and reviewer, first for *Burton's Gentleman's Magazine* and then, after failing in an attempt to establish a magazine of his own, for *Graham's Lady's and Gentleman's Magazine*. After quarreling with William E. Burton, Poe endured a long illness before being hired as editor of *Graham's*, but he resigned after thirteen months, traveling to Washington DC to seek a government appointment, but without success. At this time, in the early 1840s, he turned to new types of stories, detective stories, which he called "tales of ratiocination." "The Murders in the Rue Morgue" (1841), "The Gold-Bug" (1843), and "The Purloined Letter" (1844) are three of the most well known. The first and third are stories that feature an amateur detective named C. August Dupin, a brilliant, reclusive gentleman, living in Paris, who assists the police in solving perplexing crimes. Dupin combines an analytical mind with a poet's imagination, and he displays a sense of superiority to mere mortals, such as his nameless companion, the narrator, and, of course, the police. With these tales, Poe developed the modern detective story (he was familiar with earlier models), and Dupin later served as a major influence on Arthur Conan Doyle's famous Sherlock Holmes and a multitude of other fictional detectives.

In 1844, Poe, Muddy, and Sissy, who was slowly dying from tuberculosis, moved back to New York City, and there Poe contributed articles, reviews, and poems to the *Evening Mirror*. The publication of "The Raven," in 1845, gained him celebrity and female admirers. It is a memorable poem with a haunting refrain that evokes melancholy thoughts. If closely analyzed, it reveals some sloppy and redundant diction, but the regular meter carries the poem forward swiftly enough that few readers even notice these deficiencies. In the following stanza, for example, the words "flirt," "stayed," and "sat" add sound but little sense:

> Open here I flung the shutter, when, with many a flirt and flutter,
> In there stepped a stately Raven of the saintly days of yore;
> Not the least obeisance made he; not a minute stopped or stayed he;
> But, with mien of lord or lady, perched above my chamber door—
> Perched upon a bust of Pallas just above my chamber door—
> Perched, and sat, and nothing more.
>
> (*Portable* 423)

William Butler Yeats, arguably the greatest poet of the twentieth century, wrote in a private letter, "Analyze 'The Raven' and you find that its subject is a commonplace and its execution a rhythmical trick. Its rhythm never lives for a moment, never once moves with an emotional life. The whole thing seems to me insincere and vulgar." Similarly, Walt Whitman, long after Poe's death, observed that Poe's verses "probably belong among the electric lights of imaginative literature, brilliant and dazzling, but with no heat." Yet Yeats later publicly praised Poe as "a great lyric poet" (qtd. Carlson 76–77), and Whitman conceded, "There is an indescribable magnetism about the poet's life and reminiscences, as well as the poems" (873). Poe's "Raven" has had remarkable staying power, not least because of its musicality and ease of memorization.

Conclusion

In the same year "The Raven" appeared, Poe became an editor of the *Broadway Journal* and used this position to attack Longfellow again as a plagiarist in a series of five articles. In 1847 Virginia died, and in the final two years of his life, Poe had several indiscreet love affairs with literary women and became engaged to his childhood sweetheart, the widowed Sarah Royster Shelton. He again tried, unsuccessfully, to launch a magazine of his own called "The Stylus." In his essays called "Marginalia," he included the well-known "Poetic Principle," which argued that the most poetic topic is the death of a beautiful woman. He also gave a failed reading of his difficult poem "Al Aaraaf" in Boston at an annual lyceum event (and afterward claimed it was a hoax, meant to mock his audience). He criticized in print James Russell Lowell's verse satire *A Fable for Critics*, which included the lines, "There comes Poe, with his raven, like Barnaby Rudge, / Two-fifths of him genius and three-fifths sheer fudge." (Barnaby Rudge is the half-witted title character of a Dickens novel.) Poe died in Baltimore on October 7, 1849 under mysterious circumstances. At age forty, he was found half conscious, lying in the street with no money or identification. Taken to a local hospital, he died there and is buried in Baltimore.

Longfellow, during the last twenty-one years of his life as a widower, translated the *Divine Comedy* of Dante, still one of the finest translations available, published several more collections of poems, and received numerous honors, including an audience with Queen Victoria and a bust in Poets' Corner in Westminster Abbey. In the wake of Poe's death, Longfellow expressed charitable remarks about the man, writing, "The harshness of his criticism I have never attributed to anything but the irritation of a sensitive nature, chafed by an indefinite sense of wrong" (qtd. Moss 189).

Longfellow's take on Poe has much to recommend it, for it goes to the heart of Poe's life and career. Unfortunately, few of Poe's contemporaries shared Longfellow's understanding and kindness. Soon after Poe's death, Rufus W. Griswold, a "trusted" friend whom "Muddy" chose as Poe's literary executor, took savage revenge upon Poe by writing an untruthful obituary that appeared in the *New-York Tribune*, and a biographical "memoir" written for an edition of Poe's published works. In both he represented Poe as a demonic, depraved, dishonest, friendless drunkard and drug addict. Griswold published portions of Poe's correspondence with emendations and forged additions to support his portrait. Soon other enemies of Poe (and he had many) elaborated upon Griswold's scurrilous portrait. This image of Poe as a mad addict persisted well into the twentieth century.

Although Longfellow managed his career wisely and achieved great success in his lifetime, his reputation fell sharply at the beginning of the twentieth century, when modernists rejected him as too genteel, conventional, and derivative. Recently, however, he has earned recognition for inventing poetry for the reading public, promoting social justice, and establishing an international context for early American literature. In 1845 he published *The Poets and Poetry of Europe,* an anthology that introduced the American public to the translated poetry of some four hundred poets of ten different nations and established a transnational context for American literature. As the scholar Lawrence Buell has pointed out,

> No one can fully comprehend the literary culture of nineteenth-century America without coming to terms with his work, and those who come to it for the first time are likely to be surprised at how absorbing the best of it is.
>
> (xxxii)

Poe's reputation, though miserable when he died, has steadily risen over the years. The French poet Charles Baudelaire translated and published a multi-volume edition of Poe's works in French, which established him as an international figure and major influence on the European symbolist movement of the 1910s and 1920s. Today, even in the United States, Poe is recognized as an innovative and brilliant writer of poetry, fiction, and critical essays, who helped shape modernist literature and contemporary tastes. Most scholars also regard him as a major contributor to American literary emergence in the antebellum period.

Suggestions for further reading

Arbour, Christoph and Robert Arbour, Eds. *Reconsidering Longfellow*. Madison: Fairleigh Dickinson University Press, 2014.

Blair, Kirstie. "Accents Disconsolate: Longfellow's Evangeline and Antebellum Politics." *Literature in the Early American Republic: Annual Studies on Cooper and His Contemporaries*, Vol. 3. Eds. Matthew Wynn Sivils and Jeffrey Walker. New York: AMS Press, 2011. 81–112.

Calhoun, Charles C. *Longfellow: A Rediscovered Life*. Boston: Beacon Press, 2004.

Charvat, William. *The Profession of Authorship in America, 1800–1870: The Papers of William Charvat*. Edited by Matthew J. Bruccoli. Columbus: Ohio State University Press, 1968.

Kennedy, J. Gerald and Liliane Weissberg, Eds. *Romancing the Shadow: Poe and Race*. New York: Oxford University Press, 2001.

Silverman, Kenneth. *Edgar A. Poe: A Mournful and Never-Ending Remembrance*. New York: HarperCollins, 1991.

Thompson, G. R. *Poe's Fiction: Romantic Irony in the Gothic Tales*. Madison: University of Wisconsin Press, 1973.

References

Auden, W. H. "Introduction." *Edgar Allan Poe: Selected Prose and Poetry*. Revised Edition. Ed. W. H. Auden. New York: Holt, Rinehart, 1950.

Buell, Lawrence. "Introduction." *Henry Wadsworth Longfellow: Selected Poems*. New York: Penguin Books, 1988. Pp. vii–xxxii.

Calhoun, Charles C. *Longfellow: A Rediscovered Life*. Boston: Beacon, 2004.

Carlson, Eric W. Ed. *The Recognition of Edgar Allan Poe*. Ann Arbor: University of Michigan Press, 1966.

Charvat, William. *The Profession of Authorship in America, 1800–1870: The Papers of William Charvat*. Ed. Matthew J. Bruccoli. Columbus: Ohio State University Press, 1968.

Douglass, Frederick. *Autobiographies: Narrative of the Life of Frederick Douglass, an American Slave; My Bondage and My Freedom; Life and Times of Frederick Douglass*. New York: Library of America, 1994.

Emerson, Ralph Waldo. *Collected Poems & Translations*. New York: Library of America, 1994.

Emerson, Ralph Waldo. *The Journals and Miscellaneous Notebooks of Ralph Waldo Emerson.* Ed. William H. Gilman, Ralph H. Orth, et al. 16 vols. Cambridge, MA: Belknap Press of Harvard University Press, 1960–1982. Abbreviated JMN.

Fuller, Margaret. *Critic: Writings from the "New-York Tribune," 1844–1846.* Eds. Judith Mattson Bean and Joel Myerson. New York: Columbia University Press, 2000.

Hawthorne, Nathaniel. *The Centenary Edition of the Works of Nathaniel Hawthorne.* Ed. William Charvat et al., 23 vols. Columbus: Ohio State University Press, 1962–1997. Abbreviated CE and volume number.

Higginson, Thomas Wentworth. *Henry Wadsworth Longfellow.* Boston: Houghton, Mifflin, 1902.

Irmscher, Christoph. "Introduction." In *Reconsidering Longfellow.* Eds. Christoph Irmscher and Robert Arbour. Madison: Fairleigh Dickinson University Press, 2014. 1–9.

Kennedy, J. Gerald. *The Narrative of Arthur Gordon Pym and the Abyss of Interpretation.* New York: Twayne, 1991.

Kennedy, J. Gerald. "'Trust No Man': Poe, Douglass, and the Culture of Slavery." In *Romancing the Shadow: Poe and Race.* Eds. J. Gerald Kennedy and Liliane Weissberg. New York: Oxford University Press, 2001. 225–257.

Lepore, Jill. "How Longfellow Woke the Dead." *American Scholar* 80, no. 2 (2011). https://theamericanscholar.org/how-longfellow-woke-the-dead.

Longfellow, Henry Wadsworth. *Poems and Other Writings.* Ed. J. D. McClatchy. New York: Library of America, 2000. Abbreviated Poems.

Longfellow, Henry Wadsworth. "Review: The Defence of Poesy by Sir Philip Sidney." *North American Review* 34, no. 74 (January 1832): 56–78.

McGettigan, Katie. "Henry Wadsworth Longfellow and the Transatlantic Materials of American Literature." *American Literature* 89, no. 4 (December 2017): 727–759.

McGill, Meredith L. *American Literature and the Culture of Reprinting, 1834–1853.* Material Texts. Philadelphia: University of Pennsylvania Press, 2003.

Moss, Sidney P. *Poe's Literary Battles: The Critic in the Context of His Literary Milieu.* Carbondale: Southern Illinois University Press, 1963.

Poe, Edgar Allan. *The Letters of Edgar Allan Poe.* Ed. John Ward Ostrom. 2 vols. 1949; rpt. New York: Gordian Press, 1966.

Poe, Edgar Allan. *The Narrative of Arthur Gordon Pym of Nantucket, and Related Tales.* Ed. J. Gerald Kennedy. New York: Oxford University Press, 2008. Abbreviated *Pym.*

Poe, Edgar Allan. *The Portable Edgar Allan Poe.* Ed. J. Gerald Kennedy. New York: Penguin, 2006.

Poe, Edgar Allan. *The Selected Writings of Edgar Allan Poe.* Ed. G. R. Thompson. Norton Critical Edition. New York: Norton, 2004.

Reynolds, David S. *Walt Whitman's America: A Cultural Biography.* New York: Knopf, 1995.

Silverman, Kenneth. *Edgar A. Poe: A Mournful and Never-Ending Remembrance.* New York: HarperCollins, 1991.

Thompson, Lawrance. *Young Longfellow: (1807–1843).* New York: Macmillan, 1938.

Thoreau, Henry David. *Journal.* Vol. 5. 1852–1853. Ed. Patrick F. O'Connell. Princeton: Princeton University Press, 1997.

Whitman, Walt. *Complete Poetry and Collected Prose: Leaves of Grass (1855), Leaves of Grass (1891–92), Complete Prose Works (1892), Supplementary Prose.* New York: Library of America, 1982.

2 Emerson, Thoreau, and transcendentalism

In New England in the late 1830s, a group of intellectuals later known as Transcendentalists came together to discuss new ideas about religion and philosophy. They included Unitarian ministers, young poets, teachers, and thoughtful men and women of various sorts. The writings of three members of this group have made major contributions to the American Renaissance and United States cultural history: Ralph Waldo Emerson (1802–1882), Henry David Thoreau (1817–1862), and Margaret Fuller (1810–1850). Although their writings differed widely, each participated not only in the Transcendentalist movement, but also major reform movements, including abolitionism and women's rights. This chapter will focus primarily on Emerson and Thoreau, while the next will feature Fuller.

To many of their contemporaries, the Transcendentalists seemed misguided and practically incoherent. Emerson, in an essay of his titled "The Transcendentalist," defined transcendentalism as "Idealism as it appears in 1842" (*Essays & Lectures* 193). He first offered this definition to an audience in Boston in January 1842, as he tried to explain the "*new views*" that had recently appeared in New England. The term "transcend" means literally "to go beyond," and what this meant for Emerson and a number of his friends was to rise above the material world filled with illusions and achieve union with spiritual reality, in short, with the divine. There is a strong mystical strain in Emerson and in Thoreau as well, and both were often viewed as pantheists, that is, persons who believe that all of creation contains sparks of the divine, including rivers, rocks, and trees, not to mention people and animals. The prefix "pan," as you may know, means "all."

The transcendentalist idea that the material world is governed by certain spiritual laws of God's making, and that it is possible for individuals to intuit these laws owes much to the Puritan practice of introspection. A constant concern for the state of one's soul was one way of knowing whether one was destined for Heaven, even though, because of Adam's fall, every human presumably deserved to go to hell. The Quakers, who became more radical than the Puritans, by doing away with a learned ministry altogether, also emphasized the individual's ability to respond to "an inner light." The Transcendentalists shared this idea with the Quakers, whose works Emerson read and admired,

DOI: 10.4324/9781315751627-2

though there is more of a sense of brotherhood among Quakers, whereas the Transcendentalists emphasized individualism. In fact, Emerson's major contribution to the intellectual history of the United States is the belief that each and every person is responsible for the life he or she lives. "Trust thyself: every heart vibrates to that iron string" (*Essays & Lectures* 260) is the way Emerson put it in his famous essay "Self-Reliance." For him, self-reliance and God-reliance were one. "Blessed is the day," he wrote in his journal in 1834, "When the youth discovers that Within and Above are synonyms" (*JMN* 4: 365).

In his book *Nature* (1836) Emerson uses a famous metaphor to explain the feeling of a transcendental moment. He writes that one day he was walking across a bare common (the pasture set aside for everyone's use in the center of many New England towns), and for no apparent reason, he suddenly felt a perfect exhilaration, which made him "glad to the brink of fear." He goes on to explain, "I become a transparent eyeball; I am nothing; I see all" (*Essays & Lectures* 10). In other words, he loses a sense of separate identity as divinity shines through him and all creation. This one image has become famous and the object of satire. Emerson's friend the painter Christopher Cranch drew a cartoon of Emerson as this huge eyeball walking around on stick-like legs, staring into space.

Whereas Emerson and the other Transcendentalists tended to be optimistic about life and their relation to a higher power, many readers regarded the Transcendentalists skeptically. Nathaniel Hawthorne was among them. Although he became friends with a number of the Transcendentalists, especially when he lived in Concord, Massachusetts, during the early 1840s, he assessed them as rather confused and misguided. He called Emerson a "poet, of deep beauty and austere tenderness," but he ridiculed the "hobgoblins of flesh and blood" (*Tales and Sketches* 1145), drawn to Emerson by his lectures and writings. ("Hobgoblins" are imaginary sprites thought to create mischief.) In his story "The Celestial Railroad" (1843), Hawthorne satirizes the influence of the movement by describing the "Giant Transcendentalist" as a terrible monster living in a cave who periodically seizes upon "honest travelers" and fattens "them for his table with plentiful meals of smoke, mist, moonshine, raw potatoes, and saw-dust." The travelers in Hawthorne's story rush past the cave but catch "a hasty glimpse" of the giant,

> looking somewhat like an ill-proportioned figure, but considerably more like a heap of fog and duskiness. He shouted after us, but in so strange a phraseology that we knew not what he meant, nor whether to be encouraged or affrighted.
>
> (*Tales and Sketches* 817)

Oddly enough, Emerson apparently found Hawthorne's story engaging, for he recommended it to Thoreau, telling him that it "has a serene strength which one cannot afford not to praise,—in this low life" (*Letters* 7: 546). Serenity, requiring a certain detachment from the material world, was a state of mind

Emerson deeply appreciated and did his best to maintain at all times, even in the face of the most challenging circumstances, such as the death of his first wife Ellen, and later, his young son Waldo. Although Thoreau and Fuller tried to match Emerson's public coolness, they showed their emotions more readily. Their journals and writings reveal their desire to remain calm about the many injustices apparent in antebellum American society, yet they often found themselves unable to do so. As Thoreau put in at the end of his essay "Slavery in Massachusetts," "Who can be serene in a country where both the rulers and the ruled are without principle? The remembrance of my country spoils my walk. My thoughts are murder to the State, and involuntarily go plotting against her" (*WMW* 872). In a dispatch from Italy, Fuller, angry at the Catholic powers of Europe, called for

> a fire that will burn down all, root and branch, and prepare the earth for an entirely new culture. The next revolution, here and elsewhere, will be radical.... Sons cannot be long employed in the conscious enslavement of their sires, fathers of their children.
>
> (*SGD* 321)

Emerson's search for a career

Emerson came from a religious family, and his philosophy, which was a new form of idealism, had a strong religious component that distinguished it. His father had been pastor of the First Church in Boston, America's oldest church, and his grandfather a minister at Concord. After his father died, when Ralph was eight years old, his mother supported her six children by running a series of boarding houses, with help from her sister-in-law Mary Moody Emerson, who tutored the children. At age nine, Emerson attended the Boston Latin School before he went off to Harvard at age fourteen where he was an average student. After he graduated, he taught school in the Boston area and studied for the ministry. While preaching at various churches, he met and married a beautiful young parishioner named Ellen Louisa Tucker, who was sixteen when he met her and nineteen when they married. Emerson was six years older at the time, and she jokingly called him "grandpa." They shared several blissful years together, as is evident from the joint journal they kept, but she suffered from tuberculosis and died at the age of twenty-one. They had no children.

Life expectancy in the United States in the 1830s was short, and tuberculosis, the infectious, incurable lung disease known as the White Death, was a prevalent killer. Poe's mother and his wife died of it, and two of Emerson's brothers did as well. Thoreau also died of the disease, and Emerson was certain he would too. The year before he met Ellen, he experienced early signs of the disease and traveled to South Carolina and Florida to recover. Lungs and breath became key images in his writings, and the idea of inspiration (literally to breathe in) held special meaning for him. He also suffered from eye problems, which may account in part for his emphasis on vision, both physical and mental.

After Ellen's death, Emerson went through a dark period in his life and became uncertain of his role as a minister. In 1832, he decided he could no longer preside over the Communion Service at Boston's Second Church, which distressed his congregation. "This mode of commemorating Christ is not suitable to me," he said (*Sermons* 4: 192). He felt it went against his belief that the essence of Christianity was freedom, particularly freedom from inflexible forms, such as Communion. He took leave of the church and the active ministry and traveled to Europe where he developed his growing interest in natural history and met a number of famous intellectuals. He began his tour in Italy and traveled north to Paris, where he visited the Cabinet of Natural History in the Garden of Plants and saw the arranged series of shells, birds and fossils, suggesting an evolutionary process at work or what he called "the upheaving principle of life" (*JMN* 4: 198–200). The experience strengthened his belief that a beneficent force was at work in the world improving the condition of mankind.

For the most part, Emerson admired all of the writers he met, especially William Wordsworth, Samuel Taylor Coleridge, and Thomas Carlyle, and the latter became a life-long friend; however, his considered response to them revealed the Puritan background of New England, with its emphasis on piety, for he confided in his journal on the way home that they all lacked insight into religious truth. He shared a number of the ideas held by the British Romantics, however, including a sense of the divinity of nature, or, at least, a belief that nature could reveal spiritual truths. As Emerson would put it in the center of his little book *Nature*, which he started writing on this trip, "Nature is the Symbol of Spirit." He also asserted that particular natural facts are symbols of particular spiritual facts. For example, "a lamb is innocence; a snake is subtle spite … Light and darkness are our familiar expression for knowledge and ignorance; and heat for love" (*Essays & Lectures* 20–21).

Nature (1836)

In seventeenth-century New England, the Bible served Puritans as a source of knowledge about God's will. Nature, especially accidents and natural disasters, were interpreted as evidence of God's judgments. The eighteenth-century Enlightenment, however, especially the writings of Sir Isaac Newton and John Locke, suggested that certain natural phenomena could be explained through an understanding of natural laws. One of the last great Puritan ministers, Jonathan Edwards (1703–1758), has been regarded as a transitional figure in America, with regard to the shift toward nature as a means of communion with God. Edwards lived in the early eighteenth century, at a time known as the Great Awakening, a period of religious revivalism that swept through the English colonies. In an unpublished notebook titled "Shadows and Images of Divine Things," Edwards anticipated Emerson's link between the natural world and a beneficent divinity. As the scholar Perry Miller pointed out years ago, Edwards worked hard "to hold in check the mystical and pantheistical tendencies of his teaching because he himself was so apt to become a mystic and a pantheist" (23). The intense piety at the heart of Emerson's understanding of the world came from his own region of the country. The religious fervor and intellectual vitality of his aunt, the feisty Calvinist Mary Moody Emerson, exerted a powerful influence on her nephew, encouraging his self-reliance and religious sensibility. As the scholar Phyllis Cole has shown, Mary Emerson's letters to her nephew "formed the matrix of his thought, both early in life and through the years of his landmark literary utterance" (5).

During the eighteenth century and the beginning of the nineteenth, Harvard College, where Emerson studied divinity, had become more and more centered upon a progressive form of religion called Unitarianism, which emphasized the importance of reason in supporting one's religious faith. Whereas the Puritans saw Jesus's role as saving humankind from damnation, the Unitarians saw it as teaching humans how to treat one another. Both Emerson and a group of other Unitarians, many of them ministers, too, subscribed to the Unitarian emphasis on self-culture, that is, individual self-improvement, yet they felt that when Puritanism had been abandoned and rational thought brought to the fore, something had been lost. To them, Unitarianism seemed too dry and uninspiring, and they wanted to regain the intense piety and emotional uplift of Puritanism but without its intolerance and superstition. Madame de Staël's *De l'Allemagne* (1810), which celebrated German spirituality, and Samuel Taylor Coleridge's *Aids to Reflection* (1825), which celebrated the spiritual intensity of seventeenth-century Anglican divines, provided inspiration to budding American Transcendentalists such as Emerson, who were seeking alternatives to rational Christianity. Emerson's early lectures and his book *Nature* stimulated any number of young people to entertain the possibility of experiencing the ecstasy of union with the divine.

Despite its short length, *Nature* is a difficult read. On the surface, it seems rather straightforward, filled with down-to-earth language. In fact, its purpose is clearly stated at the beginning: to answer the question of what are the uses of nature. There then follow a number of sections corresponding to Emerson's answers to this question. For example, nature gives us commodities, language, beauty, and so on. Eventually it teaches about Spirit and the appeal of Idealism. The difficulty in reading *Nature* is that the paragraphs are rather confusing, mainly because of the unfamiliar concepts Emerson sets forth. His style of writing also makes his argument difficult to follow, as is true for many of his essays as well. For example, at the beginning of *Nature*, he declares, "To speak truly, few adult persons can see nature," which seems obviously absurd in a conventional sense. Yet the difficulty in understanding the statement lies in Emerson's unusual perspective and the biblical features of his prose. That is, he does not put forth a logical argument, but rather, expresses a series of original insights or truths, in declarative sentences, which tend to be striking and memorable. As a result, Emerson is one of the most quote-worthy of authors, as any book of quotations can show. Carlyle described Emerson's style as "a beautiful square *bag of buckshot* held together by canvas!"

(Carlyle 2: 81–82.). In other words, you can imagine Emerson's sentences as singular pellets, which do not stick together except though the pressure of their container, the paragraph. Emerson obviously puts great demands upon his auditor or reader—intentionally—, but if one exerts sufficient mental effort, there is great delight in discovering the brilliant insights he intentionally half hides from view. His truths dazzle gradually, as Emily Dickinson would say.

Emerson's publication of *Nature* caused a sensation by its synthesis of the idealism emerging from major European intellectuals, including Victor Cousin in France, Immanuel Kant in Germany (whom Coleridge translated and popularized in his *Biographia Literaria)*, and Carlyle in Scotland. Emerson included a host of idealistic ideas in *Nature* that ran counter to the prevailing utilitarianism in the United States. He explains that the process by which one experiences union with the divine is by one's SOUL (which Emerson calls the ME) rising above the material world or NATURE (which Emerson calls the NOT-ME and includes one's body) to join SPIRIT (which he also calls at various times the Over-soul, ALL, the Creator, and God). Drawing upon Coleridge's somewhat inaccurate translation from Kant, Emerson makes a distinction between the two faculties of mind that everyone possesses: Understanding and Reason. The first deals with sense impressions, with properties of matter, weight, inertia, density, that allow us to arrive at general principles useful for dealing with the natural world, within and around us. Engineers, scientists, inventors obviously rely upon the Understanding. For Coleridge and Emerson, Reason is a higher, intuitive faculty of mind that perceives analogies between matter and spiritual realities such as Justice, Truth, Love, Beauty, and Goodness. In *Nature*, Emerson explains, "That which, intellectually considered, we call Reason, considered in relation to nature, we call Spirit. Spirit is the Creator" (*Essays & Lectures* 15–16). Later, in his essay "The Transcendentalist," he explains,

> The Idealism of the present day acquired the name of Transcendental, from the use of that term by Immanuel Kant, of Konigsberg, who replied to the skeptical philosophy of Locke, which insisted that there was nothing in the intellect which was not previously in the experience of the senses, by showing that there was a very important class of ideas, or imperative forms, which did not come by experience, but through which experience was acquired; that these were intuitions of the mind itself; and he denominated them *Transcendental* forms.
>
> (*Essays & Lectures* 198)

While Emerson drew upon Kant's formal philosophy, his system of thought had at its foundation spiritual sentiment rather than logic.

Emerson and subjective reality

Perhaps the most radical idea found in *Nature*, an idea that Cranch also satirized with a cartoon, is that as you enhance your spiritual being, the world itself responds by becoming a better place. As Emerson puts it, when you conform your life to the pure idea in your mind, things in the world will change for the better: "So fast will disagreeable appearances, swine, spiders, snakes, pests, madhouses, prisons, enemies, vanish" (*Essays & Lectures* 48). The ultimate use of nature then is to reveal to each of us the state of our own soul, that is, how far we have come in perfecting ourselves. Nature is "the present expositor of the divine mind. It is a fixed point whereby we may measure our departure. As we degenerate, the contrast between us and our house is more evident" (*Essays & Lectures* 42). In other words, if we see imperfections in others, or horrible things happening in the world, they are the product of our own imperfections. Herman Melville's response to this idea, when he encountered it in one of Emerson's essays, "Spiritual Laws," was to argue in the margins of his book, "A perfectly good being, therefore, would see no evil.—But what did Christ see?—He saw what made him weep" (*Log* 2: 648).

Melville's remark assumes that the objective world of persons and things exists independent of the person seeing them; however, Emerson believed that the world you see is determined by the person you are. He was supported in this notion by the revolution in the field of optics that was occurring in the first half of the nineteenth century. As Jonathan Crary has shown, studies of optics, vision, and visuality by Goethe, Schopenhauer, Ruskin, and others argued that the observer was not a passive receiver, but rather the autonomous producer of visual experience. Emerson's self-identification as a "transparent eyeball," that is, a clear lens that sees all but is nothing, is related to this development in the field of optics.

In his book *Theory of Colours* (1810), Johann Wolfgang von Goethe posits the importance of the optical phenomenon of the retinal afterimage, which severs the link between the external referent and the sensory perception, with the mind alone creating motion where there is none. New optical devices for studying afterimages verified this theory and in the 1830s made their way into popular culture in the form of machines with unusual names, such as the thaumatrope, phenakistiscope, and zootrope, which were the beginning of today's cinema and allowed the viewer to realize motion when there was actually just a series of static images. Study of binocular vision also led to the conclusion that the sense of an object's three-dimensional unity was a "reality" created in the mind of the observer, and the stereoscope verified this theory as well. (To demonstrate, you can hold a finger up about a foot from your face. Close one eye and look at it, then try the same with the other. With both eyes open, you can now recognize that it is the mind that merges the two images into one reality.)

The Transcendentalists fully appreciated these developments in the study of vision, and understood subjectivity as having both limiting and liberating forms. Emerson pointed out that one kind of subjectivity turned the individual inward in self-indulgent, solipsistic ways, teaching us nothing about nature, ourselves, or spirit. The second, however, by focusing on what is true for everyone gives us expansive knowledge that, if perceived, redeems us. "A man may say I, and never refer to himself as an individual"—such is the valid subjectivity that arises from the perception that "there is One Mind, and that all the powers and privileges which lie in any, lie in all" (qtd. Matthiessen 9). It is the spiritual development of the person, then, that determines whether his or her subjectivity is of the high or low sort.

Melville was also skeptical of Emerson's optimistic belief that each person has an inherent divinity that can be awakened if approached in the right way. In the essay "Prudence," Emerson wrote, "Trust men, and they will be true to you" (*Essays & Lectures* 365). Melville responded, "God help the poor fellow who squares his life according to this" (*Log* 2: 648). Despite such negative reactions, a select group of Emerson's contemporaries, mostly idealistic young people, found him inspirational, and they traveled to Concord to be near him and to learn from him. Thoreau even moved into the Emerson house as a handy man and became not only a disciple for a while but also a caretaker of the Emerson children when their father left on his extended lecture tours.

Emerson's lectures

Emerson was one of the most successful lecturers of his day. He traveled the country giving talks in cities and small towns, usually as part of the lyceum movement, a form of adult education open to the public. In 1846–1848, he traveled to Great Britain and Europe, being away for some ten months. He had a strong, slightly nasal, baritone voice and pleasing expression, and he deployed striking metaphors and stunning assertions, called aphorisms, such as, "books are for the scholar's idle times" (*Essays & Lectures* 58), and "the first lesson of history is the good of evil" (*Essays & Lectures* 1083). Although audiences often emerged from the lecture hall uncertain about what Emerson had said and meant, they nevertheless felt better about themselves and the world. The way in which Emerson constructed his lectures, which he revised regularly, was a bit unusual and may explain some of the difficulty we have following his arguments. He kept a journal, starting at the age of sixteen, and in it he entered ideas, reflections, and insights that came to him on various topics, such as Character, Genius, Worship, Health, and so on. Sometimes he commented on specific individuals and events, but usually he showed more interest in general matters. Occasionally, he would go through his journals adding topics to the top of the page of certain entries, and he also constructed separate master indices. Then, when it came time to write a new lecture, he would go through his journals and extract relevant entries or paragraphs and, adding new thoughts, weave them into an oral performance. After he had a group of lectures, he would polish them and make them into a collection, which he published. Thus, two of his most famous books are *Essays, First Series* (1841) and *Essays, Second Series* (1844).

He also delivered a series of lectures about prominent historical figures, including Plato, Shakespeare, Napoleon, and Goethe. These he collected in a volume titled *Representative Men* (1850). The reason he called his subjects "representative" was because they were examples of those who excelled in certain vocations. Shakespeare represented the poet, for example, Napoleon, the man of the world, and Goethe, the writer. Emerson's Scottish friend Thomas Carlyle, not coincidentally, had written an earlier book titled *Heroes and Hero-Worship* (1841), which included figures who had distinguished themselves as men of action. Emerson's men, however, were not heroic in a conventional sense. In fact, the one military person he included, Napoleon, was described as too worldly, too interested in power and glory. Emerson's other figures stood out for their intellectual achievements, the ideas they expressed. Time and again, Emerson argued that ideas are far more powerful than military might as far as improving the state of mankind.

Scholars have seen a progression in the emphases of Emerson's writings, from the early ones to later ones. To put it simply, the early Emerson seems to be more transcendental, more concerned with the ability of the individual to achieve spiritual elevation, whereas the later Emerson tends to focus on all those constraints that stand in the way of such an achievement, that have to be overcome in one way or another and sometimes cannot be. Actually, though, one can find a mixture of idealism and practicality in most of Emerson's writings. Even in his essay "Fate" (1860), he declares that fate "is a name for facts not yet passed under the fire of thought; for causes which are unpenetrated" (*Essays & Lectures* 958), suggesting that whatever material circumstances restrain you or oppress you, such as illness, poverty, slavery, can be overcome by powers of the mind.

Emerson's essays for the most part focus on how his readers can change themselves and the world for the better, mainly through self-reliance, insight into spiritual truths, and the forthright expression of these truths. His goal was to lift others up. "Keep thyself pure from the race," he wrote to himself in his journal. "Come to them only as savior, not as companion" (*JMN* 8:186). You can see that in many ways although Emerson gave up being a minister and became a lecturer and essayist, he still preached in a way. It's just that he did not preach using the *Bible*, but rather, his own ideas and insights.

"The American Scholar" (1837)

Two of Emerson's early essays are his most transcendental and famous: "The American Scholar" (1837) and "The Divinity School Address" (1838). The first asks the scholar to ponder what is most important in life and how to attain it. If you believe the way to happiness and fulfillment is to acquire wealth, power, and status, then Emerson challenges your value system and tries to persuade you that ideals such as truth, goodness, and beauty, especially inward beauty, are far more important. There is a wholeness, as well, that Emerson asserts should be primary in one's life. That is, he warns about letting your vocation narrow and define you. The person who farms should avoid becoming just a farmer; the person who teaches should avoid becoming just a teacher. Likewise, the scholar should strive to be a person thinking, not just a thinker or bookworm. Such well-roundedness, of course, characterized eighteenth-century gentlemen like Jefferson, but by the late 1830s, Emerson had seen the rise of specialization within all social classes and the attendant narrowness that accompanied it.

Emerson delivered his lecture "The American Scholar" to a small group of Phi Beta Kappa students who had invited him to Harvard to speak. A widespread and devastating financial panic had just occurred in the northeastern United States and the panic, some scholars have suggested, inspired Emerson to challenge the prevalent value system of commercial America, which was becoming more and more intent on getting and spending (see Milder). Rampant speculation coupled with an absence of bank regulation led to the panic, which occurred when banks called in loans and suspended cash payments. Investors who had borrowed heavily in order to purchase land, railroad stock, and goods, had to sell all they had or go bankrupt if they could not cover their loans. Many banks in the northern United States failed and depositors lost their money. The panic, which lasted some five years, 1837–1843, resulted in widespread poverty and unemployment.

The financial struggles gave Emerson the opportunity to put forward his own value system and to encourage the young Phi Beta Kappa scholars to adopt it as their own. (Emerson, by the way, had inherited quite a bit of money from his first wife's estate and had invested it wisely.) He gave his lecture in a meetinghouse across from Harvard Yard to an audience of about 200 members of the college and guests, including his new friend Margaret Fuller, the poet James Russell Lowell, and Massachusetts governor Edward Everett. First a band played, a minister gave a prayer, and then Emerson gave his oration, which lasted an hour and fifteen minutes. As he was giving it, he could sense its success, and later he said he felt he was playing on his listeners as on an organ. One undergraduate, however, reported that "afterwards men and women freely said [Emerson] was crazy" (Hale 50).

Many of the main points of the essay remain relevant to today's college student, because Emerson, like Longfellow before him, encouraged a spirit of independence, and directed attention to the importance of the intellect. "Not he is great who can alter matter," he said, "but he who can alter my state of mind" (*Essays & Lectures* 65), which is a brilliant insight. In his conclusion, he addresses the problem Americans faced in the decades following the American Revolution; that is, how to achieve intellectual independence from England comparable to the political independence already achieved. In an attempt to assert the importance of democratic subjects and American writers, Emerson claimed to see signs of change in the literature of his country, a new positive emphasis on the common, the familiar, the lowly, and in a famous proclamation he declared, "We have listened too long to the courtly muses of Europe" (*Essays & Lectures* 70). As the poet Oliver Wendell Holmes would later recall, Emerson's address was "our intellectual Declaration of Independence" (Holmes 88). When printed, the lecture was exceptionally popular and within a month the 500 copies of it had sold out.

"Divinity School Address" (1838)

A year later, Emerson gave another address at Harvard that was far less popular, at least among the college administration and conservative faculty. In fact, it resulted in his not being invited back to his alma mater for almost thirty years. "The Divinity School Address" was shocking at the time, for it offered an entirely new understanding of Jesus. In fact, modern readers with a profound Christian faith, who believe that Jesus was the one and only son of God and performed miracles and rose from the dead, will be offended by what Emerson contends. He delivered his address in a small chapel on the second floor of Divinity Hall (now open to visitors to the campus) at the invitation of six members of the graduating class who were about to become Unitarian ministers. The room, which held perhaps 100 or so, was crowded. Emerson began with an observation with which few could disagree: what a beautiful summer it was and how one's moral sentiment responds favorably to the beauty of the natural world. He then suggests a higher pleasure, the delight in perceiving divine laws, such as justice and truth and the good. Once he has his audience agreeing with him, he turns to the Christian Church and its failure to recognize that the divinity of Jesus resides in everyone to more or less degree. He then quotes Jesus as saying, "I am divine. Through me, God acts; through me, speaks. Would you see God, see me; or, see thee, when thou also thinkest as I now think" (*Essays & Lectures* 80).

Of course, nowhere in the New Testament will you find this quotation. Emerson made it up. He had become familiar with the Higher Criticism conducted by German scholars beginning in the eighteenth century. Using rigorous textual methods, they postulated that the first three overlapping written Gospels of the Bible began as inconsistent oral recollections based on an earlier primitive gospel no longer extant. For Emerson, this meant it was better to focus on the spirit, rather than the letter, of the apostles' words, and he felt justified in offering his interpretation of what Jesus had preached. As for the reported miracles, he claims that Jesus felt that life was a miracle, whereas Christian churches had made the word Miracle into a supernatural "monster." He laments that this unnatural "Miracle" "is not one with the blowing clover and the falling rain" (*Essays & Lectures* 80), that is, with the naturally miraculous.

He also faults the Christian Church for dwelling too much on the person of Jesus, the man whose character and powers are almost mythic and so unlike those of mere human beings. He claims that the soul knows no person, and that Jesus serves us by his holy thoughts, which remain vital and accessible in the present. Most preachers, he says, speak as if God were dead and revelation given long ago. He gives as an example his local minister who gave a boring and lifeless sermon in the church, oblivious to the beautiful snow falling outside. "The snow storm was real," Emerson declares, "the preacher merely spectral … He had lived in vain" (*Essays & Lectures* 84). As for the new minsters before him, Emerson advises them to live boldly and fully, to breathe new life into old forms, and to see and teach that the world mirrors the soul.

Obviously, his advice to the divinity students was very similar to his advice to the young scholars. He wanted to inspire them, to make them Transcendentalists who appreciated the importance of the present moment, of being able to perceive and feel the joy and wonder and goodness that surrounds us in this world, but also to perceive what the world signifies, that is, an animating spirit that abounds throughout creation and within each person. The furor the Address set off surprised Emerson a bit, though it should not have. His most harsh and hostile critic was the president of the Harvard Divinity School, the distinguished Andrews Norton, who wrote a long article calling Emerson a dangerous heretic. Emerson chose not to defend himself, but several of his friends did.

"Experience" (1845)

For the most part, Emerson succeeded in not taking human relations personally. One exception was the loss of his five-year-old son Waldo, a precocious child who died in January of 1842 from scarlet fever. The death of Waldo tested Emersion's transcendental idealism by becoming one of those material facts it seemed impossible to render illusory by the power of the intellect. In a memorial poem of mourning, titled "Threnody," Emerson depicts Waldo as an angelic guest sent to earth to show men by his brief stay what love, laughter, and goodness exists in Heaven. It's a strong and touching poem, which begins:

> The South-wind brings
> Life, sunshine and desire,
> And on every mount and meadow
> Breathes aromatic fire;
> But over the dead he has no power,
> The lost, the lost, he cannot restore;
> And, looking over the hills, I mourn
> The darling who shall not return.
>   (*Collected Poems* 117)

In 1845, Emerson wrote a well-known essay titled "Experience" about the loss of Waldo and other setbacks and griefs he and others encounter in life. In it he strives to rise above his grief by arguing that such sentiments are shallow and respond to illusions, not reality. He insists that grief should make us idealists: "In the death of my son, now more than two years ago, I seem to have lost a beautiful estate,—no more. I cannot get it nearer to me" (*Essays & Lectures* 473). Despite this apparent philosophical detachment, Emerson's journals reveal that he never completely recovered from the loss of Waldo and the sadness it evoked. In fact, what one discovers if one compares Emerson's journals with his published essays is that the former are filled with more human emotion—anger, frustration, depression, doubt—while the latter are more calm, certain, and serene. In his journal, for example, he calls the abolitionists and other philanthropists "an altogether odious set of people" (*JMN* 9: 120), yet in his essays, he praises their anti-slavery efforts. In other words, his writings, like those of many authors, feature an "I" that differs from the actual person doing the writing.

The "Newness" and social change

Emerson's notoriety and intellectual vitality drew many to him, and he became a spokesperson for what became known as the "Newness" in New England. Slowly a group of innovative thinkers surrounded Emerson and began to get together periodically to discuss the new ideas in the air. At first, they called themselves Hedge's Club, because they met when Henry Hedge was in town from his ministry in Maine. Later, they became known as the Transcendental Club. As the scholar Lawrence Buell has pointed out, "for a premodern movement, Transcendentalism was striking in its openness to the participation of women and to feminist critiques of patriarchy" ("Introduction" xii). In addition to Emerson, Thoreau, and Fuller, the members included Elizabeth Peabody, George and Sophia Ripley, Sarah Ripley, and Bronson Alcott, among others. They began a small periodical called the *Dial*, which Fuller edited for two years, 1840–1842, before Emerson took over for two more. Even though its circulation was small, it created a stir because of its originality. As the *Dial*'s subtitle, "A Magazine for Literature, Philosophy, and Religion," suggests, it sought submissions on a wide range of topics. Fuller initially invited members of the Transcendental Club to provide copy for publication, but few did so. She had more success when she turned to her circle of personal friends. This circle, also known as a coterie, had privately shared packets of materials, printed and in manuscript, including poetry, journals, and letters to and from one another. For the most part, they did not author novels or short stories, because they considered fiction rather trivial. Emerson, in fact, gave his friend Hawthorne a back-handed compliment by observing that "Hawthorne's reputation as a writer is a very pleasant fact, because his writing is not good for anything, and this is a tribute to the man" (*JMN* 7: 465). Spiritual autobiography, based on journal entries, became quite important to the *Dial* contributors and was often combined with travel narratives or excursions. In 1840 Thoreau, just back from a trip with his brother John on the Concord and Merrimack Rivers placed his first publications, an essay and a poem, in the *Dial*. Emerson, who admired the originality and promise of Thoreau, his new young friend, urged Fuller to accept his compositions, many of which she did. Some, though, she rejected, giving him good advice about being less rugged and more polished in his offerings.

In addition to starting the *Dial*, the Transcendentalists inspired several other endeavors, including Elizabeth Peabody's bookshop on West Street in Boston, which contributed to the new intellectual movement by importing foreign periodicals and books. In 1839–1843, Fuller offered "Conversations," a series of paid group lessons, for prominent Boston women in the parlor of Peabody's shop. And in 1841 the utopian community Brook Farm was founded by two members of the Transcendental Club, George Ripley, a restless Unitarian minister, and Sophia Ripley, his brilliant, well-educated wife. Located on 200 acres of land near the Charles River in West Roxbury, Massachusetts, some nine miles west of Boston, Brook Farm, despite its unique transcendental origins, became one of a number of communities that emerged in the early 1840s, in part because the financial panic of 1837–1843. The new market economy and emerging industrialism were changing the landscape and the lives of working people, but not always for the better. Unemployment and poverty came in the wake of the new boom and bust economy. As a result, many Americans sought alternative forms of living.

During the first half of the nineteenth century, the United States was transforming from a small, slow-paced agricultural nation into a rapidly growing, urban, highly competitive, industrialized one. The proportion of Americans living in cities grew from six percent to twenty percent of the total. Textile mills and railroads with their smoke-spewing engines grew in number, evoking considerable ambivalence among observers. Some painters included the smoke from factories in their landscape paintings as a picturesque feature, signifying progress. Even Thoreau, in *Walden*, as he describes the train that shatters the silence at the pond, is both repulsed and awed by the power and noise of the iron horse flying by:

> All day the fire-steed flies over the country, stopping only that his master may rest, and I am awakened by his tramp and defiant snort at midnight, when in some remote glen in the woods he fronts the elements incased in ice and snow.
>
> (*WMW* 95)

Several chapters later, however, he calls it "a bloated pest" (*WMW* 156), and he wishes someone would stab it with a spear.

Brook Farm was an idealistic enterprise that sought to resist the ills that accompanied the rapid urbanization and industrialization in the United States at this time, including unemployment, exploitation, poverty, alcoholism, homelessness, crime. The Farm offered a new form of agricultural life for the 70 to 80 young men and women struggling to find uplifting work. Its initial organization was as a joint-stock company, a socialist co-op of sorts, whose members bought one or more shares, worked at the farm, received free room and board, and then shared in whatever profits accrued through the sale of produce. The evenings and weekends were set aside for social and creative activities, such as singing, readings, musical performances, *tableaux vivants* (staged static poses), and trips into Boston to hear a concert or see a play. There were also hayrides and picnics and lots of flirting among younger members.

Hawthorne bought shares in the Farm, with the intention of bringing his young bride to live with him there, but after seven months he left, finding the onerous farm work leaving him too tired in the evening to think or write.

Emerson, Thoreau, and Fuller visited the farm but did not live there. Ripley tried his best to persuade Emerson to join, but he declined saying it would compromise his independence. "I do not wish," he asserted, "to remove from my present prison to a prison a little larger. I wish to break all prisons" (*JMN* 7: 408). The Farm struggled for a while, eventually trying some of the ideas of the French Socialist Charles Fourier, dividing the cooperative community into groups called phalanxes, adding dormitories, workrooms, and a large central building to be known as the Phalanstery, which burned down in 1846.

The Alcotts

One member of the Transcendental Club, Bronson Alcott (1799–1888), decided to invest in another commune, named Fruitlands. Alcott was perhaps the most idealistic of the Transcendentalists. He grew up in Connecticut, spent time peddling wares through the South, acquiring impeccable manners, meeting and marrying Abby May, starting a progressive school, and raising a family of five girls, including Louisa May Alcott, who, by becoming a best-selling author, supported her family and made it possible for her father to pursue his philosophical interests. Louisa idolized Emerson, who helped the family through a series of bouts with poverty, caused mostly by Bronson's poor business sense. Although Bronson was self-educated, Emerson found him profound, and encouraged him to publish his "Orphic Sayings" in the *Dial*, which he did; however, they were ridiculed in the newspapers and satirized by wits. On the surface they appear to be nonsense, due to their unfamiliar terms and ideas, yet on close reading, they can almost seem nuggets of pure genius. For example, here is one titled "INCARNATION":

> Nature is quick with spirit. In eternal systole and diastole, the living tides course gladly along, incarnating organ and vessel in their mystic flow. Let her pulsations for a moment pause on their errands, and creation's self ebbs instantly into chaos and invisibility again. The visible world is the extremist wave of that spiritual flood, whose flux is life, whose reflux death, efflux thought, and conflux light. Organization is the confine of incarnation,—body the atomy of God.
> (Alcott, "Days from a Diary" 423–424)

Although the saying seems somewhat nonsensical, it also seems to anticipate the wave-particle duality foundational to modern quantum mechanics.

Before trying his luck establishing a small utopian community, Alcott established an innovative school for children at the Masonic Temple in Boston. It was based on new principles he had acquired from the great Swiss educator Johann Pestalozzi, who emphasized the goodness of children and their innate ability to discern spiritual truths. Alcott created an open space in the classroom and surrounded the children with books, pictures, paintings, and busts of notable teachers, including Jesus and Socrates. He did not insist upon memorization or harsh discipline, just kindness, curiosity, and thoughtfulness. Elizabeth Peabody assisted Alcott by teaching Latin, arithmetic, and geography, while Alcott, using a Socratic method of teaching, led discussions with his young charges on a variety of challenging topics. He allowed the students to question his ideas, and, at times, they got the better of him, especially young Josiah Quincey, age six, who later became a prominent Boston intellectual. Peabody recorded some of the conversations with the children, publishing them in *Conversations with Children on the Gospels* (1836–1837), and they are fascinating, because the children are so precocious. Some scholars, however, discern considerable coercion in Alcott's form of questioning and believe he forced his own ideas upon his unsuspecting students. Despite its innovations and apparent success, the school failed because Alcott allowed the students, both boys and girls, ages six to thirteen, to discuss human reproduction. When parents learned of this, they became outraged, finding it not a fit subject for children. A year later, in 1839, Alcott tried to open a similar school in his own home, but when he enrolled a young black girl as a student, white parents withdrew their children.

After his schools failed, Alcott took a trip to England where others had adopted his methods, and he returned to the United States with two admirers, Charles Lane and Henry G. Wright, along with Lane's son. Together they determined to establish a new kind of living arrangement, which they called a consociate family, one replacing a family based on blood ties. Alcott's wife did not approve of the venture, but she and her five daughters went along with it. Lane purchased a farm about twenty miles west of Concord near a town called Harvard (not to be confused with the college of that name). Because there were fruit trees on the property, they called their experiment Fruitlands. They planned to maintain the purest form of living possible. All members were to remain celibate, that is, to refrain from sexual relations. They were to drink only water and to eat only vegetables, preferably those that aspired by growing upward not downward. No animals were to be made to work on the farm, and the clothing was to be free from the taint of exploitation. Thus they avoided cotton, because of slavery, and silk, because it was taken from silkworms, and of course, leather. They wore only linen garments, though one member, Samuel Bower, a nudist, went without clothes altogether for a while.

Louisa May Alcott, who was only a little girl at Fruitlands, later wrote a satire called *Transcendental Wild Oats* (1873), where Lane (named Lion) and her father (named Lamb) are blamed for doing no work on the farm and causing it to fail. The two spent much of their time traveling, trying to recruit new members and manpower. Louisa's mother, Abby (named Sister Hope in the book), and her small daughters were stuck with all the chores, including bringing in the barley before a heavy rain. When winter came and no food was left, Abby packed her children in a borrowed wagon and departed for the east. Bronson, who had taken to his bed in despair, finally got up and followed. Lane and his son joined the Shaker community down the road.

When the Alcotts lived in Concord during 1845–1852, Bronson Alcott and Thoreau became good friends, influencing one another. Alcott did not pay his poll tax in 1842, years before Thoreau in 1845 decided to do the same, which led to his night in jail and his famous essay "The Relation of the Individual to the State" (1849), better known as "Civil Disobedience." Alcott appears in *Walden*, where Thoreau describes him as "A blue-robed man, whose fittest roof is the overarching sky which reflects his serenity. I do not see how he can ever die; Nature cannot spare him" (*WMW* 216). Alcott was known as an eloquent speaker, but he never wrote anything that achieved much success, other than the annual reports he compiled as superintendent of Concord's schools. Emerson, soon after he met Alcott, in 1836, wrote to his brother William, "He is a great genius. So thoroughly original that he seems to subvert all you know and leave only his own theories" (*Letters* 2: 29–30), yet four years later, he privately called him "a tedious archangel" (*JMN* 7: 539).

Young man Thoreau

Emerson tended to bestow exaggerated praise on new people who sought him out, and later to lose his enthusiasm for them, becoming critical. Although he and Thoreau were close friends for many years, and Thoreau lived his life according to the value system Emerson set out in "The American Scholar," Emerson expressed reservations about Thoreau in the eulogy he delivered about him, saying

> with his energy and practical ability, he seemed born for great enterprise and for command; and I so much regret the loss of his rare powers of action, that I cannot help counting it a fault in him that he had no ambition. Wanting this, instead of engineering for all America, he was the captain of a huckleberry party.
>
> ("Thoreau" 278)

There's great irony in the fact that Thoreau, whom Emerson charges with no ambition, has had a greater impact on the advancement of civil rights and environmental justice in the world than anyone else in his generation.

Thoreau was born in Concord, Massachusetts, the third child of John Thoreau and Cynthia Dunbar Thoreau. Thoreau's father held a number of jobs, and the family moved often. John ran a grocery store, taught school, and finally took over a pencil-making business in Concord, which Henry later made profitable through his inventions. Thoreau's father was mild-mannered and unassuming, while his mother was outgoing, witty, and energetic. She took in borders to help the family's income, and engaged in charity work and reform activities, exerting a major influence on her son Henry's social activism. A year before the family again took up residence in Concord in 1823, Thoreau saw Walden Pond for the first time as a five-year-old while visiting his grandmother. He later recalled, "That woodland vision for a long time made the drapery of my dreams" (*Journal* 2: 173–174). As the most scholarly of the four children, Henry was sent to Harvard at age sixteen, while his sister Helen and brother John taught school to help with family finances.

At Harvard, Thoreau was an average student due to disinterest and periodic illnesses (perhaps related to the tuberculosis that eventually killed him), graduating nineteenth in a class of fifty. He was most engaged intellectually reading Homer in the original Greek and studying German with the intense Unitarian minister Orestes Brownson, during a six-week leave of absence from Harvard. He later reported, those weeks "were an era in my life—the morning of a new *Lebenstag* [a day of rebirth]. They are to me as a dream that is dreamt, but which returns from time to time in all its original freshness" (*Correspondence* 1: 30). In 1836, the summer before his senior year, he spent six weeks in a hut on the shores of nearby Flint Pond with a college friend, Charles Stearns Wheeler, and sold pencils with his father in New York City. Upon graduation he briefly taught school in Concord but after being told he was expected to use flogging to maintain discipline, he flogged six students at random and quit.

Because of the financial panic of 1837, work was hard to find, and when his search for a teaching job in Maine did not pan out, he opened a private school in his parents' home in June of 1838, enrolling four students. In September of that year, he was hired as head of the Concord Academy, and his brother John joined him the next spring. John, who was two years older than Henry, was much beloved, not just by Henry but by all who knew him. He was handsome, kind, smart, and humorous. By all accounts, the children adored John. The brothers combined rigorous academic study with weekly field trips, often devoted to the study of natural and human history, including the lives of the Indians who once lived in the area. Together they developed new teaching methods. As biographer Laura Dassow Walls has pointed out:

> On Saturday afternoons, Henry's long stride would lead the students on weekly field trips, to the *Yeoman's Gazette* to see how newspapers were made; to the gunsmith's to try making their own gunflints; on long walks to Walden, Fairhaven, or Sleepy Hollow for field lessons in botany, geology, and natural history; or boating on the rivers in the *Musketaquid*, the new boat Henry and John built their first spring at the academy, which the students helped to keep clean and watertight.
>
> (99)

Louisa May Alcott was one of their young students, and she recalled the experience fondly.

During summer vacation in August 1839, Thoreau and John left for a two-week trip on the Concord and Merrimack rivers. The journey they took included a climb of Mt. Washington, in northern New Hampshire, before they returned on the same river route. A year after the brothers returned, both proposed to and were rejected by a charming young woman named Ellen Sewall, who had boarded with the Thoreau family briefly. Her father disapproved of both brothers. Somewhat adrift, Thoreau turned to helping his father with the pencil business, and teaching himself surveying, a skill that gave him all the income he required the rest of his life. In 1840 he closed the

Concord Academy and moved into the Emerson household for two years as their handyman and gardener. Although Thoreau was a new college graduate with no vocational prospects, Emerson found him interesting and promising: "I delight much in my young friend, who seems to have as free & erect a mind as any I have ever met," Emerson wrote in his Journal (*JMN* 5: 452).

In the same month that Emerson's son Waldo died, January 1842, Thoreau lost his brother John, who cut his finger with a razor while shaving. John replaced the skin and wrapped it in a soiled rag, but the finger soon became infected, and ten days later, at age twenty-seven, he died of lockjaw. Henry was devastated by this tragedy and almost died himself from a sympathetic reaction. Following John's death, Thoreau fell into a deep depression, lasting several months. That summer he met Nathaniel Hawthorne and sold him the boat that he and John had built. In his Notebook, Hawthorne describes Thoreau as

> a young man with much of wild original nature still remaining in him... He was educated, I believe, at Cambridge, ... but for two or three years back, he has repudiated all modes of getting a living, and seems inclined to lead a sort of Indian life among civilized men—an Indian life, I mean, as respects the absence of any systematic effort for a livelihood.
>
> (*CE* 8: 354)

Hawthorne put Thoreau in touch with editors he knew, and Thoreau inspired several characters in Hawthorne's work, notably the faun-like Donatello in *The Marble Faun* (1860). The two authors became friends, and when Thoreau brought his boat to the Concord River running behind Hawthorne's home, called the Manse, the two of them, as Hawthorne wrote, "voyaged further up the stream, which soon became more beautiful than any picture, with its dark and quiet sheet of water, half shaded, half sunny, between high and wooded banks... . Mr. Thorow managed the boat so perfectly, either with two paddles or with one, that it seemed instinct with his own will, and to require no physical effort to guide it." The next day, Hawthorne took a lesson in rowing and paddling, with his wife looking on, and Thoreau apparently pranked him. Hawthorne reported,

> Mr. Thorow had assured me that it was only necessary to will the boat to go in any particular direction, and she would immediately take that course, as if imbued with the spirit of the steersman. It may be so with him, but certainly not with me; the boat seemed to be bewitched, and turned its head to every point of the compass except the right one.
>
> (*CE* 8: 355–356)

One suspects Thoreau smiled at the scene. As Hawthorne would learn, Thoreau had a sly sense of humor and was a trickster of sorts, much less stoic and dour than the first chapters of *Walden* suggest. In fact, *Walden* is filled with inside jokes, as Michael West has pointed out. For example, when Thoreau writes that on his walks, he has helped farmers by watering the trees on their property, "which might have withered else in dry seasons" (*WMW* 17), the reader should guess how he did so.

Thoreau enjoyed his work as Emerson's handyman and gardener, but Emerson apparently wearied of his presence and in 1843 arranged for him to become a tutor to Emerson's nephew on Long Island (a task Thoreau did not care for, because he missed his friends and rambling in Concord woods). Thoreau often served as a surrogate father for Emerson's children while Emerson traveled on his lecture trips, and he very much enjoyed the company of Emerson's second wife, Lidian. The children loved Thoreau, for unlike their father, he would romp and play with them. Lidian, too, bonded with Thoreau, causing some scholars to suggest a romantic relationship between them. One letter of his to her from Staten Island, New York, in 1843 seems especially suggestive. He writes:

> I have only read a page of your letter, and have come out to the top of the hill at sunset, where I can see the ocean to prepare to read the rest ... You seem to me to speak out of a very clear and high heaven, where any one may be who stands so high. Your voice seems not a voice, but comes as much from the blue heavens, as from the paper ... Such a voice is for no particular time nor person, but it makes him who may hear it stand for all that is lofty and true in humanity. The thought of you will constantly elevate my life, it will be something always above the horizon to behold, as when I look up at the evening star. I think I know your thoughts without seeing you, and as well here as in Concord.
>
> (*Correspondence* 1: 195–196)

Emerson's letters to his wife, in contrast, were seldom so romantic or personal. When she suggested they should be, he wrote her from Europe, "A photometer cannot be a stove" (*Letters* 4: 33), suggesting that a seer who registers light cannot be expected to give off heat.

When Thoreau returned to Concord in 1844, he helped his father's business by devising a drilling machine that revolutionized the making of pencils. He also accidentally burned down some 300 acres of Concord woods, while camping with a friend, annoying his neighbors, who saw him watching them battle the flames after he had run to town, alerted a fire brigade, and returned to the scene. In 1845, Emerson let Thoreau build a cabin on his woodlot on the shore of Walden Pond, and in exchange, Thoreau cleared and planted an adjacent field, gave the Emersons a portion of the vegetables he grew, and agreed to sell his house back to Emerson when he left. The plan was for Thoreau to use the cabin as a study where he would write. The venture was not as original or as unusual as it sounds today, for several of Thoreau's acquaintances had tried similar retreats before, and, as previously mentioned, he had spent the summer of 1837 living in a hut on the shores of nearby Flint's

Pond with a college schoolmate. Nevertheless, Walden Pond, as a result of Thoreau's book about his life there, has become a sacred site for many. When Thoreau lived there, it was a depopulated rural area, whose previous inhabitants had been poor whites and struggling freed slaves (see Lemire).

Means of transcendence

The book Thoreau tackled first while living at the pond focused on the journey he and his brother John had taken in the summer of 1839. Thoreau never mentions his brother in *A Week on the Concord and Merrimack Rivers* or in *Walden*, but both books are impelled by an effort to overcome Thoreau's grief and to gain a sense of spiritual renewal. *A Week* is a pastoral elegy of sorts, an idyllic remembrance of the brothers' boat trip, coupled with digressions on books Henry had read and ideas they evoked. There are sections on friendship and religion, and Colonial encounters with Indians, and other topics. One of the most innovative and transcendental episodes occurs in the "Monday" chapter, when the brothers camp for the night. Thoreau tells of hearing someone playing a drum at a distance and how it transports him and reveals "the actual glory of the universe" (*Week* 174): he writes, "I see, smell, taste, hear, feel, that everlasting Something to which we are allied, at once our maker, our abode, our destiny, our very Selves" (*Week* 173). The experience seems clearly to inform his famous advice near the end of *Walden*: "If a man does not keep pace with his companions, perhaps it is because he hears a different drummer. Let him step to the music which he hears, however measured or far away" (*WMW* 261).

Thoreau delighted in all of his senses, but sound was the primary medium of his correspondence with nature. The trill of the song sparrow, the carol of the wood-thrush, the pattering of rain drops, the chirp of the cricket, the roar of wind in the trees, and even the hum of the telegraph wire, all stimulated his outward and inward senses and allowed him to achieve mystical union with a spiritual reality. As Sherman Paul has indicated, Thoreau viewed nature "as a harp at rest, like the soul, passively awaiting the divine inspiration; the vibrating harp produced the Aeolian music, the celestial harmony Thoreau heard. Both the soul and nature were harps" (520).

Just as Emerson valued the distant panoramic view as the best condition for inspiration, so Thoreau valued the distant, diffused sound. In *Walden* he explains that

> all sound heard at the greatest possible distance produces one and the same effect, a vibration of the universal lyre, just as the intervening atmosphere makes a distant ridge of earth interesting to our eyes by the azure that it imparts to it.
>
> (*WMW* 100)

Similarly, in *A Week*, while describing his moment of transcendence initiated by the beating of the distant drum, he explains that music reminds me of a passage of the Vedas, and I associate with it the idea of infinite remoteness, as well as of beauty and serenity, for to the senses that is farthest from us which addresses the greatest depth within us. It teaches us again and again to trust the remotest and finest as the divinest instinct, and makes a dream our only real experience.

(*Week* 174–175)

Ultimately, then, physical reality for Thoreau was primarily a means to an end, and while he accorded nature, including the material self, more acute and detailed attention than Emerson, he insisted upon the subordination of natural facts to spiritual facts, and particularly of Body to Soul. He was, at times, an ascetic, someone who abstained from sensual pleasures, as the "Higher Laws" chapter of *Walden* reveals. There he declares that "we are conscious of an animal in us, which awakens in proportion as our higher nature slumbers," and he goes on to proclaim that "he is blessed who is assured that the animal is dying out in him day by day, and the divine being established" (*WMW* 177–178). Despite the grumpiness found in the first half of *Walden*, where Thoreau takes his neighbors to task for their excesses with regard to food, clothing, and shelter, the second half of the book becomes more positive and features the inspiration and joy his life at the pond provided. In these chapters the reader encounters a persona, an "I," much closer to the actual Thoreau.

Close friends and young children especially found Thoreau likable and fun to be around. He took them on nature walks, played his flute for them, even dancing as he did so. There's a delightful story an observer told about Thoreau and the Emerson children coming home from a successful huckleberry-picking party. Little Edward Emerson, carrying his basket, tripped, fell, and scattered his berries on the ground, making him cry in despair. Thoreau came up, put his arm about the boy, and comforted him by telling him that Nature had planned for little boys to stumble so that more huckleberries would grow on that spot for other children to pick in the future. Edward then stopped crying and began to smile (Conway 1: 133–134).

In the second chapter of *Walden*, Thoreau declares:

I went to the woods because I wished to live deliberately, to front only the essential facts of life, and see if I could not learn what it had to teach, and not, when I came to die, discover that I had not lived.

(*WMW* 74)

He thus gives the impression that he lived an austere life, alone in nature, engaged in serious thought and action. Some students thus find it annoying to learn that Thoreau did not actually live a solitary life in the woods far from everyone, but daily walked the short distance into town to visit his family and eat dinner with them or with the Emersons or Alcotts. When it got very cold at the pond, he stayed in his room at his parents' home, where he was warm and cozy. He also had many visitors at his cabin. His friend Ellery Channing even stayed there with him several weeks in August of 1845. In other words, the "I" who relates his life in the woods in *Walden* is an idealized "Thoreau," a stoic, contemplative monk of sorts. Channing dubbed him "the holy hermit," perhaps in jest. Once one understands that the selves that all of us present to the public differ from who we actually are, assuming we can discover this, then it becomes easier to accept writings that pretend to be reliably autobiographical. Of course, the difference between two or more selves one constructs can lead to problems such as hypocrisy or deceit, which can be debilitating, as Hawthorne shows in *The Scarlet Letter* (1851).

Walden (1854)

Although Thoreau lived at the pond for two years and two months, *Walden* condenses his experiences to one year, a cycle of the seasons. The book began as an account told to his neighbors about what life was like living in the woods and why he was there. Over the years, he added to this account, drawing from journal entries written even after he left the pond. In a book called *The Making of "Walden"*, the scholar Lynden J. Shanley traces seven different versions of the book, and notes that Thoreau even made corrections in his printed copy, which was published in 1854. In the sense that he persistently sought to improve his manuscript, Thoreau resembled the artist of Kouroo, described in his "Conclusion" as creating a whole new world by taking the time to make a perfect staff:

> As he made no compromise with Time, Time kept out of his way, and only sighed at a distance because he could not overcome him ... When the finishing stroke was put to his work, it suddenly expanded before the eyes of the astonished artist into the fairest of all the creations of Brahma. He had made a new system in making a staff, a world with full and fair proportions; in which, though the old cities and dynasties had passed away, fairer and more glorious ones had taken their places. And now he saw by the heap of shavings still fresh at his feet, that, for him and his work, the former lapse of time had been an illusion, and that no more time had elapsed than is required for a single scintillation from the brain of Brahma to fall on and inflame the tinder of a mortal brain. The material was pure, and his art was pure; how could the result be other than wonderful?
> (*WMW* 262–263)

No scholar has found a source for this wonderful fable, and it most likely allegorizes Thoreau's writing of his book. If you have worked intently and long on any project, you probably understand the subjectivity it describes.

The opening chapters of *Walden* come across as rather self-righteous as Thoreau chides his neighbors for their materialism, their getting and spending, and their failure to distinguish between wants and needs, the trivial and the profound; however, he gradually shifts his emphasis from chiding his neighbors to tracing his own spiritual development. *Walden* begins, like Emerson's *Nature*, with practical facts, answers to such questions as What kind of house did he build? What did it cost? What did he eat? What did he do there? His first chapter, the longest, titled "Economy," tries to answer these questions, focusing on food, clothing, shelter, and his belief in keeping these as simple as possible. In the process, he criticizes the luxuries his neighbors take for necessities. You have probably heard the famous quotation, "simplify, simplify, simplify." That is the idea he sets out to argue for, often taking it to humorous extremes. His business, he puns, is with the celestial empire (by which he means not China, as his readers may have assumed, but Heaven above).

In the second chapter of the book, "Where I Lived, and What I Lived For," he uses the metaphor of being struck by a sword, "a cimeter" (also spelled scimitar), to explain the effect of penetrating the illusions that surround us:

> If you stand right fronting and face to face to a fact, you will see the sun glimmer on both its surfaces, as if it were a cimeter, and feel its sweet edge dividing you through the heart and marrow, and so you will happily conclude your mortal career. Be it life or death, we crave only reality.
>
> (*WMW* 80)

In other words, to confront ultimate Reality is like being overcome by the presence of the divine. Thoreau's observation echoes moments of divine revelation found in Christian and Hindu texts in traditional religions. For example, there's a sculpture by Gian Lorenzo Bernini called *The Ecstasy of Saint Teresa* (1647–1652), showing an angel piercing the heart of Saint Teresa that captures such a visionary moment. As Teresa herself described it:

> In his hands I saw a great golden spear, and at the iron tip there appeared to be a point of fire. This he plunged into my heart several times so that it penetrated to my entrails. When he pulled it out I felt that he took them with it, and left me utterly consumed by the great love of God.
>
> (210)

Similarly, in one of Thoreau's favorite books, the *Bhagavad Gita*, the poet describes the moment the god Krishna, pretending to be a mere charioteer, reveals himself and becomes "a supreme and heavenly form; of many a mouth and eye; many a wondrous sight; many a heavenly ornament; many an upraised weapon" (Wilkins 90) and the effect is that of the sun rising into the heavens with a thousand times more than usual brightness. The vision stuns and frightens the young warrior Arjoon, but it represents, as does Thoreau's scimitar metaphor, the experience of a divine revelation.

An argument for revelation through contemplation runs throughout *Walden*, especially in the "Sounds" chapter, where Thoreau sits for hours on his doorstep and just listens. "I grew in those seasons like corn in the night" (*WMW* 91), he declares. The metaphor suggests the silent, slow, almost invisible way in which spiritual growth can occur. The central chapter of the book, "Ponds," marks the division between nature and spirit, earth and heaven, and provides a wonderful analogy for the transcendental experience through an account of midnight fishing. Thoreau floats along in his boat, throwing his hook down into the water below, yet its reflection makes it seem as if it drops into the sky above.

> It was very queer, especially in dark nights, when your thoughts had wandered to vast and cosmogonal themes in other spheres, to feel this faint jerk, which came to interrupt your dreams and link you to Nature again ... Thus I caught two fishes as it were with one hook.
> (*WMW* 143)

That is, he took home as his catch actual fish as well as profound thoughts.

Thoreau was very attracted to Eastern philosophy, and by the ideas found in sacred texts such as the *Gita* and the *Vedas*, religious texts from ancient India. He works ideas from them into a number of chapters of *Walden*, especially those near the end, "The Pond in Winter," "Spring," and "Conclusion." The borrowings allow him to suggest how an understanding of nature leads to an understanding of one's self and of that which is divine, or Real, with a capital "R." The final chapters use anecdotes, fables, and natural facts to convey how a spiritual awakening marks the possibility of new life, in this world and the next. In his "Conclusion," he relates the story of a bug in an old table of apple-tree wood, which, warmed by the heat of an urn, gnawed its way out and came forth as a beautiful winged creature. "Who does not feel his faith in a resurrection and immortality strengthened by hearing of this?" (*WMW* 267), he asks.

The Maine Woods (1864) and *Cape Cod* (1865)

Thoreau has been categorized as a mystic and as a naturalist; in *Walden*, the reader finds a unique combination of the two. As Thoreau grew older, especially after he realized his writings would not achieve commercial success, he devoted more time and effort to his journal entries, many of them weighted with scientific observations. It has been argued that beginning around 1851, he began to consider his journal his major work, more important even than his published books. At this time, he stopped removing leaves from the journal to use in lectures or essays.

Although Thoreau spent much of his life in Concord, he did take walking tours with friends, and he wrote two other books about his travels, *The Maine Woods* (1864) and *Cape Cod* (1865), both edited by his devoted sister Sophia and published posthumously. The first is based on three trips he took to Maine, in 1846, 1853, and 1857. Scholars have been most interested in how the trips reveal his evolving attitude toward nature and toward the native Penobscot Indians, who were hired as guides on the trips. In the first section of *The Maine Woods*, a fascinating moment occurs when Thoreau is shocked out of his sense of union with nature near the top of Mount Katahdin, which he finds "vast, Titanic, and such as man never inhabits" (*WMW* 320). Coming down the mountain and passing an area of burned over land, he is moved to declare:

> I stand in awe of my body, this matter to which I am bound has become so strange to me ... What is this Titan that has possession of me? Talk of mysteries!—Think of our life in nature,—daily to be shown matter, to come in contact with it,—rocks, trees, wind on our cheeks! The *solid* earth! The actual world! The *common sense! Contact! Contact! Who* are we? *Where* are we?
>
> (*WMW* 326)

Critics have disagreed about whether the passage describes a traumatic experience or a sublime one. Because he wrote about the experience at his desk after the fact, it is probable he sought to suggest its sublimity (Hoag 32–36). In either case, it is a unique moment in Thoreau's writings.

In the opening sections of *The Maine Woods*, Thoreau regards the Native Americans he encounters with mild contempt and condescension. On his third trip, however, he comes to revere his Penobscot Indian guide Joe Polis, who becomes a heroic figure in Thoreau's eyes, based on his character and skills. At one point he even compares Polis to the Greek god Prometheus, the former of man and fire-giver in classical mythology. Thoreau and Polis agree to share knowledge (though Joe withholds some at times to tease Thoreau), and Thoreau learned not only Indian lore but so many new words that he constructed a "List of Indian Words" to be included as an appendix to his book. Thoreau's interest in Native Americans was lifelong. He and his brother John played Indians as young men and addressed each other as braves. Thoreau even imagined himself an Indian at times, and at his death, he had more than 2,800 pages of handwritten notes and quotations in his "Indian Books," which remain unpublished. Scholars do not know for certain what he planned to do with this material, beyond drawing upon it for *The Maine Woods*.

Whereas *Walden* features an environmental consciousness that merges the self with a deep and pure body of water, *The Maine Woods* takes narrator and reader into more rugged and alienating scenes. Throughout the later book, Thoreau expresses sympathy and respect for the land and its wild animals, especially moose, who are wantonly killed for their hides. In his account of his second trip to Maine titled "Chesuncook," he writes about his revulsion at his Indian guide's wounding and killing a cow moose, whose calf runs away. Thoreau describes her butchering:

> a tragical business it was; to see that still warm and palpitating body pierced with a knife, to see the warm milk stream from the rent udder, and the ghastly naked red carcass appearing from within its seemly robe, which was made to *hide* it.
>
> (*WMW* 360)

Soon afterward he relates,

> Other white men and Indians who come here are for the most part hunters, whose object is to slay as many moose and other wild animals as possible. But, pray, could not one spend some weeks or years in the solitude of this vast wilderness with other employments than these—employments perfectly sweet and innocent and ennobling? For one that comes with a pencil to sketch or sing, a thousand come with an axe or rifle. What a coarse and imperfect use Indians and hunters make of Nature!
> (*WMW* 364)

Thoreau especially laments the widescale logging of the stately white pines, valued for their use as masts on sailing ships.

When he sent "Chesuncook" to the 1858 *Atlantic Monthly*, the editor, James Russell Lowell, accepted the essay but removed a sentence without Thoreau's permission, apparently finding it sacrilegious. The sentence about the pine tree reads, "It is as immortal as I am, and perchance will go to as high a heaven, there to tower above me still" (*WMW* 365), thus equating human claims upon the sacred with those of the natural world. Thoreau returned the proofs, indicating the sentence should be left in, but Lowell removed it again, and when Thoreau received the published essay, he angrily observed that the omission was "very mean and cowardly" (*CHDT* 515), and he refused to deal with Lowell subsequently.

Thoreau has often been praised as a keen naturalist and an influential proto-environmentalist. This "green Thoreau," who so obviously advocated protecting the wilderness and its non-human species, has been both praised and criticized. His admirers have used his example in support of both local and global environmental projects. Yet some critics have dismissed Thoreau's reverence for the natural world and attacked his failure to realize the social and global consequences of privileging the non-human. At times, Thoreau's individualism, his love of nature, and his disdain for the mass of mankind, has run counter to the goals of those environmentalists committed to environmental and economic justice. For example, the protection of wildlife, even predators, can harm those whose farms and livestock suffer as a result. Despite his critics, Thoreau will remain a canonical figure, as Lawrence Buell has pointed out: "If literary history is to be reimagined under the sign of environment, Thoreau will certainly continue to be one of the key points of reference, even by those who expose his feet of clay" (*Environmental Imagination* 367).

Three years after his first trip to Maine and the climbing of Mount Katahdin, Thoreau visited Cape Cod with his friend Ellery Channing. He would visit the Cape two more times, and his posthumous book *Cape Cod* (1865) combines the three trips into one narrative. There are a number of pleasant descriptions and humorous tales in the book, especially one featuring an old Wellfleet oysterman who regales Thoreau and Channing at breakfast, while occasionally spitting near or on their food baking on the hearth. Thoreau recalls,

I ate of the apple-sauce and the doughnuts, which I thought had sustained the least detriment from the old man's shots, but my companion refused the apple-sauce, and ate of the hot cake and green beans, which had appeared to him to occupy the safest part of the hearth. But on comparing notes afterward, I told him that the buttermilk cake was particularly exposed, and I saw how it suffered repeatedly, and therefore I avoided it; but he declared that, however that might be, he witnessed that the apple-sauce was seriously injured, and had therefore declined that.

(*Cape Cod* 77–78)

Despite such light-hearted moments in *Cape Cod*, considerable death and destruction are featured, which represents a new development in Thoreau's relation to nature. The first chapter, "The Wreck," has echoes of the "Ktaadn [*sic*]" section of *The Maine Woods*, for he describes how the ocean has caused a shipwreck and cast corpses upon the shore which relatives must claim. He describes in detail the "livid, swollen and mangled body of a drowned girl—who probably had intended to go out to service in some American family" (*Cape Cod* 5).

In 1850, before he completed *Cape Cod*, Thoreau had gone to Fire Island, New York, at Emerson's request, to find the body of their friend Margaret Fuller along with her belongings, for she, her husband, and their child had just died in a shipwreck as they returned from Europe. Their ship had been caught in a hurricane and run aground and broken to pieces in sight of the shore. Although Thoreau never found Fuller's body, he incorporated his experience of looking for it into a chapter in *Cape Cod*, and there tried to argue for detachment from such human tragedy. Like Emerson in "Experience," Thoreau sought, sometimes successfully, sometimes not, to rise above worldly events, including death and destruction, in order to focus on matters of the spirit. After finding a button from Fuller's husband Count Ossoli, he wrote in a letter to a friend,

Held up, it intercepts the light,—an actual button,—and yet all the life it is connected with is less substantial to me, and interests me less, than my faintest dream. Our thoughts are the epochs in our lives: all else is but as a journal of the winds that blew while we were here.

(*CHDT* 265)

While this may seem unfeeling, Thoreau wanted to believe, like Emerson, that the mind is an active, not a passive agent, in the world we experience through our senses.

Transcendentalism and slavery

Politics, especially the slavery controversy, was one issue Thoreau could not consistently rise above. The summer of 1844 was a turning point for the Transcendentalists, for not only was Thoreau preparing to undertake his experiment in living at Walden Pond, but Fuller, visiting in Concord, was about to go to New York City and begin a career as a columnist for Horace Greeley's *New-York Tribune*. Meanwhile, the Concord Female Anti-Slavery Society had arranged for a major event to take place in the town, on August 1, a celebration of the tenth anniversary of emancipation of slaves in the British West Indies. They had persuaded Emerson to participate as a speaker, along with the former slave Frederick Douglass, the abolitionist Samuel May, and others. Although Emerson, Thoreau, Fuller, and Alcott had kept their distance from the abolitionists, finding them too fanatical in their devotion to the immediate abolition of slavery, they were becoming more sympathetic to the movement. Lidian Emerson, Thoreau's mother and two sisters, plus other women in Concord had become activists after a visit of two Southern abolitionists, Sarah and Angelina Grimké.

Leading members of Concord were opposed to any abolitionist meeting because the abolitionists were viewed as too fanatical and too critical of Christian defenders of slavery. Although the ministers in Concord refused to allow a church to be used for the meeting, Hawthorne, who lived at the Manse and had become friends with Emerson, Thoreau, Fuller, and others, offered the use of his yard. It rained on the day of the meeting, so the decision was made to hold the meeting in the courthouse. No one would ring the Unitarian meetinghouse bell to announce the event, so Thoreau entered and did it himself. The event proved inspirational. Fuller, in particular, was impressed with Emerson's speech, writing in her journal, "It was true happiness to hear him; tears came to my eyes ... I felt excited to new life and a nobler emulation by Waldo this day" ("The Impulses of Human Nature" 107).

Emerson's 1844 anti-slavery address has gained the attention of many scholars in recent years. It combines support of social activism, which he had tried to avoid, with his own ideas about the power of the intellect to change the world one inhabits. The success that the British had getting rid of slavery in their West Indian plantations in 1833 was the occasion of the event, but obviously many New Englanders believed that the United States needed to follow Britain's example. So the talks on August 1, 1844 in Concord celebrated West Indian emancipation on the one hand and argued against slavery in the Southern United States on the other. Emerson's essay is filled with praise, sarcasm, outrage, hope, and prophecy. "There is a blessed necessity," he declares, "by which the interest of men is always driving them to the right; and, again, making all crime mean and ugly" (*AW* 33).

Emerson had been impressed with Frederick Douglass, the fugitive slave from Virginia who had become a well-known abolitionist lecturer. In his journal, Emerson praised him as the Anti-Slave. (Emerson had a low opinion of black people in general, as did most white citizens at the time.) He included the figure of the Anti-Slave in his talk, but without mentioning Douglass by name. Afterward, Emerson wrote Thomas Carlyle, who was an ardent racist, and told him he felt ashamed of having gone public with his speech:

> Though I sometimes accept a popular call, & preach on Temperance or the Abolition of slavery, as lately on the First of August, I am sure to feel before I have done with it, what an intrusion it is into another sphere & so much loss of virtue in my own.
>
> (Carlyle 2: 85)

It is hard to tell if Emerson meant this or was just adapting his remarks to Carlyle's prejudices, which he tended to do with some persons. Thoreau, who was in the audience that day, made sure to take the lecture to the printers in Boston, and he and members of the Female Anti-Slavery Society distributed it widely. The abolitionists were elated that Emerson seemed to have joined their ranks. Two years later, on August 1, 1846, Thoreau hosted the meeting of the Society at his hut near Walden Pond.

In 1846, Thoreau became quite distressed when he learned that the United States government had annexed Texas and gone to war with Mexico. Like many others in the North, he saw this as an attempt to extend slavery territory. In protest, he refused to pay his poll tax, spent a night in jail, and then lectured and wrote about his experience. His essay known as "Civil Disobedience" has become an inspiration to those practicing civil disobedience to protest injustice, including Mahatma Gandhi and Martin Luther King. Although the essay seems rather radical, and Thoreau has been seen as an anarchist, he does not declare in the essay that he favors no government, but rather, that he wants a better one. He also does not suggest that one break all those laws one finds unjust, but just those that oblige you to harm another. As he puts it,

> If I have unjustly wrested a plank from a drowning man, I must restore it to him though I drown myself. This, according to Paley, would be inconvenient. But he that would save his life, in such a case, shall lose it. This people must cease to hold slaves, and to make war on Mexico, though it cost them their existence as a people.
>
> (*WMW* 733)

Perhaps the greatest misinterpretation of the essay has to do with the reading of it as supporting only passive resistance. While refusing to pay one's taxes is indeed non-violent and passive, notice that Thoreau does not rule out resorting to bloodshed, for he believes there are some things worse. As he puts it, "Is there not a sort of blood shed when the conscience is wounded? Through this wound a man's real manhood and immortality flow out, and he bleeds to an everlasting death. I see this blood flowing now" (*WMW* 740). Some ten years later, in 1859, when John Brown shed blood at Harpers Ferry in an attempt to free slaves, Thoreau praised his efforts.

Emerson also opposed the Mexican War, yet he believed that in the long run, it would not matter how Anglo-Saxon racial superiority triumphed, because he saw it as inevitable. In a journal entry of 1844, he observed,

It is very certain that the strong British race which have now overrun so much of this continent, must also overrun that tract [Texas], & Mexico & Oregon also, and it will in the course of ages be of small import by what particular occasions & methods it was done. It is a secular question.

(*JMN* 9: 74)

Later, in an 1860 essay "Considerations by the Way," he observed with regard to the expansion of the United States, "most of the great results of history are brought about by discreditable means" (*Essays & Lectures* 1085).

Activism

During the 1850s, both Emerson and Thoreau became less serene about the state of the nation and more and more engaged in the anti-slavery movement, mainly because of the passage of the Compromise of 1850, containing the Fugitive Slave Act, which required those in the North to assist in the capture of fugitive slaves, or face a $1000 fine and six months in prison. Almost everyone in the North found the Fugitive Slave Act offensive, yet it passed in Congress because many found it a necessary evil to prevent Southern succession and civil war. There were also a number of wealthy investors who supported the Compromise because it was in their financial interest. The industrial mills that turned out clothing needed cheap Southern cotton provided through slave labor. The employees in the mills were poorly paid women, and the male owners were allied to the Whig party and known as "Cotton Whigs." Their political leader was Daniel Webster, a United States senator from Massachusetts.

Despite opposition, the Fugitive Slave Act passed 109–76 in the House, 27–12 in the Senate. Afterward, Emerson gave several speeches expressing his outrage and attacking Webster. In his journal, he fumed, "The word *liberty* in the mouth of Mr. Webster sounds like the word *love* in the mouth of a courtezan" (*JMN* 11: 346). Thoreau expressed his outrage in his journal when the first fugitive slave case occurred, involving Thomas Sims, a fugitive from Georgia who was arrested in Boston on April 12, 1851 and taken under armed guard to a ship in Boston Harbor. Upon arrival in Savannah, Georgia, he was flogged in the public square. Thoreau felt deep contempt for the state and local officials who participated in the remission of Sims, and in his journal wrote,

> I wish you to consider this who the man was—whether he was Jesus christ [*sic*] or another—for in as much as ye did it unto the least of these his brethren ye did it unto him. Do you think *he* would have stayed here in *liberty* and let the black man go into slavery in his stead?
>
> (*Journal* 3: 203)

Several years later, in 1854, another fugitive slave, Anthony Burns, was arrested in Boston and returned to his Virginia owner, with federal troops taking him down to the harbor to the awaiting ship, as almost all of Boston silently protested with black flags draped from the windows of office buildings. On July 4 of that year, Thoreau gave a fiery speech expressing his shame at his government and his desire to blow it to bits. The speech was published as "Slavery in Massachusetts," and the slavery it refers to is the way in which the South had enslaved the people of Massachusetts by making them participate in returning fugitives. In a startling statement in his journal, Thoreau raged,

> Rather than thus consent to establish Hell upon earth—to be a party to this establishment—I would touch a match to blow up earth & hell together. I will not accept life in America or on this planet on such terms.
> (*Journal* 8: 165–166)

That fall, *Walden* was published, and Sandra Harbert Petrulionis has argued that "Slavery in Massachusetts" would have been even more radical, if Thoreau had not wanted to protect sales of his book.

Defending John Brown

Throughout the 1850s, Thoreau, Emerson, and other Transcendentalists they knew, including Alcott, Thomas Wentworth Higginson, and Theodore Parker, became more and more willing to condone violence in the fight against slavery. A group of six men, including Higginson and Parker, became supporters of John Brown, the famous abolitionist who would lead a raid on the federal arsenal at Harpers Ferry, Virginia in the fall of 1859. Although Brown was captured and hanged, along with many of his men, a number of Southern states began forming armed militias and saw themselves under threat of invasion by radicals in the North. Emerson and Thoreau gave speeches in support of Brown, and the publicity generated gave the impression that indeed the entire North was ready to go to war to end slavery.

The Transcendentalists celebrated Brown as a contemporary saint and viewed his actions as responding to what they called "a higher law"; that is, God's law, as opposed to the laws of the land. In Emerson's two short speeches about Brown, he presents him as an illustrious patriot, not unlike Emerson himself. "I do not wonder," he says, "that gentlemen find traits of relation readily between him and themselves" (*AW* 117). For Emerson, Brown is an idealist and a gentleman, adding, "For what is the oath of gentle blood and knighthood? What but to protect the weak and lowly against the strong oppressor?" (*AW* 123). Thoreau's blistering speech "A Plea for Captain John Brown" is more extensive and animated. Written at breakneck speed, in October 1859, it is almost breathless in its urgency, and filled with anger, disgust, defiance, and adoration. "Some eighteen hundred years ago Christ was crucified," he declares, "this morning, perchance, Captain Brown was hung. These are the two ends of a chain which is not without its links" (*WMW* 942). Alcott in his journal was one of the first to point out the similarities between Thoreau and Brown: "[They] have much in common: the sturdy manliness, straight-forwardness and independence" (*Journals*, 321). One could add that they were fellow surveyors, natives of New England, men of Spartan habits, and admirers of Oliver Cromwell. In many respects, Thoreau's "Plea" can also be read as a defense of his own nonconformity and sanctity, especially when he describes Brown as "A man of rare common sense and directness of speech, as of action; a transcendentalist above all, a man of ideas and principles,—that was what distinguished him" (*WMW* 925).

Conclusion

Emerson once said that his writings all put forth "one doctrine, namely, the infinitude of the private man" (*JMN* 7: 342), and in *Nature* and his other essays, one finds variations on this theme, which is one reason readers find his writings so uplifting, so encouraging. He writes about individualism and self-reliance, not because he is advocating selfishness or egotism (though he has been misinterpreted as doing such), but rather because he believed that first one had to elevate one's self before trying to do good for others. Thoreau shared this belief, which is why he, too, has been criticized as self-centered and anti-social, even though his writings have exerted a lasting influence on the struggle for civil rights in the United States, India, and elsewhere. His contribution to environmental consciousness has also attained sway across the planet. Although both Emerson and Thoreau supported the righteous violence of John Brown, they later became more moderate, expressing admiration for Brown's commitment to the ideal of freedom, rather than for the actions of the man himself.

Suggestions for further reading

Buell, Lawrence. *Emerson*. Cambridge, MA: Belknap Press of Harvard University Press, 2003.

Howarth, William L. *The Book of Concord: Thoreau's Life as a Writer*. New York: Viking, 1982.

McAleer, John. *Ralph Waldo Emerson: Days of Encounter*. Boston: Little, Brown, 1984.

Matteson, John. *Eden's Outcasts: The Story of Louisa May Alcott and Her Father*. New York: Norton, 2008.

Packer, Barbara L. *The Transcendentalists*. Athens, GA: University of Georgia Press, 2007.

Petrulionis, Sandra Harbert. *To Set This World Right: The Antislavery Movement in Thoreau's Concord*. Ithaca, NY: Cornell University Press, 2006.

Richardson, Robert D. *Emerson: The Mind on Fire*. Berkeley: University of California Press, 1995.

References

Alcott, Amos Bronson. "Days from a Diary." *Dial* 2 (April 1842): 409–436.

Alcott, Amos Bronson. *The Journals of Bronson Alcott*. Ed. Odell Shepard. Boston: Little Brown, 1938.

Buell, Lawrence. *The Environmental Imagination: Thoreau, Nature Writing, and the Formation of American Culture*. Cambridge, MA: Belknap Press of Harvard University Press, 1995.

Buell, Lawrence. "Introduction." *The American Transcendentalists: Essential Writings*. Ed. Lawrence Buell. New York: Modern Library, 2006. xi–xxviii.

Carlyle, Thomas. *The Correspondence of Thomas Carlyle and Ralph Waldo Emerson: 1834–1872*. 2 vols. London: Chatto & Windus, 1883.

Cole, Phyllis. *Mary Moody Emerson and the Origins of Transcendentalism: A Family History*. New York: Oxford University Press, 1998.

Conway, Moncure Daniel. *Autobiography: Memories and Experiences of Moncure Daniel Conway*. 2 vols. London: Cassell, 1904.

Crary, Jonathan. *Techniques of the Observer: On Vision and Modernity in the Nineteenth Century*. Cambridge, MA: MIT Press, 1990.

Emerson, Ralph Waldo. *Collected Poems & Translations*. New York: Library of America, 1994.

Emerson, Ralph Waldo. *Complete Sermons of Ralph Waldo Emerson*. 4 vols. Ed. Albert J. von Frank et al. Columbia: University of Missouri Press, 1989–1992.

Emerson, Ralph Waldo. *Emerson's Antislavery Writings*. Eds. Len Gougeon and Joel Myerson. New Haven: Yale University Press, 1995. Abbreviated AW.

Emerson, Ralph Waldo. *Essays & Lectures*. New York: Library of America, 1983.

Emerson, Ralph Waldo. *The Journals and Miscellaneous Notebooks of Ralph Waldo Emerson*. Ed. William H. Gilman, Ralph H. Orth, et al. 16 vols. Cambridge, MA: Belknap Press of Harvard University Press, 1960–1982. Abbreviated JMN.

Emerson, Ralph Waldo. *The Letters of Ralph Waldo Emerson*. Eds. Ralph L. Rusk and Eleanor M. Tilton. 10 vols. New York: Columbia University Press, 1939–1995.

Emerson, Ralph Waldo. "Thoreau." *Ralph Waldo Emerson and Margaret Fuller: Selected Works*. Ed. John Carlos Rowe. Boston: Houghton Mifflin, 2003. 264–280.

Fuller, Margaret. "'The Impulses of Human Nature': Margaret Fuller's Journal from June through October 1844." Eds. Martha L. Berg and Alice de V. Perry. *Massachusetts Historical Society Proceedings* 102 (1990): 38–126.

Fuller, Margaret. *"These Sad but Glorious Days": Dispatches from Europe, 1846–1850*. Eds. Larry J. Reynolds and Susan Belasco Smith. New Haven: Yale University Press, 1991. Abbreviated SGD.

Hale, Edward Everett. *Ralph Waldo Emerson: Together with Two Early Essays of Emerson*. Boston: American Unitarian Association, 1902.

Hawthorne, Nathaniel. *The Centenary Edition of the Works of Nathaniel Hawthorne*. Ed. William Charvat et al., 23 vols. Columbus: Ohio State University Press, 1962–1997. Abbreviated CE and volume number.

Hawthorne, Nathaniel. *Tales and Sketches*. New York: Library of America, 1982.

Hoag, Ronald Weley. "The Mark on the Wilderness: Thoreau's Contact with Ktaadn." *Texas Studies in Literature and Language* 24 (Spring 1982): 23–46.

Holmes, Oliver. *Ralph Waldo Emerson, John Lothrop Motley*. Boston: Houghton, 1906.

Lemire, Elise. *Black Walden: Slavery and Its Aftermath in Concord, Massachusetts*. Philadelphia: University of Pennsylvania Press, 2009.

Matthiessen, F. O. *The American Renaissance: Art and Expression in the Age of Emerson and Whitman*. New York: Oxford University Press, 1941.

Melville, Herman. *The Melville Log: A Documentary Life of Herman Melville, 1819–1891*. Ed. Jay Leyda. 2 vols. New York: Harcourt, Brace, 1951.

Milder, Robert. "The American Scholar as Cultural Event." *Prospects* 16 (1991): 119–147.

Miller, Perry. "From Edwards to Emerson." 1940. Rpt. *Ralph Waldo Emerson: A Collection of Critical Essays*. Ed. Lawrence Buell. Englewood Cliffs, NJ: Prentice Hall, 1993. 13–31.

Paul, Sherman. "The Wise Silence: Sound as the Agency of Correspondence in Thoreau." *New England Quarterly* 22 (1949): 511–527.

Shanley, J. Lyndon. *The Making of "Walden": With the Text of the First Version*. Chicago: University of Chicago Press, 1957.

Teresa of Avila. *The Life of Saint Teresa of Avila by Herself*. Trans. J. M. Cohen. New York: Penguin, 1988.

Thoreau, Henry David. *Cape Cod*. Ed. Joseph J. Moldenhauer. Princeton: Princeton University Press, 1988.

Thoreau, Henry David. *The Correspondence of Henry David Thoreau*. Eds. Walter Harding and Carl Bode. New York: New York University Press, 1968. Abbreviated CHDT.

Thoreau, Henry David. *The Correspondence. Vol 1: 1834–1848*. Ed. Robert N. Hudspeth. Princeton: Princeton University Press, 2013.

Thoreau, Henry David. *Journal. Vol. 2. 1842–1848*. Ed. Robert Sattelmeyer. Princeton: Princeton University Press, 1984.

Thoreau, Henry David. *Journal. Vol. 3. 1848–1851*. Eds. Robert Sattelmeyer, Mark R. Patterson, and William Rossi. Princeton: Princeton University Press, 1990.

Thoreau, Henry David. *Journal Vol. 8. 1854*. Ed. Sandra Harbert Petrulionis. Princeton: Princeton University Press, 2002.

Thoreau, Henry David. *A Week on the Concord and Merrimack Rivers*. Eds. Carl F. Hovde, William L. Howarth, and Elizabeth Hall Witherell. Princeton: Princeton University Press, 1980.

Thoreau, Henry David. *Walden, The Maine Woods, and Collected Essays & Poems*. College Edition. New York: Library of America, 2007. Abbreviated WMW.

Walls, Laura Dassow. *Henry David Thoreau: A Life*. Chicago: University of Chicago Press, 2017.

West, Michael. "Scatology and Eschatology: The Heroic Dimensions of Thoreau's Wordplay." *PMLA* 89 (1974): 1043–1064.

Wilkins, Charles, Trans. *The Bhagvat-Gita*. 1785. Rpt. Gainesville, FL: Scholars' Facsimiles & Reprints, 1959.

3 Fuller, Fern, and women's rights

Over the past fifty years, Margaret Fuller (1810–1850) has become an established figure in the American Renaissance, due not only to her central role in the transcendental movement, but also to her influence on United States cultural and political history. Her *Woman in the Nineteenth Century* (1845) is widely regarded as a founding text of the women's rights movement, and her journalism for the *New-York Tribune* has been credited with inspiring a number of social reform movements. More recently, Fanny Fern (born Sara Payson Willis) (1811–1872) has made her way into the American Renaissance, at least in the opinion of many scholars. Her popular columns and her best-selling novel *Ruth Hall: A Domestic Tale of the Present Time* (1855), feature dramatic examples of the oppression of women by men and complement the earlier work of Fuller and other feminists. Both Fuller and Fern established new, distinctive models of womanhood and advanced the cause of women's social and political equality. In the process, they created literary works that remain surprisingly relevant to social and political issues of the twenty-first century.

During the antebellum period, as the United States transformed from an agrarian-artisanal society to a commercial and early industrial one, new possibilities opened up for women; however, as Carroll Smith-Rosenberg has pointed out, the new freedoms met strong resistance as men "developed elaborate justifications for women's separateness and inferiority, clothed in the new language of science and biology" (159). A common male assertion was that women were naturally emotional beings and that only men possessed the reason and restraint necessary to succeed outside the home. As a result, a preponderance of single, educated women either became teachers and tutors or remained at home, often caring for their parents. If they were single, uneducated, and poor, they sought work as servants, seamstresses, mill workers, and worse. In almost all cases, women were denied the rights and opportunities afforded men. In Fern's newspaper column "The Working-Girls of New York" (1867), she gives a powerful account of the miserable lives of the young women who work in an urban factory, with no opportunity to better their lives. She asks the reader to

> follow them to the large, black-looking building, where several hundred of them are manufacturing hoop-skirts ... You could not stay five minutes

DOI: 10.4324/9781315751627-3

in that room, where the noise of the machinery used is so deafening, that only by the motion of the lips could you comprehend a person speaking. Five minutes! Why, these young creatures bear it, from seven in the morning till six in the evening; week after week, month after month, with only half an hour at midday to eat their dinner of a slice of bread and butter or an apple ... Pitiful! Pitiful, you almost sob to yourself, as you look at these young girls. *Young?* Alas! It is only in years that they are young.

(Fern 348)

This account is but one example of Fern's disclosing the invisible misery of oppressed women.

While Fuller and Fern both advocated social equality for women, they were not political activists, in the sense that they did not join organizations, attend meetings, give speeches, or participate in organized political activities. Instead, they sought to advance reform through their writings and, in Fuller's case, through her Boston "Conversations," held during the winters of 1839–1844. Drawing upon the European model of salon culture, Fuller wrote to a friend that she envisioned the Conversations as a "point of union to well-educated and thinking women in a city which ... boasts at present nothing of the kind" (*Letters* 2: 86). Led by Fuller, the group of twenty-five to thirty women explored ethics, religion, education, Greek and Roman mythology, and questions about human nature, especially what it meant to be a woman and how a woman should live her life. In the second year of the Conversations, men were invited, but the experiment proved fraught, for obvious reasons, and the invitation was not extended again.

Although Fuller and Fern were born a year apart, Fuller achieved literary success before 1850, the year she died, while Fern did not begin her writing career in earnest until the spring of 1851, and she continued writing until her death in 1872. The two women, who apparently never met, both had domineering fathers and supportive mothers; both came from middle-class families and received private schooling; both were intellectually adventuresome and skeptical of organized religion; both suffered financially and psychologically at the hands of men; and both gained wide audiences by becoming professional journalists employed by newspapers in New York City.

The key distinctions between the two women were primarily behavioral. Fuller was a voracious reader, someone deeply interested in intellectual history and the work of major authors throughout the world. Her interests were international and global in scope, and she thrived on travel and cultural diversity. She was reading Latin and Greek by the age of nine, and as a young adult, assisted male friends attending Harvard with their studies. She also acquired an enthusiasm for German literature, and her first major publication was a translation of *Eckermann's Conversations with Goethe* (1839). Fern, on the other hand, had more local interests and excelled as a keen observer of the social life around her, not only of individuals with their humorous habits and speech, but also of all the material objects that one encountered indoors and out. Like Walt

Whitman, whom she championed, she was fascinated by the concrete world of people and things, and these often shone with significance in her writings. Fuller, while engaged by human relations, had a strong mystical bent, and her stories and poems are filled with visionary romantic imagery. Fern was more of a realist, who described her observations with a sharp ironic wit.

Fern delighted in revealing how ridiculous certain romantic notions were, especially when it came to landing a perfect husband. Her column "Aunt Hetty on Matrimony" (1851) features a wise older woman who explains that love is a farce, matrimony a humbug, and husbands domestic tyrants. Aunt Hetty warns,

> Think of carrying eight or nine children through the measles, chicken pox, rash, mumps, and scarlet fever … Oh, you may scrimp and save, and twist and turn, and dig and delve, and economise *and die*, and your husband will marry again, take what you have saved to dress his second wife with, and she'll take your portrait for a fireboard.
>
> (Fern 221)

Fern's "Hints to Young Wives" (1852) likewise satirizes the "poor little innocent fool" who dotes on her husband and thereby becomes his house servant whom he ignores, snubs, and cheats on with other women.

Fuller also wrote about naïve young women and obtuse husbands satirically, but some young women she saw as hopeless:

> you whose whole character is tainted with vanity, inherited or taught, who have early learnt the love of coquettish excitement, and whose eyes rove restlessly in search of a "conquest" or a "beau." You who are ashamed *not* to be seen by others the mark of the most contemptuous flattery or injurious desire. To such I do not speak.
>
> (*WNC* 79)

Fuller emphasized the power and influence unmarried women had achieved throughout human history. The main targets of her hostility, however, at least in her later years, were not husbands, but political leaders such as Pope Pius IX and Louis Napoleon, whom she charged with crimes against the people under their sway.

Fuller's career

Fuller has often been described as a Romantic, and her life was filled with fascinating and unusual features. As a result, her biography has gained as much attention as her writings. During the past twenty-five years, eight major biographies of her have appeared, all quite impressive. Most begin with her own autobiographical sketch, written in 1840–1841, in which she explained how her father treated her as a son and made severe demands upon her with regard to her early education, which generated considerable psychological stress. She describes herself as "a victim of spectral illusions, nightmare, and somnambulism [sleep walking], which at the time prevented the harmonious development of my bodily powers and checked my growth, while, later, they induced continual headache, weakness and nervous affections, of all kinds" (*WNC* 144). Fuller felt, in retrospect at least, that her father harmed her natural development. In *Woman in the Nineteenth Century*, however, she includes an episode featuring a young woman named Miranda, based on herself and named after Prospero's gifted daughter in Shakespeare's *The Tempest*, who benefits from the demanding instruction of her father. Fuller's Miranda

> was early led to feel herself a child of the spirit. She took her place easily, not only in the world of organized being, but in the world of mind. A dignified sense of self-dependence was given as all her portion, and she found it a sure anchor. Herself securely anchored, her relations with others were established with equal security. She was fortunate in a total absence of those charms which might have drawn to her bewildering flatteries, and in a strong electric nature, which repelled those who did not belong to her, and attracted those who did.
>
> (*WNC* 21)

In many respects, Miranda represents Fuller's idealization of her upbringing.

Born in Cambridgeport, Massachusetts, Fuller was the oldest surviving child of six children born to Timothy Fuller and Margaret Crane Fuller. As a teenager, Fuller attended Miss Prescott's Young Ladies Seminary, where she had some difficulty due to her awkward social manner; in particular, an off-putting air of superiority and condescension. Later an older female friend gave her excellent advice about gaining admirers, and she eventually had a large circle of good friends, both men and women. In 1836, Fuller had plans to go abroad, but the sudden death of her father left her responsible for her family's welfare. Although her Uncle Abraham stepped in and presumed to dictate to Fuller and her mother how to manage his late brother's estate, Margaret was able to resist his total control. She advised two of her brothers in their businesses, financed the education of another, arranged for the care of her mentally disabled brother, and provided financial and emotional support to her mother and her sister. (This sister, Ellen, married the transcendentalist poet Ellery Channing, who deserted her and their child.)

At this time, Fuller became focused on the writings of the eminent German intellectual Johann von Goethe, whose expansive mind, commitment to self-culture, and creation of pure, thoughtful, and refined women in his plays impressed her a great deal. "From his poetic soul," she writes, "grew up forms new and more admirable than life has yet produced, for whom his clear eye marked out paths in the future" (*WNC* 74). She translated several of Goethe's works and made plans to write a biography of him, yet soon realized she did not have access to the materials she needed to do so. To earn money for herself and her family, Fuller taught briefly at Bronson Alcott's elementary school in

Boston and then spent eighteen months teaching young women at the Greene Street School in Providence, Rhode Island, but without much reward or satisfaction. Her young students found her too demanding, and she found them lacking in preparation and intellectual ambition. In 1839, she sold her family's farm in Groton and moved to Jamaica Plain, just outside of Boston, and undertook editing the *Dial,* for which she earned almost nothing. She also began her series of Boston "Conversations" for a group of adult well-educated women.

By all accounts, Fuller excelled in conversation. She had an extensive vocabulary, a quick wit, penetrating intelligence, an entertaining satirical bent, and the ability to express herself eloquently and persuasively. Too often, male commentators have compared her conversational skills to her written work in order to denigrate the latter, but her digressive, allusive prose style challenges her readers to view conventional topics from unconventional perspectives. In this sense, she joins Emerson in trying to break through the boundaries of received knowledge to acquire new ways of thinking and being. Unlike Emerson, however, Fuller was willing to use romantic and, at times, mystical erotic imagery, to explore prophetic experience and the world of the occult.

She was fascinated by omens, gemstones, and spiritual visitations. In 1840 she recorded a transcendental experience of hers that occurred on Thanksgiving Day 1831. After attending church, where she felt lonely and sad, she took a long walk, stopping at last by a dark pool where she sat cold and still, until a beam of sunlight sparked a revelation:

> I saw there was no self; that selfishness was all folly, and the result of circumstance; that it was only because I thought self real that I suffered; that I had only to live in the idea of the ALL, and all was mine. This truth came to me, and I received it unhesitatingly; so that I was for that hour taken up into God. In that true ray most of the relations of earth seemed mere films, phenomena.
>
> (Buell 160)

As her career progressed, Fuller's moments of ecstasy and exaltation infused a unique feminism, less personal and more committed to inspiring other women.

One of her first contributions to the *Dial* was the poetical short story "Leila" (1841), which presents the female title character as a powerful, almost unknowable force of nature, able to terrorize and comfort. "Leila, with wild hair scattered to the wind, bare and often bleeding feet, opiates and divining rods in each over-full hand, walked amid the habitations of mortals as a Genius, visited their consciences as a Demon" (*WNC* 171). Yet, Leila also becomes "the mild sunset," who "puts you to rest on a love-couch of rosy sadness, when on the horizon swells up a mighty sea and rushes over you till you plunge on its waves, affrighted, delighted, quite freed from earth" (*WNC* 169). Obviously, Fuller self-identified with Leila, and Emerson in his journal paid tribute to Fuller's visible growth, in comparable terms: "She rose before me at times into heroical & godlike regions, and I could remember no superior women, but thought of Ceres, Minerva, Proserpine, and the august ideal forms of the Foreworld" (*JMN* 8: 368–369).

In the late 1830s, Fuller, as one of several well-educated women who joined the transcendentalist movement, shifted its focus to matters beyond philosophy and religious sectarianism toward literature, art, and human relations. Soon after meeting Emerson in 1836, Fuller became his valued correspondent, and in September 1837, he invited her to join the Transcendental Club, which she did, making a favorable impression. The two became close friends, though Fuller sought a level of intimacy Emerson was unable to understand or provide. In a journal entry of 1840, he wrote,

> You would have me love you. What shall I love? Your body? The supposition disgusts you. What you have thought & said? Well, whilst you were thinking & saying them, but not now. I see no possibility of loving any thing but what now is, & is becoming; your courage, your enterprize, your budding affection, your opening thought, your prayer, I can love,—but what else?
> (*JMN* 7: 400)

The two obviously viewed their relationship from different points of view. In the summer of 1842, while Fuller was visiting the Emersons for several weeks, the two writers took a walk at night to the Concord River, where they looked at reflections of the moon in the water. In her journal, Fuller recorded that Emerson observed that

> each twinkling light breaking there summons to demand the whole secret, and how "promising, promising nature never fulfils what she thus gives us a right to expect." I said I never could meet him here, the beauty does not stimulate me to ask *why*?, and press to the centre, I was satisfied for the moment, full as if my existence was filled out, for nature had said the very word that was lying in my heart. Then we had an excellent talk: We agreed that my god was love, his truth.
> ("1842 Journal" 320)

Although Fuller agrees to a dichotomy here between love and truth, or heart and head, such a distinction, which Emerson had publicly endorsed, was having a harmful effect on women at the time. In his lecture "Human Life" (1838), Emerson had asserted, "Man represents Intellect whose object is Truth, Woman Love whose object is goodness ... Man goes abroad into the world and works and acquires. Woman stays at home to make the house beautiful" (*Early Lectures* 3: 62). This notion of separate spheres provided a rationale for excluding women from the so-called male professions of law, medicine, the ministry, higher education, and politics.

It was such exclusion that inspired Fuller to try to enlighten and empower well-educated women in Boston. Her Conversations were paid seminars that she proposed to lead. As she put it in a letter to a friend, she hoped "to ascertain what pursuits are best suited to us in our time and state of society, and how we may make best use of our means for building up the life of thought upon the life of actions" (*Letters* 1: 87). Her Conversations had a ripple effect with regard to the women's rights movement, for she encouraged her students to think about and put into words the current plight of women, that is, how it came about, and how it was to be relieved. While her *Woman in the Nineteenth Century* (1845), became a manifesto of sorts, it was informed by the give and take she encouraged in her classes. As Charles Capper has pointed out,

> in this period, Fuller was no advocate of political activism. But she was a most powerful advocate of an activism of the mind and, to some extent, the social mind. And there was no other woman in America who came close to filling that role.
>
> (523)

In response to her request for a written paper on the intellectual differences between men and women, one of her "assistants," as she called them, Sally Gardner, wrote,

> I recognize between man & woman a necessary difference of position, of which the results are accidental or arbitrary. It was founded, in the origin of society, on the difference of physical strength, when materials were scanty & the labour which procured & made them available was all-important ... Now we vastly overrate the progress we have made since those early times. Still *might* makes *right* & other remnants of barbarism linger amongst us.
>
> (qtd. Peabody 283)

Other participants in the Conversations offered similar sound arguments for social change.

Woman in the Nineteenth-Century (1845)

The relations between men and women fully engaged Fuller's attention in the early 1840s. Her 1843 *Dial* essay "The Great Lawsuit: Man *versus* Men, Woman *versus* Women" (1843) draws upon her conversations with Emerson about the oppression endemic to the institution of marriage. In the country at large, others were exploring alternatives to traditional marriage as well. There was a free love commune set up at Oneida, New York, the utopian cooperative at Brook Farm and the Shakers' celibate communities at various sites in New England. More consequentially, there was the small but growing religious group of Mormons who practiced polygamy and were persecuted for doing so. Even Emerson for a time fantasized about having an open marriage in the early 1840s and persuaded his wife Lidian to accept his intense emotional relations with a small group of friends, including Fuller and her former student Caroline Sturgis, who was a rich and gifted young poet.

By 1843, Fuller realized how harmful male attitudes toward women had become, and in "The Great Lawsuit" (1843) she rejects the idea of gender duality. She points out,

> Nature provides exceptions to every rule. She sends women to battle, and sets Hercules spinning; she enables women to bear immense burdens, cold, and frost; she enables the man, who feels maternal love, to nourish his infant like a mother.
>
> (419)

While Fuller was developing her progressive notions about gender fluidity, Emerson remained committed to the concept of separate spheres. For him, the solution to any discontent a woman might feel was to find a man to be her guardian.

Based on her observations of friends, including the Emersons, Fuller became highly critical of conventional marriages. Like Fanny Fern, Fuller found the institution of marriage fraught with disadvantages for women. According to the law at the time, a married woman could not own her own property, earn wages, or obtain a formal education without her husband's permission. And, of course, she could not vote. Fuller declared that the goal in life for a man or a woman was "to grow," and she thought the traditional concept of a woman's "sphere," prohibited such growth. In *Woman in the Nineteenth Century* (an expanded version of "The Great Lawsuit"), she stages a conversation with a businessman, who makes the argument that his wife is happy in her own domestic sphere and enjoys more leisure than he has. After he is asked whether the wife has actually said she's happy, the following conversation ensues:

> "No, but I know she is. She is too amiable to wish what would make me unhappy, and too judicious to wish to step beyond the sphere of her sex. I will never consent to have our peace disturbed by any such discussions."
>
> "'Consent—you?' it is not consent from you that is in question, it is assent from your wife."
>
> "Am not I the head of my house?"
>
> "You are not the head of your wife. God has given her a mind of her own."
>
> "I am the head and she the heart."
>
> (*WNC* 15–16)

Although Fuller herself once subscribed to such a binary concept, most of her book works to show how simplistic and harmful it is.

As Fuller expanded her "Great Lawsuit" into *Woman* in the fall of 1844, she described the kinds of marriages she had seen which prevented a woman from growing. First is the mere household partnership, which has no love sustaining it; second is mutual idolatry, in which the wife and husband are so infatuated with one another, they become detached from all else; third is intellectual companionship, based on friendship and esteem, but not love. For Fuller, the best form of marriage was a spiritual union wherein both husband and wife are on a pilgrimage toward a common goal. Before one can enter such a relationship, however, it must be as equals. As she puts it, "Union is only possible to those who are units. To be fit for relations in time, souls, whether of man or woman, must be able to do without them in the spirit" (*WNC* 71). She cautions individual women not to subordinate themselves to a man, even at the risk of remaining forever single. In fact, she celebrates the single life, rejects the notion of "being taught and led by men," and declares she would have woman become like the Indian girl of Chippewa history who dreamt in youth that she was betrothed to the Sun, "the Sun of truth" (*WNC* 70).

As scholars have pointed out, Fuller draws upon examples of famous females from mythology, history, and literature to expand available models of female power for her readers. These include the Virgin Mary, Minerva, Isis, Ceres, Proserpine, Diana, Queen Elizabeth, Madame de Staël, and Mary Wollstonecraft. As Jeffrey Steele has observed, her numerous portraits "of great women and powerful female types enabled her to chart undeveloped areas of female being, at the same time they demonstrated that energy and creativity were not only masculine attributes" ("Rhetoric" 286). Ultimately, Fuller advocates what Emerson does—self-reliance—yet the key difference in their thought is that Fuller reveals all the obstacles contemporary women face, which are invisible to Emerson and other men, who take their freedoms and privileges for granted. She attributes to Goethe the idea, shared by all the male Transcendentalists, that "A man can grow in any place, if he will," yet she points out that "bad institutions are prison walls and impure air that make him stupid, so that he does not will" (*WNC* 74). In other words, institutions such as the family, schools, churches, marriage, the courts, and legislatures can prevent girls and women in both visible and invisible ways from developing their full potentials. Fuller asks not for special treatment for women, but rather, for the removal of arbitrary barriers. Responding to the question of what vocations should be open to women, she famously declares, "any. Let them be sea-captains, if you will" (*WNC* 102).

At the conclusion of her book, Fuller asks the question when will the woman appear "who shall vindicate their birthright for all women; who shall teach them what to claim, and how to use what they obtain?" (*WNC* 104–105). She does not assume such a role for herself, but with what appears sincere modesty, envisions her future in allegorical terms:

> I stand in the sunny noon of life. Objects no longer glitter in the dews of morning, neither are yet softened by the shadows of evening. Every spot is seen, every chasm revealed. Climbing the dusty hill, some fair effigies that once stood for symbols of human destiny have been broken; those I still have with me, show defects in this broad light. Yet enough is left, even by

experience, to point distinctly to the glories of that destiny; faint, but not to be mistaken streaks of the future day. I can say with the bard,

"Though many have suffered shipwreck, still beat noble hearts."
(*WNC* 104–105)

Because Fuller would die in a shipwreck five years later, her final words seem sadly prophetic.

Summer on the Lakes, in 1843 (1844)

Poe, among other reviewers, was impressed by Fuller's argument in *Woman*, calling it "nervous, forcible, thoughtful, suggestive, brilliant, and to a certain extent scholar-like." Nevertheless, he questioned whether all women had the same attributes and potential that Fuller did. "She judges *woman* by the heart and intellect of Miss Fuller, but there are not more than one or two dozen Miss Fullers in the whole face of the earth" (*Literati* 224). What Poe could not envision was the day that educational and vocational opportunities would allow a multitude of women to match Fuller's ambition and brilliance. For Poe, Fuller's "high genius" appeared most clearly in her *Dial* essays and her travel book *Summer on the Lakes, in 1843* (1844), which she wrote after a trip to the Illinois and Wisconsin Territory. *Summer* is both more and less than an account of her journey to the Great Lakes; it includes multiple digressions including stories, poems, imaginary dialogues, autobiography, and commentary on books she has read and ideas she has pondered, such as the fate of the displaced Native Americans she saw. As the scholar Susan Belasco Smith has observed, "Fuller used the opportunity of visiting the frontier to meditate on the state of her own life and of life in America" (xx). She supplemented her journal and letters by researching contemporary travel books in the Harvard College Library and was the first woman to be granted such a privilege.

A large section of *Summer* is dedicated to a book she had read just before leaving on her trip to the West, *Die Seherin von Prevorst* (*The Seerest of Prevorst*) written by Dr. Justinius Kerner which tells the story of Frederika Hauffe, a German seeress able to have visions, discern spirits, and presumably leave her body during magnetic trances. Fuller, in an attempt to defend the authenticity and importance of Hauffe's life, introduces a dialogue between herself as *Free Hope* and three skeptics, *Old Church, Good Sense, and Self-Poise*, the latter two sounding much like Emerson. *Good Sense* rejects the effort to know what lies beyond life as we know it: "let us be completely natural, before we trouble ourselves with the supernatural. I never see any of these things but I long to get away and lie under a green tree and let the wind blow on me" (*Summer* 79). Fuller, as *Free Hope*, declares, "I never lived, that I remember, what you call a common natural day. All my days are touched by the supernatural, for I feel the pressure of hidden causes, and the presence, sometimes the communion, of unseen powers" (*Summer* 79). What the dialogue reveals is Fuller's adventuresome spiritualist bent, which lifted her far above religious dogma, deference to a learned ministry, and masculine notions of rationality. The dialogue in *Summer* echoes others that Fuller and Emerson had, as found in their journals and writings, even unpublished ones. At its heart, the debate is the matter of going beyond conventional bounds, or limitations. Fuller prefers extravagance, in Thoreau's Latin sense of the term, *extra* (outside) *vagary* (to wander) while Emerson did not. As *Free Hope* says, "Thou art greatly wise, my friend, and ever respected by me, yet I find not in your theory or your scope, room enough for the lyric inspirations, or the mysterious whispers of life" (*Summer* 81). Some of those whispers came out of a spiritual mist whose extent Fuller had yet to discern.

Horace Greeley, the editor of the *New-York Tribune* was impressed by *Summer on the Lakes* as was his wife, Mary Chaney Greeley, who had attended Fuller's Boston Conversations and become a huge admirer. Consequently, Greeley offered to publish Fuller's next book, *Woman in the Nineteenth Century*, and to hire her as literary editor and cultural commentator on the *Tribune*. She accepted both offers. When Fuller moved to New York City in the fall of 1844, she took with her the inspiration of not only Emerson and Goethe with regard to self culture and self reliance, but also a reforming spirit from her female students and innovative ideas about gender relations and the visionary powers of certain women. In *Woman in the Nineteenth Century*, she identifies "the especial genius of woman" as "electrical in movement, intuitive in function, spiritual in tendency" (*WNC* 68), and then argues that "male and female represent the two sides of the great radical dualism. But, in fact, they are perpetually passing into one another ... There is no wholly masculine man, no purely feminine woman" (*WNC* 68–69). As Bruce Mills has shown, this concept of gender fluidity drew upon Fuller's interest in and study of mesmerism, also known as animal magnetism, a theory that invisible energy can be transmitted immaterially between humans, plants, and animals. The practice of mesmerism was closely allied with the spiritualist movement, and it eventually evolved into modern verbal hypnosis.

Writer on the *New-York Tribune*

Fuller argued on behalf of open-mindedness when it came to communications beyond the conventional means of sight and sound. In an essay for the *Tribune*, she asserted, "As to the power of holding intercourse with spirits enfranchised from our present sphere, we see no reason why it should not exist, and do see much reason why it should rarely be developed, but none why it should not *sometimes*. Those spirits are, we all believe, existent somewhere, somehow, and there seems to be no good reason why a person in spiritual nearness to them, whom such intercourse cannot agitate, or engross so that he cannot walk steadily in his present path, should not enjoy it, when of use to him." As Phyllis Cole and Albert Von Frank have pointed out, "This passage was often quoted, during and after the Civil War, in England and America, in defense of Spiritualism" (74). Moreover, as Ann Braude has argued,

> What distinguished spirit mediums from other religious women who rose to public roles at certain moments of enthusiasm within their religious communions was their commitment to women's rights ... Spiritualism formed a major—if not *the* major—vehicle for the spread of women's rights ideas in the mid-nineteenth century.
>
> (xx)

The movement encouraged female leadership and gave women a respected public voice. As Paul Crumbley has pointed out, "Female trance speakers, especially, attracted public attention by speaking from elevated platforms and regularly addressing large gatherings of several hundred persons while in a trance state" (237–238).

When Fuller first moved to New York City to work on the *Tribune*, she lived with the Greeleys in their rural home north of Manhattan and commuted to the *Tribune* offices downtown. Greeley was a likeable workaholic and devoted all of his energy to growing the *Tribune* and supporting progressive causes, including abolition, socialism, and women's rights. He and Fuller had far different personalities; he being rather impatient, slovenly and politically engaged and she being careful, scholarly, and politically detached. Nevertheless, they influenced each other and developed a fond partnership that experienced only a few tensions.

Fuller, like many brilliant women, suffered from migraine headaches, which at times debilitated her (the "vulture with the iron talons" took her in its grasp, as she put it), and when she would have to stay home from work, Greeley recalled that before he left for the office he would "look her in the face and exclaim with marked emphasis,—quoting from her 'Woman in the Nineteenth Century,'—'*Let them be sea-captains if they will!*'" (qtd. Fuller, *Memoirs* 2: 155–156). Fuller took such teasing in stride, and in the spring of 1845, she told her brother Eugene, "Mr Greeley I like, nay more, love. He is, in his habits, a slattern and plebeian, and in his heart, a nobleman ... We are true friends" (*Letters* 4: 56). Greeley in turn praised Fuller publicly as "one of the most independent, free-spoken and large-souled of the [female] sex ... a gifted, earnest and thoroughly informed woman—an embodied Intellect" (Greeley 143).

At the *Tribune*, Fuller became one of Greeley's most productive and valuable columnists, writing some 250 articles on a variety of topics during her stay in New York City during 1844–1846. As contributor to and editor of the *Dial*, she had advocated for self-culture, but on the *Tribune* she became more socially engaged and advocated reform efforts on behalf of women, slaves, prisoners, Indians, the poor, and Irish immigrants. (Her friend William Henry Channing, a Unitarian minister and Christian socialist, encouraged her in these efforts.) As Jeffrey Steele has pointed out, in the United States,

> Women imprisoned for prostitution, the mentally ill, the blind, the urban poor, and African Americans had all fallen beneath the threshold of respectability and even social visibility. Like other urban reformers, [Fuller]

knew that it was all too easy to forget about the inmates at Sing-Sing Prison or the Bloomingdale Asylum for the Insane ... On the streets of New York, the poor were often treated as an alien species, while churches and public institutions often excluded or marginalized impoverished and black members of the population. Functioning as New York's public conscience, Fuller documented her visits to the city's institutions, while she testified to the morally fragmenting effects of social, class, and racial prejudices.

(*Transfiguring* 258–259)

As cultural critic for the *Tribune*, Fuller reviewed books by both American and foreign authors, and she spoke out against American imperialism and the Mexican war, as well as slavery and the oppression of women.

She had her detractors, of course, especially among those threatened by women demanding more freedom and equality. Orestes Brownson, for example, a former Unitarian minister and recent Roman Catholic convert, declared that

> God, and not man, has assigned her the appropriate sphere; and, moreover, we must be ungallant enough to question Miss Fuller's leading doctrine of the perfect social and political equality of the sexes. She says man is not the head of the woman. We, on the authority of the Holy Ghost, say he is.
>
> (215)

Brownson, like a number of men, relied upon St. Paul's command in Ephesians 5:22, that wives submit themselves unto their husbands, as unto the Lord.

Reform activism

The number of women in the 1840s who were challenging this command was growing. In the summer of 1848, Fuller was living in Italy and serving as a foreign correspondent for the *Tribune*, when the first Women's Rights Convention was held in Seneca Falls, New York. The organizers of the Convention had been provoked by the exclusion of women from the London World Anti-Slavery Convention in 1840. The early New England Anti-Slavery Society organized by William Lloyd Garrison in 1831 included many women and supported their various activities, including public speaking. The Society sponsored the controversial lecture tour of the abolitionists Sarah and Angelina Grimké, who inspired a number of local female antislavery societies. In 1839, however, a split developed within the National Anti-Slavery Society when Maria Weston Chapman, Abby Kelley, Lydia Maria Child, and Lucretia Mott were elected to the Society's executive board, shocking a number of male members and prompting a permanent division into two societies. One prominent leader, Lewis Tappan, declared that to put a woman on the committee with men was "contrary to the usages of civilized society." In 1840 Tappan and others formed an alternative organization, the American and Foreign Anti-Slavery Society. Garrison and Frederick Douglass remained strong supporters of women's rights, and Douglass was one of the few men to sign the Declaration of Sentiments introduced at the Seneca Falls Convention. Its preamble began, "We consider these truths to be self-evident, that all men and women have been created equal."

Elizabeth Cady Stanton, a key organizer of the Convention, late in life acknowledged Fuller's influence upon her and upon the Seneca Falls event. As Phyllis Cole has shown, Stanton, who had attended Fuller's Conversations, was indebted to her for urging the virtues of self-trust and persistence in battle. In Stanton's first address following the Seneca Falls Convention, she quoted the final poem of Fuller's *Woman in the Nineteenth Century*:

> Then fear not thou to wind the horn,
> Though elf and gnome thy courage scorn.
> As for the castle's King and Queen,
> Though rabble rout may rush between,
> Beat thee senseless to the ground,
> In the dark beset thee round,
> Persist to ask and it will come,
> Seek not for rest in humbler home
> So shalt thou see what few have seen
> The palace home of King and Queen
> (Cole 533–534)

Although the poem uses aristocratic imagery, its underlying point seems to be that women should rise above those who would harm or humble them. Some seven years later, Stanton also extended praise to Fanny Fern, especially her depiction of female independence in her novel *Ruth Hall*, pointing out that the "great lesson it taught" was "that God has given to woman sufficient brain and muscle to work out her own destiny unaided and alone" (qtd. Warren 140).

The reaction in the press to the women's rights initiatives was to stigmatize the participants as dangerous radicals, not unlike the women of the 1789 French Revolution, who marched to the palace at the Tuileries with the heads of jailers on stakes. One New York City newspaper observed,

> the work of revolution is no longer confined to the Old World, nor to the masculine gender ... a solemn league and covenant has just been entered into by a Convention of women at Seneca Falls ... Little did we expect this new element to be thrown into the cauldron of agitation which is now bubbling around us with such fury.
> (qtd. Stanton et al. 805)

As the Seneca Falls Convention was taking place, a revolution had just occurred in France, with the king and his family fleeing to England, and workers demanding changes from the new provisional government. Soon other revolutions broke out across Europe, due to poverty, starvation, exploitive working conditions, and oppression from absolutist governments, including those in Italy, where Fuller was residing.

Fuller abroad

Fuller had dreamed of going to Europe since she was a child, and in the spring of 1846, she was saving money to go when her friends Marcus and Rebecca Spring offered to take her abroad with them, as a tutor to their twelve-year-old son. Greeley agreed to help finance her trip by paying her for each dispatch she sent him. Though concerned about her physical and mental health, Fuller accepted the offers. She had been visiting a male mesmerist, Dr. Théodore Léger, who helped her manage her painful spinal curvature. A friend, who witnessed one session, said the doctor transmitted a healing magnetic "fluid" to Fuller's back by moving his hand up and down her spine without touching her but willing power from himself to his patient, which she received. According to the friend, he thus straightened Fuller's back and caused her to grow three inches taller. She often met by arrangement, her would-be lover, James Nathan, in the good doctor's office after her sessions, which may have contributed to her new posture. Nathan, a Jewish, German-born businessman, courted Fuller while she was in New York City, got her help editing and placing his overseas letters in the *Tribune*, and then left the country with his mistress, going to Germany where, unbeknownst to Fuller, he would marry a woman of wealth and eventually sell Fuller's love letters, even after she asked for their return.

When Fuller arrived in England, she contacted Nathan, who was in Germany, asking him to join her for a tour in Scotland, but he sent her a letter announcing his engagement to another woman. Fuller destroyed the letter and apparently fell into a depression, riding on the top of a coach in a driving rain on a journey to Loch Katrine and Ben Lomond. She also became lost in the fog during a hike up Ben Lomond, and in one of her most powerful dispatches to the *Tribune*, she describes her near-death experience high on the mountain during the night:

> I saw far below me a light that looked about as big as a pin's head, that I knew to be from the inn at Rowardennan, but heard no sound except the rush of the waterfall, and the sighing of the night-wind.
>
> For the first few minutes that I perceived I had got to my night's lodging, such as it was, the prospect seemed appalling. I was very lightly clad—my feet and dress were very wet—I had only a little shawl to throw round me, and a cold autumn wind had already come, and the night-mist was to fall on me, all fevered and exhausted as I was. I thought I should not live through the night, or if I did, live always a miserable invalid ... For about two hours I saw the stars, and very cheery and companionable

they looked; but then the mist fell and I saw nothing more, except such apparitions as visited Ossian on the hill-side when he went out by night and struck the bosky shield and called to him the spirits of the heroes and the white-armed maids with their blue eyes of grief.—to me, too, came those visionary shapes; floating slowly and gracefully, their white robes would unfurl from the great body of mist in which they had been engaged, and come upon me with a kiss pervasively cold as that of Death. What they might have told me, who knows, if I had but resigned myself more passively to that cold, spirit-like breathing!

(SGD 75–76)

In the morning a search party of shepherds found Fuller, and it took several days for her to recover. (Ossian, whom Fuller mentions, was a fictitious ancient Gaelic warrior poet invented around 1760 by Scottish poet James Macpherson, who presented his writings as "translations.")

Fuller's account of her traumatic experience, which impressed her readers when it appeared in the *Tribune*, marked a change in her coverage of her travels. She started writing less about notable authors and landscapes and more about those suffering from despair, especially women. She soon reported from Glasgow, "I saw here in Glasgow persons, especially women, dressed in dirty, wretched tatters, worse than none, and with an expression of listless, unexpecting woe upon their faces, far more tragic than the inscription over the gate of Dante's *Inferno*" (SGD 79). In Lyons, France, she wrote about the victimized young silk weavers, who worked long hours for low wages. After a companion explained that weaving or prostitution was the only way for young girls in the city to avoid starvation, Fuller declared,

And there are those who dare to say that such a state of things is *well* enough, and what Providence intended for man—who call those who have hearts to suffer at the sight, energy and zeal to seek its remedy, visionaries and fanatics! To themselves be woe, who have eyes and see not, ears and hear not, the convulsions and sobs of injured Humanity!

(SGD 128)

Fuller thus anticipated the 1848 revolutions that were soon to break out all over Europe, and she suggested that her own country might face a similar crisis.

In the United States, slavery was crushing the lives of millions, while in Europe, the potato blight of 1846–1847 had caused widespread famine among the working classes. Poor wheat harvests, the high price of bread, and a slump in manufacturing had also inflicted hunger and unemployment upon thousands. In the search for food and work, masses of people moved to the cities, where most found only increasing crime, misery, and social injustice, all aggravated by the suppression of dissent by absolutist governments. In her *Tribune* column "First of January" (1846), Fuller observed that "the caldron simmers, and so great is the fire that we expect it soon to boil over, and new Fates appear for

Europe" (*Critic* 327). As she traveled in Britain and Europe later that year, she saw more signs of political upheaval ahead.

The Italian dispatches

Fuller parted with the Springs in Italy in the spring of 1847 having met and fallen in love with Giovanni Angelo Ossoli, a handsome, modest, poorly educated Italian nobleman. By the end of December 1847, while living in Rome, Fuller learned she was pregnant and during the summer of 1848, she tried to avoid the shame heaped on unwed mothers by leaving her apartment in Rome and staying in the nearby countryside. Her baby Angelo was born on September 5, 1848, in the mountain town of Rieti, Italy, and Fuller returned to Rome, leaving him in the care of a wet nurse, a woman hired to nurse the infant. In Angelo's baptism papers, Fuller and Ossoli signed as husband and wife, though no evidence of their marriage has been found. In the fall of 1848 and spring of 1849 Fuller wrote dispatches describing the revolution that drove the Pope from the Papal States. He had shown himself more loyal to the Catholic rulers of Austria than to the people of northern Italy who had rebelled against Austrian oppression. In Rome, the revolution established a triumvirate led by Fuller's friend, the political radical Giuseppe Mazzini, whom she had met in London where he was living in exile.

Fuller's dispatches are exciting and compelling. In fact, as the scholar Barbara Packer has pointed out, they are "one of the most absorbing, brilliant, and far-ranging of all texts written by the transcendentalists" (544). Ultimately, the Italian dispatches constitute a tragedy, in the sense that the French army came to the aid of the Pope and laid siege to Rome, ultimately driving the republican revolutionaries from the city and restoring the Pope to power. During the battle of Rome, Fuller nursed the wounded in a hospital on Tiber Island, while Ossoli (a captain in the civic guard) manned a post on the Pincian Hill. During the bombardment of the city Fuller reported that "men are daily slain, and this state of suspense is agonizing," adding,

> In the evening 'tis pretty, though a terror, to see the bombs, fiery meteors, springing from the horizon line upon their bright path, to do their wicked message. 'Twould not be so bad, meseems, to die of one of these, as wait to have every drop of pure blood, every child-like radiant hope, drained and driven from the heart by the betrayals of nations and of individuals, till at last the sickened eyes refuse more to open to that light which shines daily on such pits of iniquity.

(*SGD* 302)

As is apparent, once Fuller saw that republican Rome would fall, her dispatches combine personal and objective reporting. As I have pointed out elsewhere, "Fuller writes poetically at times, polemically at others, and prophetically at still others; she creates colorful and romantic scenes; yet she also pens stark and restrained descriptions of the fighting and dying around her" (Reynolds 68).

In June of 1849, when the French army was on the verge of restoring Pope Pius IX to power, Fuller, a harsh critic of the Pope, reported as both witness and partisan. "What shall I write of Rome in these sad but glorious days?" she asks. "Plain facts are the best; for my feelings I could not find fit words" (*SGD* 285). She then describes a recent battle:

> The attack began before sunrise and lasted all day. I saw it from my window, which, though distant, commands the Gate St. Pancrazio. Why the whole force was bent on that part, I do not know. If they could take it, the town would be cannonaded and the barricades useless; but it is the same with the Pincian Gate. Small parties made feints in two other directions, but they were at once repelled. The French fought with great bravery, and this time it is said with beautiful skill and order, sheltering themselves in their advance by moveable barricades. The Italians fought like lions, and no inch of ground was gained by the assailant. The loss of the French is said to be very great: it could not be otherwise. Six or seven hundred Italians are dead or wounded, among them were many officers, those of Garibaldi especially, who are much exposed by their daring bravery, and whose red tunic makes them the natural mark of the enemy.
> (*SGD* 291–292)

After Republican Rome fell, Garibaldi left Rome with four thousand men, pursued through the mountains by Austrian, French, Spanish, and Neapolitan armies. Almost all of Garibaldi's men were killed or captured, but he made it across the Apennines into Piedmont with one follower and eventually made his way to London and then New York City. Meanwhile, Fuller and Ossoli fled to Florence with their child, where they lived for ten months, becoming friends with the poets Elizabeth Barrett Browning and her husband Robert Browning.

Fuller's dispatches from Italy to the *Tribune* made her an international figure and influenced abolitionists in the United States. In fact, her support of political violence in Europe prefigured a major change in antislavery thinking, inspiring a number of abolitionist leaders, including Emerson, to accept violence as a valid means to effect political change. In one of her last dispatches, Fuller declared,

> The next revolution, here and elsewhere, will be radical. Not only Jesuitism must go, but the Roman Catholic religion must go ... Not only the Austrian, and every potentate of foreign blood, must be deposed, but every man who assumes an arbitrary lordship over fellow man, must be driven out ... The New Era is no longer an embryo; it is born; it begins to walk—this very year sees its first giant steps, and can no longer mistake its features.
> (*SGD* 321)

The New Era would include the Civil War and the end of slavery in the United States.

When Fuller, Ossoli, and their child were returning to America in the summer of 1850, a hurricane caused their ship to wreck off the coast of Fire Island, New York, fifty yards from shore. Emerson sent Thoreau to see if he could retrieve any of the bodies or any of Fuller's writings (she had been working on a manuscript about the Italian Revolutions, which she considered her *magnum opus*). Thoreau found very little, because scavengers had made off with most of the wreckage. The child Angelo's body was recovered and buried in Mount Auburn Cemetery in Cambridge, Massachusetts, but the bodies of Fuller and Ossoli were never found. The Fuller family later erected a stone monument in the cemetery as a memorial to Fuller and her husband.

After Fuller's death, Emerson lamented that he had lost in her his audience, and his later essays reveal her influence upon him, although his attitude toward women's rights remained more permissive than supportive. That is, he was willing to let women become voters if they wished, but asserted in an 1855 lecture before the Woman's Rights Convention held in Boston, "I do not think it yet appears that women wish this equal share in public affairs" ("Woman" 255). He explained, "Man is the will, and Woman the sentiment. In this ship of humanity, Will is the rudder, and Sentiment the sail. When Woman affects to steer, the rudder is only a masked sail" ("Woman" 246). In his view, women were still guided by their emotions, not reason: "They have tears, and gayeties, and faintings, and glooms and devotion to trifles" ("Woman" 252). Needless to say, the lecture was not well received by many in his audience.

As Phyllis Cole has shown, Fuller's spectacular death in a shipwreck at age forty allowed her to become a romantic and symbolic figure within the women's rights movement during the last half of the nineteenth century. "Early advocates claimed Fuller in 1850;" and "in 1901, New York and Boston women united to dedicate a memorial to her on Fire Island. Margaret Fuller was part of the movement's usable past" (Cole 2). With each passing decade in the present, Fuller's life and writings have been providing inspiration for the struggle for women's rights.

Fern's career

Unlike Fuller, Fanny Fern, the pseudonym for Sarah Payson Willis, found that her independence, irreverence, and scandal-ridden life set her apart at times from other women. In a column about the 1851 Women's Rights Convention, Fern asked, "Where is the woman, who, when a sister is unjustly slandered, or spoken against, does not oftener circulate the story than seek to defend or excuse her?" (qtd. Warren 97). Fern admired activists like Lucy Stone, and she supported the quest for women's suffrage and social equality, but was a sceptic when it came to human nature, male and female. Some women, she felt, could be as cruel as some men.

During the years that Fuller was writing for the *Tribune* in New York City and then Europe, Fanny Fern was enjoying a rather conventional and comfortable middle-class life that seemed almost idyllic. However, the future held a series of losses that shattered her financially and almost psychologically. Although she would become one of America's most popular and wealthiest writers of the nineteenth century, she had to suffer considerable distress before she had such success.

Fern was born in 1811, in Portland, Maine, the fifth of nine children. At the time, her father, Nathaniel Willis, had recently converted to Calvinism, which Fern came to resent, for she recalled him as joyless, stern, and self-righteous. He apparently treated Fern's mother, Hannah Parker Willis, with rudeness and brutality. Fern wrote about her mother as patient, long-suffering, and talented, someone who could have been a writer were it not for raising so many children and having so little time of her own. Soon after Fanny was born, the family moved to Boston, where her father became a deacon of the Park Street Congregational Church and editor of a religious newspaper and later a children's newspaper. As a youth, Fanny rebelled against her father's strict conservatism, but she helped him with his newspaper work, even writing short pieces for his newspaper *The Youth's Companion*.

Although Fern became a committed free thinker and rejected the notion of original sin, there is a severity even within her humorous columns, which often have a cynical tone, revealing her low opinion of her fellow man. A reader once wrote her praising her sense of humor and asking how she could be so funny, and she replied that "it's a way I have when I can't find a razor handy to cut my throat" (qtd. Warren 100). Fern's father sought to correct for his daughter's lack of piety by sending her to several boarding schools, including Catharine Beecher's Hartford Female Seminary, known for its high moral tone. During her three years there, many who knew her later recalled her pranks and playfulness, yet Fern, like Fuller, was something of an outsider, due to her nonconformity and high spirits. She later wrote about the "over-dressed, vain, vapid, brainless" girls whose parents sent them to such schools because it was the fashionable thing to do. Future author Harriet Beecher Stowe, a fellow pupil and sometime teacher remembered Fanny as a "bright, laughing witch of a half saint half sinner" (qtd. Warren 275).

At age eighteen, Fern returned to her parents' home in Boston, and six years later, she married Charles Harrington Eldredge, a bank cashier with whom she had three daughters, in 1838, 1841, and 1844. The family apparently enjoyed a happy conventional life on a beautiful fifteen-acre country estate outside of Boston. In 1844, however, Fern's world began to collapse. Her younger sister, Ellen, became ill and died, and within weeks, Fern's mother died as well. The following year, Fern's oldest daughter, Mary, died, and then the next year her husband died of typhoid fever, at age thirty-five. When Fern discovered that her husband had made a number of bad investments, leaving her and her two surviving children destitute, she turned to her family and her husband's family for help, but received very little. Her father had remarried a widow with two daughters and gave Fern only a small allowance. Although he was well off, he was notoriously stingy. (For example, he removed the false teeth from the body of his first wife before her burial and sold them.) Fern's in-laws blamed her for her husband's debts and refused to provide any financial help.

Fern Leaves and *Ruth Hall*

Fern was forced to move into a boarding house with her children and tried to find work. She applied for a job as a schoolteacher but was turned down. She then tried to earn money as a seamstress, but could not earn enough to provide for herself and her children. At her father's urging, she remarried in 1849, to Samuel P. Farrington, a friend of her father's and a widower with two young daughters. The marriage proved unhappy. Farrington became extremely jealous and sexually abusive. After Fern fled with her daughters, he spread rumors accusing her of adultery, refused to support her, and obtained a divorce on the grounds of desertion. Meanwhile, Fern was shunned by friends and relatives, who refused to give her any more financial support. In her semi-autobiographical novel *Ruth Hall*, she does not mention Farrington, but draws upon her pathetic life living with her two children in a cheap rooming house and existing on milk and bread. One of her early columns, "Little Mary's Story" (1852), features a conversation between two little girls who are cold, poor, and hungry. The older one tells the younger about the time "before papa went to heaven," when on "Thanksgiving-day we were *so* happy; we sat around such a large table, with so many people,—aunts and uncles and cousins,—I can't think why they *never* come to see us *now*, Letty" (Fern 241). The mother overhears the conversation and cries. This affecting riches-to-rags story has a basis in the facts of Fern's life, which helps it rise above mere contrived sentimentality.

In 1851, Fern determined to try to earn a living as a creative writer. A number of women had achieved success at writing for the periodicals, and because Fern's essays at school had received praise, she determined to try to earn money through her writing as well. Her prospects were favorable because the reading public was growing rapidly and the periodical press was as well. In fact, there were over 2500 newspapers in the country and a high demand for engaging material. Fern's brother N.P. Willis had launched a successful career as a poet, travel writer, and editor, but when Fern turned to him for help in placing her essays, he responded by telling her, essentially, she had no talent, and he could not assist her. Later in a newspaper column and in *Ruth Hall,* she satirized her brother as a pretentious dandy named Hyacinth. In her column, she describes how he clings to friends

> as long as he can use them; but let their good name be assailed, let misfortune once overtake them, and his 'moral excellence' compels him, at once, to ignore their existence, until they have been extricated from all their troubles, and it has become perfectly safe and *advantageous* for him to renew the acquaintance.
>
> (Fern 260)

Because all of us have encountered such fair-weather friends, Fern's skewering of her brother is a delight to read. By all accounts it was also accurate, for readers recognized N. P. Willis right away.

Fern was encouraged when her first essay, "The Model Husband" (1851), was published pseudonymously in a Boston newspaper, and pirated by other papers as well. Her description of the husband, Mr. Smith, includes the following:

> He always laces on his wife's boots, lest the exertion should make her too red in the face before going out to promenade Washington St. He never calls any woman "*pretty*," before Mrs. Smith. He never makes absurd objections to her receiving bouquets, or the last novel, from Captain this, or Lieutenant that ... He never takes the newspaper and reads it, before Mrs. Smith has a chance to run over the advertisements, deaths, and marriages, etc. He always gets into bed *first*, cold nights, to *take off the chill* for his wife.
>
> (Fern 215–216)

Although Fern's humor is a bit dated, her contemporary readers responded happily to it. By the fall of 1851, she was writing regularly for two papers, the *Olive Branch* and *True Flag*, and her columns were reprinted widely.

Soon a New York paper *Musical World and Times* offered her an exclusive contract, and in early 1853, her career took off in earnest with the publication of a collection of her newspaper pieces titled *Fern Leaves from Fanny's Portfolio*, which sold some 80,000 copies in less than a year. With the success of Fanny Fern's writings, Sara Willis adopted her pen name as her official name, and she used her columns to address a variety of contemporary social issues, many involving husbands' ill treatment of wives, and, more generally, men's ill treatment of women. In these columns, satire, sarcasm, and racy humor predominate; however, Fern also wrote a number of heavily sentimental columns featuring suffering children, struggling widows, and tearful losses of various kinds.

Such sentimental pieces caused some twentieth-century literary historians to dismiss Fern's newspaper work as lightweight and ephemeral; in recent decades, however, as sentimentalism itself has received sophisticated critical attention, Fern's reputation has enjoyed a renaissance. Her sentimentalism, it has been argued, should not be regarded as merely a means of allowing readers to indulge in emotions at no cost to themselves, but rather, as an effective device, a ploy according to some, meant to change social norms. As Jaime Harker has observed, "With all of its limitations, Fern's progressive sentimentalism shows an active commitment both to social change and to Christianity, as well as a willingness to use Christianity for progressive causes" (63). The success of Harriet Beecher Stowe's *Uncle Tom's Cabin* in helping bring an end to slavery in the United States stands as a model for this type of influence.

Fern wrote *Ruth Hall* after she moved in 1853 to New York City from Boston, which she despised for its conservatism. The novel sold more than 50,000 copies within eight months, and sales were helped by the disclosure of her identity by a former editor trying to damage her reputation. Although she received criticism for the spirit of revenge impelling the book, the news that the book was heavily autobiographical made it all the more engaging to the public. Fern drew repulsive characters based on her brother, father, and especially her in-laws, directing satire at their heartlessness and cruelty. Fern had allowed her in-laws to take her oldest daughter from her, because she could not care for her, and in *Ruth Hall*, she describes a version of the verbal and physical abuse they subjected the child to. In one scene the mother-in-law, called "the old lady," determines to cut off the curls of the grandchild, Katy:

> "*Papa* liked them," said Katy, shrinking back.
>
> "No, he didn't," replied the old lady; "or, if he did, 'twas only to please your foolish mother; any way they are coming off; if I don't like them that's enough; you are always to live with me now, Katy; it makes no difference what your mother thinks or says about anything, so you needn't quote *her*, I'm going to try to make a good girl of you, *i.e.* if she will let you alone; you are full of faults, just as she is, and I shall have to take a great deal of pains with you. You ought to love me very much for it, better than anybody else in the world—don't you?"
>
> (No response from Katy.)
>
> "I say, Katy, you ought to love me better than anybody else in the world," repeated the old lady, tossing a handful of the severed ringlets down on the carpet. "Do you, Katy?"
>
> "No, ma'am," answered the truthful child.
>
> "That tells the whole story," said the doctor, as he started up and boxed Katy's ears; "now go up and stay in your room till I send for you, for being disrespectful to your grandmother."
>
> "Like mother—like child," said the old lady, as Katy half shorn, moved like a culprit out of the room; then gathering up in her apron the shining curls, she looked on with a malicious smile, while they crisped and blackened in the glowing Lehigh fire.
>
> (138–139)

In both the novel and in Fern's life, the child rejoined her mother, once the latter earned enough money to support them.

Although there is little that is subtle about *Ruth Hall,* its structure, style, and plot are innovative and modern. The chapters are brief and fast-paced, with few transitions between them, and the prose is breezy and sharp. Fern's plot, the growing self reliance and financial independence of its spunky heroine, makes no move toward a romantic happily-ever-after marriage. At the novel's end, Ruth is rich and single. After reviewers objected to this unusual plot, especially its emphasis on a woman's financial success, Fern wrote in an 1861 column,

> There are few people who speak approbatively of a woman who has a smart business talent or capability. No matter how isolated or destitute her

condition, the majority would consider it more "feminine" would she unobtrusively gather up her thimble, and, retiring into some out-of-the-way place, gradually scoop out her coffin with it, than to develop that smart turn for business which would lift her at once out of her troubles; and which, in a man so situated, would be applauded as exceedingly praiseworthy.

(qtd. Warren 140)

Fern, of course, had her admirers as well as her detractors among the literary class. Nathaniel Hawthorne once famously complained to a friend that "America is now wholly given over to a damned mob of scribbling women, and I should have no chance of success while the public taste is occupied with their trash—and should be ashamed of myself if I did succeed." He followed this complaint, however, with his reaction to Fern's *Ruth Hall:*

> The woman writes as if the devil was in her, and that is the only condition under which a woman ever writes anything worth reading ... Can you tell anything about this Fanny Fern? If you meet her, I wish you would let her know how much I admire her.
>
> (CE 7: 307–308)

Fern's devilish satire and overt sentimentalism make a potent combination in *Ruth Hall*. As Samuel Otter has shown, Fern manipulates her reader's emotions skillfully, using objects and gestures to evoke feelings. He gives as an example the understated death scene of Ruth's little daughter Daisy, followed by the affecting handling of Daisy's little half-worn shoe, "with the impress of a tiny foot, upon which [Ruth's] tears were falling fast." As Otter observes, "Daisy's tiny foot has left a heavy print. Her half-worn shoe is creased with desire and longing" (235). Another object that Fern uses is far different, a bank certificate that appears near the novel's end showing that Ruth owns ten thousand dollars' worth of stock. Some critics have questioned this indicator of Ruth's success, saying it justifies the nation's "sordid, sexist, exclusionary economic foundation" (see Temple). Otter, however, points out that with the stock certificate, Fern is seeking "to alter the structures of feeling that define female and male achievement in mid-nineteenth-century America" (236). Fern wants both male and female readers to feel pride and delight in Ruth's economic success, which mirrors Fern's own.

Although *Ruth Hall* draws upon the death of Fern's daughter, the death of her first husband, her poverty and struggles to make a living, and the meanness of her relatives, it leaves out both her second marriage and her relationship with the editor and writer James Parton, who would become her third husband. Parton was eleven years younger than Fern, and she had him sign a prenuptial agreement before their marriage, which proved to be a long and happy one, except for the hostility of Parton's family, who disapproved of the marriage and of Fern, mainly because of her scandalous reputation. The former slave Harriet Jacobs, a servant in Fern's brother's house, was, according to Fern "one of the few people who stuck by her when others did not" (qtd. Warren 223), and after Fern achieved success, she brought Jacobs's beautiful young daughter Louisa in as a houseguest for many months. Fern's in-laws claimed that Louisa eventually left because Fern became jealous of her. Thomas Butler Gunn, once a friend of Fern and her husband, described Louisa as having a "soft, timid voice, beautiful hair and gentle demeanor," and he reported that Fern in "some transitory spasm of jealousy" verbally abused the girl (qtd. Yellin 133). Gunn got this story from Fern's sister-in-law Mary Parton Rogers, and, as biographer Joyce Warren points out, "Given their animosity toward Fern, the Rogerses are hardly a reliable source of information" (Warren 351 n. 20).

Despite the slander that came Fern's way from reviewers, gossips, and family members, her career continued to prosper after the publication of *Ruth Hall* in 1855, and her weekly columns for the *New York Ledger* made her the highest paid newspaper writer of the time. The next seventeen years she published six more collections of her columns along with the conventional novel *Rose Clark* (1856), based in part on her disastrous second marriage. In 1856, the British prime minister, Lord Palmerston, supposedly told President James Buchanan that he wanted to settle their differences because he did not want to be deprived of "my New York Ledger. I could give up Central America and the other points but the Ledger I must have—especially now that Fanny Fern writes for it exclusively" (qtd. Warren 149).

Fern and feminism

Initially Fern's feminism was rather conservative, at odds with the demands being made by women's rights activists. In her column "A Little Bunker Hill" (1852), she argues that it was a waste of breath for women to demand their rights; they needed to use gentle persuasion instead. As she puts it,

> Appear not to have any choice, and as true as gospel you'll get it. Ask *their* advice, and they'll be sure to follow *yours*. Look *one* way, and *pull another*! Make your reins of silk, *keep out of sight, and drive where you like*!
>
> (Fern 244)

Yet, Fern's advice altered over the course of her career, aligning more closely with the work of active feminists. In 1856, she heaped praise on Walt Whitman's *Leaves of Grass*, in part because of the democratic themes of the work, especially as they related to equality of men and women. Apparently, she saw in Whitman everything a man should be, "a large-hearted, untainted, self-reliant, fearless son of the Stars and Stripes," a poet who "dared speak out his strong, honest thoughts, in the face of pusillanimous, toadeying, republican aristocracy; dictionary-men, hypocrites, cliques and creeds" (Fern 275). She especially liked and quoted these lines of his:

> The wife—and she is not one jot less than the husband,
> The daughter—and she is just as good as the son,
> The mother—and she is every bit as much as the father.
>
> (qtd. Fern 277)

In a column titled "Independence" published in 1859, Fern listed all the ways women did not enjoy the freedom of men, asking,

> Can I go out of an evening without a hat at my side? Can I go out with one on my head without danger of a station-house [being arrested for wearing a hat]? Can I clap my hands at some public speaker when I am nearly bursting with delight?
>
> (Fern 314)

The unspoken answer of course was "No!" Fern did not dismiss the value of domestic work, or criticize women who were good mothers, wives, housekeepers, and cooks; rather, she argued one could do all those things in the home and yet be informed, intellectual, and politically engaged. In her column "Bogus Intellect" (1865), she attacks the assumption that domestic work is beneath an enlightened woman: "My dear woman," she writes,

> I have washed and ironed, and baked and brewed, and swept and dusted, and washed children, and made bonnets, and cut and made dresses, and mended old coats, and cleaned house, and made carpets, and nailed them down, and cleaned windows, and washed dishes, and tended the door-bell, and done every "menial" thing you can think of. ... No woman of true intellect ever felt such duties beneath her.
>
> (Fern 332–333)

Despite such support for women in the home, Fern, unlike Fuller, did not believe all professions should be open to women. As Kevin McMullen has pointed out, Fern, in an October 1857 column titled "Lady Doctors" (her second with this title), suggests there are physical and biological barriers that limit a woman's ability to perform as doctors. She explains this idea by writing:

> I think—and I won't fib for anybody—that there are physical impediments in the way of a woman's practice of medicine, which are insurmountable. I believe it is conceded that a female doctor must of necessity forego the blessed names of wife and mother. Poor thing! but let that pass. Suppose she weds a mortar and pestle—suppose she be a single woman—I can't see that this changes her sex, or exempts her from its ails and aches, which, when under the influence of, I will persist, render her unfit, by their effects upon the nervous system, to cope successfully and continuously with responsible medical emergencies; and this is true of "healthy women," so called, who, by the way, are as scarce as angels' visits.
>
> (qtd. McMullen 147)

As McMullen points out, "This over-looked column thus serves as a crucial reminder that Fern's feminism does not easily map onto our twenty-first-century conception of the term" (149).

Near the end of her career, Fern became more sympathetic to single women who choose not to marry. In her 1869 column "The Modern Old Maid," she celebrates the new single woman:

> She has sense as well as freshness, and conversation and repartee as well as dimples and curves. She carries a dainty parasol, and a natty little umbrella, and wears killing bonnets, and has live poets and sages and philosophers in her train, and knows how to use her eyes, and don't care if she never sees a cat, and couldn't tell a snuff-box from a patent reaper, and has a bank-book, and dividends: yes, sir! And her name is Phoebe or Alice; and Woman's Rights has done it.
>
> (Fern 361)

Conclusion

When Fern died in 1872, she was the most popular writer in America, but despite her success, her reputation faded in the twentieth century, as literary historians grouped her with more sentimental female writers who dominated the literary scene in the 1850s. After her novel *Ruth Hall* was reprinted in 1986 and Joyce Warren's biography appeared in 1992, a series of articles and book chapters took a closer look at the nature of her work, finding there not only exceptional insight into human character, but also a willingness to bring to public attention topics others had avoided, such as prostitution, venereal disease, birth control, and divorce, all with a distinctive and captivating style of writing.

Fuller, now considered America's first major female intellectual, anticipated Fern in advocating for prison reform, especially on behalf of women, and she has gained recognition for far more than her editorship of the *Dial* and participation in the transcendental movement. Her advocacy for women's rights, with her Conversations, her *Woman in the Nineteenth Century,* and her columns for the *New-York Tribune*, is now recognized as having had a deep and lasting effect on the current status of women in the United States and beyond. In the last several decades, it has also become clear that her words and deeds in Europe on behalf of revolutionary violence influenced the prowar attitudes of key American abolitionists and led to support for the Civil War itself.

Suggestions for further reading

Marshall, Megan. *Margaret Fuller: A New American Life*. Boston: Houghton Mifflin Harcourt, 2013.

Myerson, Joel, Ed. *Fuller in Her Own Time*. Iowa City: University of Iowa Press, 2008.

Reynolds, Larry J. and Susan Belasco Smith. "Introduction." *"These Sad but Glorious Days": Dispatches from Europe, 1846–1850.* Eds. Larry J. Reynolds and Susan Belasco Smith. New Haven: Yale University Press, 1991. 1–35.

Smith, Susan Belasco. "Introduction." *Ruth Hall: A Domestic Tale of the Present Time.* By Fanny Fern. New York: Penguin Books, 1997. xv–xlv.

Tonkovich, Nicole. *Domesticity with a Difference: The Nonfiction of Catharine Beecher, Sarah J. Hale, Fanny Fern, and Margaret Fuller.* Jackson: University Press of Mississippi, 1997.

Warren, Joyce W. *Fanny Fern: An Independent Woman*: New Brunswick: Rutgers University Press, 1992.

Warren, Joyce W. "Introduction." *Ruth Hall and Other Writings.* By Fanny Fern. Ed. Joyce W. Warren. New Brunswick: Rutgers University Press, 1994. ix–xxxix.

References

Braude, Ann. *Radical Spirits: Spiritualism and Women's Rights in Nineteenth-Century America.* Second Edition. Bloomington: Indiana University Press, 2001.

Brownson, Orestes A. "Miss Fuller and Reformers." 1845. Rpt. *Woman in the Nineteenth Century.* Ed. Larry J. Reynolds. A Norton Critical Edition. New York: Norton, 1988. 213–216.

Buell, Lawrence, Ed. *The American Transcendentalists: Essential Writings.* New York: Modern Library, 2006.

Capper, Charles. "Margaret Fuller as Cultural Reformer: The Conversations in Boston." *American Quarterly* 39, no. 4 (1987): 509–528.

Cole, Phyllis. "Stanton, Fuller, and the Grammar of Romanticism." *New England Quarterly* 73, no. 4 (December 2000): 533–559.

Cole, Phyllis and Albert J. Von Frank. "Margaret Fuller: How She Haunts." *ESQ: A Journal of Nineteenth-Century American Literature and Culture* 64, no. 1 (2018): 66–131.

Crumbley, Paul. "Dickinson's Uses of Spiritualism: The 'Nature' of Democratic Belief." In *A Companion to Emily Dickinson.* Eds. Martha Nell Smith and Mary Loeffelholz. Malden, MA: Blackwell, 2014. 235–257.

Emerson, Ralph Waldo. *The Early Lectures of Ralph Waldo Emerson: Volume III: 1838–1842.* Eds. Robert El Spiller and Wallace E. Williams. Cambridge, MA: Belknap Press of Harvard University Press, 1972.

Emerson, Ralph Waldo. *The Journals and Miscellaneous Notebooks of Ralph Waldo Emerson.* Ed. William H. Gilman, Ralph H. Orth, et al. 16 vols. Cambridge, MA: Belknap Press of Harvard University Press, 1960–1982. Abbreviated JMN.

Emerson, Ralph Waldo. "Woman." *Ralph Waldo Emerson and Margaret Fuller: Selected Works.* Ed. John Carlos Rowe. Boston: Houghton Mifflin, 2003. 244–256.

Fern, Fanny. *Ruth Hall and Other Writings.* Ed. Joyce W. Warren. New Brunswick: Rutgers University Press, 1986.

Fuller, Margaret. *Critic: Writings from the "New-York Tribune," 1844–1846.* Eds. Judith Mattson Bean and Joel Myerson. New York: Columbia University Press, 2000.

Fuller, Margaret. "The Great Lawsuit: Man *versus* Men. Woman *versus* Women." 1843. Rpt. *Transcendentalism: A Reader.* Ed. Joel Myerson. New York: Oxford University Press, 2000. 383–427.

Fuller, Margaret. *The Letters of Margaret Fuller.* 6 volumes. Ed. Robert Hudspeth. Ithaca: Cornell University Press, 1983–1994.

Fuller, Margaret. "Margaret Fuller's 1842 Journal: At Concord with the Emersons." Ed. Joel Myerson. *Harvard Library Bulletin* 21 (1973): 320–340.

Fuller, Margaret. *Memoirs of Margaret Fuller Ossoli.* Eds. R. W. Emerson, W. H. Channing, and J. F. Clarke. 2 vols. Boston: Phillips, Sampson & Company, 1852.

Fuller, Margaret. *"These Sad but Glorious Days": Dispatches from Europe, 1846–1850.* Eds. Larry J. Reynolds and Susan Belasco Smith. New Haven: Yale University Press, 1991. Abbreviated *SGD*.

Fuller, Margaret. *Summer on the Lakes, in 1843.* 1844. Rpt. Urbana: University of Illinois Press, 1991.

Fuller, Margaret. *Woman in the Nineteenth Century.* Ed. Larry J. Reynolds. 1845. Rpt. Norton Critical Edition. New York: Norton, 1998. Abbreviated WNC.

Greeley, Horace. "Notice: *Woman in the Nineteenth Century.* By S. Margaret Fuller. 1 vol. 12 mo., pp 280. Greeley & M'Elrath, New York." *Graham's Magazine* 27 (March 1845): 143.

Harker, Jaime. "'Pious Cant' and Blasphemy: Fanny Fern's Radicalized Sentiment." *Legacy,* 18, no. 1 (2001): 52–64.

Hawthorne, Nathaniel. *The Centenary Edition of the Works of Nathaniel Hawthorne.* Ed. William Charvat et al., 23 vols. Columbus: Ohio State UP, 1962–1997. Abbreviated CE and volume number.

McMullen, Kevin. "Turning Over Fresh Leaves: A Reconsideration of Fanny Fern's Periodical Writing." *Legacy: A Journal of American Women Writers* 35, no. 2 (2018): 141–165.

Mills, Bruce. *Poe, Fuller, and the Mesmeric Arts: Transition States in the American Renaissance.* Columbia: University of Missouri Press, 2006.

Otter, Samuel. *Melville's Anatomies.* Berkeley: University of California Press, 1999.

Packer, Barbara. "The Transcendentalists." *Prose Writing, 1820–1865. Vol. 2. The Cambridge History of American Literature.* Ed. Savan Bercovitch. Cambridge: Cambridge University Press, 1995. 329–604.

Peabody, Elizabeth Palmer. "[Woman], 'The Conversations of Margaret Fuller." *Transcendentalism: A Reader.* Ed. Joel Myerson. New York: Oxford University Press, 2000. 280–289.

Poe, Edgar Allan. "The Literati of New York City—No. IV: Sarah Margaret Fuller." 1846. Rpt. Margaret Fuller, *Woman in the Nineteenth Century.* Ed. Larry J. Reynolds. Norton Critical Edition. New York: Norton, 1998. 223–226.

Reynolds, Larry J. *European Revolutions and the American Literary Renaissance.* New Haven: Yale University Press, 1988.

Smith, Susan Belasco. "Introduction." In Margaret Fuller, *Summer on the Lakes, in 1843.* 1844. Rpt. Urbana: University of Illinois Press, 1991. vii–xxii.

Smith-Rosenberg. Carroll. *Disorderly Conduct: Visions of Gender in Victorian America.* New York: Oxford University Press, 1985.

Stanton, Elizabeth Cady, Susan B. Anthony, and Matilda Joslyn Gage. Eds. *History of Woman Suffrage. Vol 1, 1848–1861.* 1881. Rpt. New York: Arno & the New York Times, 1969.

Steele, Jeffrey. "Margaret Fuller's Rhetoric of Transformation." In Margaret Fuller, *Woman in the Nineteenth Century.* Ed. Larry J. Reynolds. Norton Critical Edition. New York: Norton, 1998. 278–297.

Steele, Jeffrey. *Transfiguring American: Myth, Ideology, and Mourning in Margaret Fuller's Writing*. Columbia: University of Missouri Press, 2001.

Temple, Gale. "A Purchase on Goodness: Fanny Fern, Ruth Hall and Fraught Individualism." *Studies in American Fiction* 31, no. 2 (Autumn 2003): 131–163.

Warren, Joyce W. *Fanny Fern: An Independent Woman*:New Brunswick: Rutgers UP, 1992.

Yellin, Jean Fagan. *Harriet Jacobs: A Life*. New York: Basic Books, 2004.

4 Hawthorne, Melville, and suffering humanity

Nathaniel Hawthorne (1804–1864) and Herman Melville (1819–1891) are often taught today side by side in college courses because of the so-called "Dark Romanticism" of their works, most famously *The Scarlet Letter* (1850) and *Moby-Dick* (1851), which feature tormented characters and tragic events. The two authors were good friends for several years and shared similar world views. They first met in the summer of 1850, when Hawthorne was forty-six and Melville thirty-one. Hawthorne had moved to Lenox, Massachusetts in the Berkshires after his firing from the Salem Custom House and the publication of *The Scarlet Letter*. Melville, a resident of New York City, and in the midst of writing *Moby-Dick*, took a summer vacation in the Berkshires, and invited his editor Evert Duyckinck and their friend Cornelius Mathews to join him, which they did. Melville and Hawthorne first met on August 5, 1850, at a picnic organized by a resident of the area. The party of ten in horse-drawn carriages ascended and climbed Monument Mountain. It became a festive occasion disrupted only briefly by a thundershower. On the mountain, Hawthorne humorously pretended to look around for a precious rock known as the Great Carbuncle, the topic of one of his tales. Melville, a former sailor, climbed out on a projecting rock, as if it were the yardarm of a ship. Mathews read a poem about the mountain. And they all drank champagne. Afterward, they had midday dinner together lasting three hours at which Oliver Wendell Holmes, the Boston poet and cultural elitist, made fun of the pretensions of Americans, and, according to various accounts, found himself challenged by Melville or Hawthorne, or both.

Melville and Hawthorne began to bond that day. One reason was their connection to the sea. Melville had written a series of books about his adventures as a sailor, including *Typee*, which Hawthorne had reviewed. Hawthorne came from a family of sailors, and he had grown up in Salem, a thriving seaport at the time. Both men lost their fathers at an early age, and both felt skeptical about the mass of mankind and American democracy. (Like Poe, they feared democracy could lead to violent mobs.) Both also admired Andrew Jackson and allied themselves with the Democratic Party. Soon after the August 5, 1850 picnic, Hawthorne invited Melville to spend several days at the Hawthornes' rented Lenox cottage. Meanwhile, Duyckinck asked Melville if he would write

DOI: 10.4324/9781315751627-4

a review of Hawthorne's *Mosses from an Old Manse* (1846), which he did, using the pseudonym "a Virginian Spending July in Vermont."

The review, which appeared in the August 17 and August 24 issues of *The Literary World*, edited by Duyckinck, overflows with praise. It celebrates Hawthorne's "great power of blackness," that is, his "appeals to that Calvinistic sense of Innate Depravity and Original Sin, from whose visitations, in some shape or other, no deeply thinking mind is always and wholly free" ("Mosses" 521). It also compares Hawthorne to Shakespeare, who awes us by "those deep far-away things in him; those occasional flashings-forth of the intuitive Truth in him; those short, quick probings at the very axis of reality" (522). In an apparent response to Holmes, Melville writes,

> Let America then prize and cherish her writers; yea, let her glorify them. They are not so many in number, as to exhaust her good-will. And while she has good kith and kin of her own, to take to her bosom, let her not lavish her embraces upon the household of an alien.
>
> (525)

Two years later, Melville would satirize such literary nationalism in his novel *Pierre* (1852).

Kindred spirits

Before he met Hawthorne and read his work, Melville knew that his own pessimism about the state of mankind and the benevolence of the Creator placed him at odds with the mass of American readers for whom optimism was the norm. The concept of Manifest Destiny was accepted by many as a belief that Americans were God's chosen people, destined to populate the American continent from the Atlantic to the Pacific. Slavery, poverty, alcoholism, child labor, the exploitation of workers, especially the Irish and free blacks, persisted as evils beneath the surface, yet for the majority of free, white American men, things were getting better, and reform efforts were improving the lives of many. Yet neither Hawthorne nor Melville shared the optimism of their dominant culture.

Most Americans were pleased that between the Revolution and the Civil War tribes of Indians had been removed as a danger to those living on the frontier, yet Hawthorne in his story "Main-Street" (1849) critiqued this "progress," and Melville in *Moby-Dick* named the *Pequod* in honor of the Pequot Indians, reminding readers not only of the tribe's doom, but also their ruthless annihilation by New England colonial settlers. While Americans celebrated the vast new western territories acquired by the US government through purchase and the Mexican War, Hawthorne and Melville viewed such imperialistic aggression skeptically. The industrial age had arrived in the country along with a rise in personal wealth and financial success, yet the families of Hawthorne and Melville had fallen into poverty, and in their fictions both authors express nostalgia for a lost aristocratic past and sympathy for characters assailed by their social inferiors.

Whereas Hawthorne viewed history as a helix of sorts, with sins of the past reappearing in the present, Melville saw life as a precarious ongoing struggle involving free will, necessity, and chance. As for God's role in one's life, he worried that the deity could not hear human suffering, or worse yet, caused it. Hawthorne had a faith in God's benevolence, stating several times that man's accidents are God's purposes. Melville studied his Old Testament closely and worried that we are all in the position of Job, subject to a multitude of pains and tragedies, because the devil has been allowed by God to do as he will with us. And if we demand to know why, we are taunted by God, who asks, "Where wast thou when I laid the foundations of the earth? declare, if thou hast understanding" (Job 38:4). Hawthorne, whose faith was founded on the New Testament, viewed human suffering as a mystery beyond the powers of man to solve. It pained him and saddened him, but it did not lead him to challenge God's benevolence or omnipotence. Melville, at times, struggled with the possibility that there is no God to believe in or even to question. *Moby-Dick* dramatizes that struggle.

Melville's interests were more metaphysical than Hawthorne's, and his literary greatness lies in the sublimity he achieved in revealing all those horrible things in life that "crack the sinews" and "cake the brain," as his narrator Ishmael puts it, and also all those ways that deeply thinking persons try to understand and cope with forms of human suffering, both physical and psychological. The range of coping responses Melville portrays includes passive aggression (as in his story "Bartleby"), revenge (as in *Benito Cereno*), displaced revenge (as in *Moby-Dick*), and apparent acceptance (as in his novella *Billy Budd*).

Perhaps the most shocking aspect of Melville's praise of Hawthorne in his review is its sexual imagery. As a "Virginian," Melville confesses,

> already I feel that this Hawthorne has dropped germanous seeds into my soul. He expands and deepens down, the more I contemplate him; and further and further, shoots his strong New-England roots in the hot soil of my Southern soul.
>
> (529)

Melville clearly was emboldened by Hawthorne's writings and friendship, and scholars have long debated the degree of influence Hawthorne exerted on *Moby-Dick*, or, at least, on Melville's decision to raise it from a romantic story of the whale fishery into the wonderful and massive epic it became. When he completed *Moby-Dick*, Melville dedicated it to Hawthorne, "in token of my admiration for his genius." Hawthorne responded with a "joy-giving and exultation-breeding" letter, moving Melville to declare:

> A sense of unspeakable security is in me this moment, on account of your having understood the book. I have written a wicked book, and feel

spotless as the lamb. Ineffable socialities are in me. I would sit down and dine with you and all the gods in old Rome's Pantheon.

(*Correspondence* 212)

Hawthorne's literary development

Hawthorne, although usually reserved and taciturn, seems to have won the affection and admiration of all who got to know him well, and positive aspects of his personality contributed to his development as a writer, especially his keen powers of observation, his deep understanding of human nature, and his compassion for those struggling with hidden distress. His knowledge of the workings of the human mind, especially dealing with guilt, exceeded that of almost all his contemporaries. Plus, the elegant, subtle, nuanced way he was able to show, as opposed to merely tell, the consequences of certain kinds of destructive behavior elevates his fiction far above the ordinary. Even though Emerson found Hawthorne's work depressing and "not good for anything" (*JMN* 7: 465), Hawthorne's daughter Rose presented one of the best explanations for her father's focus on sin and guilt in his writings. She recalled, "He wrote with temperateness and in pitying love of human nature, in the instinctive hope of helping it to know and redeem itself" (Lathrop 478).

Hawthorne was born in Salem, the second of three children. He seems to have known from an early age that he would become a writer, and his home life proved conducive to the imaginative and creative personality he acquired. The most wrenching event he experienced was the death of his father when he was four years old. His father had been a sea captain, who died of yellow fever off the coast of Surinam. Hawthorne's mother, left without means to support herself and her children, moved into her mother and father's house, the Mannings, in Salem. The absent father would become a key element in Hawthorne's greatest fiction, as it is in Melville's. In his youth, Hawthorne did not care for school much; in fact, he played hooky as often as he could. After he injured his foot playing ball, he did not return for three years, being privately tutored in the meantime. At home, he and his brilliant older sister, Elizabeth, started their own periodical, which they called *The Spectator* and circulated among the family. The eighteenth-century essayists Joseph Addison and Richard Steele were early influences, contributing to Hawthorne's distinctive prose style, marked by clarity, unhurried pace, and descriptive density. Later, he got more excited by romantic authors such as Sir Walter Scott and especially wild and wooly Gothic writers like the American John Neal, who loved lots of blood and mystery, such as magic portraits, clanging chains, ghosts, and so on. Hawthorne never went for the Gothic of pure sensation, however, and included a strong moral element in all he wrote as an adult. He had a good sense of humor, almost silly and slapstick at times, especially in some of his early stories, which are seldom assigned in college classes.

Two of the most influential books Hawthorne read in his youth were Edmund Spenser's *Faerie Queene* (1590) and John Bunyan's *Pilgrim's Progress*

(1678), both of which gave him an affinity for allegorical techniques in his own writings. That is, he learned to use characters, settings, and objects as representative of ideas or concepts that moved through time in relation to one another. For example, Pilgrim, the protagonist of *Pilgrim's Progress*, carries a burden on his back, which represents the sins he has committed, and he makes his way through life toward the Celestial City (Heaven) but must travel through places named Vanity Fair, the Slough of Despond, and so on. Hawthorne's use of allegory was seldom so obvious or didactic, yet his notebooks do show that his narratives often began with an idea that he wished to carry forward. For example, *The Scarlet Letter* began with the following entry in one of Hawthorne's notebooks: "The life of a woman, who, by the old colony law, was condemned always to wear the letter A, sewed on her garment, in token of her having committed adultery" (*CE* 8: 254). This was the germ of the romance he wrote five years later, yet he endowed Hester Prynne's letter A with rich multiplicity. Whether in the Puritan marketplace or the forest, its meaning varies depending on the viewer.

Hawthorne acquired an affinity for the wilderness as a young man. At age fourteen, he moved with his mother from the Manning house in Salem to a family home on Sebago Lake in Raymond, Maine. He later recalled it as a liberating place, where he spent hours hunting, fishing, and enjoying himself with a few companions. In Salem, the most influential male figure in Hawthorne's life during his youth was his uncle Robert Manning, a no-nonsense businessman, who ran a stage-coach line and conducted horticultural experiments with fruit trees. He and Nathaniel had a rather antagonistic relationship and perhaps it is not surprising that several of Hawthorne's villains spend time with plants and poisons. At age seventeen, Hawthorne went to New Brunswick, Maine, to attend the new inexpensive Bowdoin College there and was a rather uninspired student. Though not as bad as Poe, he did gamble and drink and skip mandatory worship service, incurring fines as a result. He also joined a literary society and made lifelong friends, in particular, Horatio Bridge (who would help him publish his first book, *Twice Told Tales* (1837), by guaranteeing the publisher against loss) and Franklin Pierce (who would become president of the United States and appoint Hawthorne as consul to Liverpool as a reward for writing his campaign biography). Hawthorne also knew Henry Wadsworth Longfellow, who later helped Hawthorne's career by writing a laudatory review of *Twice-Told Tales* and bringing Hawthorne to the attention of the public.

After college, Hawthorne returned to Salem and spent the next twelve years in his old bedroom, writing stories and sketches for the magazines, annuals, and gift books. He also traveled about New England and New York on his own, collecting scenes, stories, and characters. As he tried to establish himself as a professional author and contribute to a national literature, he read histories about the American past, from the founding of the Massachusetts Bay colony through the Provincial period (when royal governors ruled the colonies) to just before the American Revolution. He did not write about the Revolution itself until near the end of his career, with an unpublished work called "Septimius

Felton." Because Hawthorne was a pacifist, he found it difficult to regard war, even the Revolution and the Civil War, as moral endeavors. For him, just because one group could defeat another in warfare, it proved nothing about the righteousness of their cause. In his nonfiction book about England titled *Our Old Home* (1863), he declares,

> in truth, the whole system of a people crowing over its military triumphs had far better be dispensed with, both on account of the ill-blood that it helps to keep fermenting among the nations, and because it operates as an accumulative inducement to future generations to aim at a kind of glory, the gain of which has generally proved more ruinous than its loss.
> (*CE* 5: 257)

As for the use of violence to right wrongs, Hawthorne insisted that "vengeance and beneficence are things that God claims for Himself. His instruments have no consciousness of His purpose; if they imagine they have, it is a pretty sure token that they are *not* His instruments" (*CE* 18: 116).

Early tales

Critiques of hypocritical self-righteousness permeate Hawthorne's fiction. In one of his early stories, "The Gentle Boy," the Puritans Tobias and Dorothy Pearson take in a hated Quaker child with the Muslim name, Ilbrahim. As Tobias tells his wife, referring to their neighbors, "'Christian men, alas! Had cast him out to die'" (*Tales and Sketches* 113). Hawthorne did not attend church as an adult, distrusted most ministers, and had no interest in religious dogma; nevertheless, he had a deep and reverent Christian faith, which he seldom discussed with others, but which informed much of his work. His tales and novels dramatize the need for sympathy and compassion, especially for those characters who are suffering, no matter their politics or social standing.

His early tale "My Kinsman, Major Molineux," for example, features the young protagonist Robin, who has come to town from the country seeking help from his high-placed kinsman, Major Molineux. Although the boy is described repeatedly as "shrewd," it becomes clear that his journey to the city is a rite of initiation, where he encounters a mob of rioters led by a fantastic figure who looks like the devil. Robin has been taught admirable values in his country home, but the city has some hellish features. At a key moment, he looks within a church, and sees a moonlit Bible reminding him of the family and values he is leaving behind:

> He pictured them assembled at the door, beneath the tree, the great old tree, which had been spared for its huge twisted trunk, and venerable shade, when a thousand leafy brethren fell. There, at the going down of the summer sun, it was his father's custom to perform domestic worship, that the neighbors might come and join with him like brothers of the

family, and that the wayfaring man might pause to drink at that fountain, and keep his heart pure by freshening the memory of home.

(*Tales and Sketches* 80)

Through such descriptive means, Hawthorne invites the reader to question the moral value of the experience Robin is acquiring. As Robin watches a colonial mob tarring and feathering his kinsman, a royal appointee, Hawthorne emphasizes that Major Molineux's main fault has been loyalty to his king. As for the colonists, "On they went, in counterfeited pomp, in senseless uproar, in frenzied merriment, trampling all on an old man's heart" (*Tales and Sketches* 86). When Robin joins in the crowd's laughter at the tale's end, Hawthorne encourages the reader to question its meaning. Robin, like the coming new nation, may "rise in the world," but the violence surrounding it threatens to stain that rise with guilt.

Hawthorne has often been linked to Puritanism, because his paternal great grandparents played significant roles in colonial society and because he used Puritan society as a major setting; however, his concerns were not primarily theological. Rather, his focus was on morality, that is, on issues of right and wrong behavior, especially in terms of how individuals treat one another. His works are filled with dramatic irony, because his characters often fail to realize that by trying to do what they consider good and positive things, they end up being harmful and destructive. Unintended consequences fascinated him. He absorbed this perspective at an early age when he learned that the people, magistrates, and ministers in Salem in 1692 thought they were driving the devil out of New England by imprisoning and hanging innocent persons accused of witchcraft. As he relates in his preface to *The Scarlet Letter*, his great-great-grandfather Judge John Hathorne was a central figure in prosecuting the accused people; he "made himself so conspicuous in the martyrdom of the witches," Hawthorne writes, "that their blood may fairly be said to have left a stain upon him" (*CE* 1: 9).

While using historical materials, Hawthorne sought to go beyond them by creating characters that struggle with psychological problems, most often related to sin and guilt. With the classic tale "The Minister's Black Veil," both the reader and Reverend Hooper's congregation must struggle to understand the meaning of the veil. It unsettles all who view the minister wearing it, and, as he preaches, "such was the effect of this simple piece of crape, that more than one woman of delicate nerves was forced to leave the meeting-house" (*Tales and Sketches* 373). A multitude of interpretations have been offered for the significance of the veil, including the minister's secret sin and the sin of all mankind. Perhaps the most useful approach to interpreting the tale is to ask why you respond to visible differences in other people you see. Is the discomfort you may feel a positive or negative response, and does that discomfort lead to social or spiritual growth? In this and his other tales, Hawthorne persistently suggests that there's a fluidity and multiplicity to human experience that can provoke understanding if one lets it.

Even though Hawthorne's early tales and sketches were greatly admired for their originality and artistry, he struggled to earn enough money to marry and start a family. He took a job he hated as Weigher and Gauger at the Boston Custom House, worked briefly as an editor on a magazine, enlisting his talented sister Elizabeth to provide copy to fill out the issues, wrote a series of children's stories, tried to enter the schoolbook market, and finally invested in the utopian community Brook Farm, in hopes that he and his fiancée, Sophia Peabody, could marry and live there together. Working on the farm, however, sapped his energy, making it difficult to write in the evenings, so he left after eight months. "It is my opinion, dearest," he wrote his fiancée, "that a man's soul may be buried and perish under a dung-heap or in a furrow of the field, just as well as under a pile of money" (*CE* 15: 545). When he and Sophia married and moved to Concord in 1842, the subjects of his tales shifted, due to the presence in the town of not only Emerson, but also the host of young poets and intellectuals attracted by Emerson.

At the Manse in Concord

The group of tales and sketches Hawthorne included in *Mosses from an Old Manse* (1846) show the influence of the Transcendentalists. Both Hawthorne and his wife Sophia found much to admire about Emerson, Thoreau, and Margaret Fuller but also regarded them critically at times. Sophia wrote in her journal a humorous account of her husband, Thoreau, and Emerson ice-skating together on the Concord River behind Hawthorne's house, the Manse:

> Henry Thoreau is an experienced skater, and was figuring dithyrambic dances and Bacchic leaps on the ice—very remarkable, but very ugly, methought. Next him followed Mr. Hawthorne who, wrapped in his cloak, moved like a self-impelled Greek statue, stately, and grave. Mr. Emerson closed the line, evidently too weary to hold himself erect, pitching headforemost, half lying on the air. He came in to rest himself, and said to me that Hawthorne was a tiger, a bear, a lion,—in short, a satyr, and there was no tiring him out; and he might be the death of a man like himself.
>
> (Lathrop, 53)

Obviously, Sophia adored her husband more than their Transcendentalist neighbors and wished to establish a certain superiority to them.

Hawthorne shared this wish, and in his preface "The Old Manse," he writes that he admired Emerson "as a poet of deep beauty and austere tenderness," but sought "nothing from him as a philosopher." He also satirizes Emerson slyly by reporting it was good to meet him "sometimes in our avenue, with that pure, intellectual gleam diffused about his presence, like the garment of a shining-one" (*CE* 10: 31).

The one Transcendentalist Hawthorne felt closest to, at least during his years at the Old Manse (1842–1845), was Margaret Fuller, who visited with his wife and spent time with him, taking walks in the woods, boat rides on the Concord River, and, at least on one occasion, spending time with him in Concord's Sleepy Hollow chatting about various subjects. As Hawthorne wrote in his notebook:

> We talked about Autumn—and about the pleasures of getting lost in the woods—and about the crows, whose voices Margaret had heard—and about the experiences of early childhood, whose influence remains upon the character after the recollection of them has passed away—and about the sight of mountains from a distance, and the view from their summits—and about other matters of high and low philosophy.
>
> (CE 8: 343)

This conversation is remarkable given Hawthorne's reputation for shyness. As for Fuller, she wrote in her journal about Hawthorne, "I love him much, & love to be with him in this sweet tender homely scene. But I should like too, to be with him on the bold ocean shore" (89). As the scholar Thomas Mitchell has pointed out, Hawthorne was fascinated by Fuller and used her as "a partial model for the most complex and provocative women characters in his fiction" (10). One of these was Hester Prynne, punished for having her lover's child.

The stories Hawthorne wrote at Concord, many of which appear in the collection *Mosses from an Old Manse,* address current issues more than those in the historical past. They also become more domestic in focus and dramatize the abuse of women by men. In stories such as "The Birth-mark" and "Rappacinni's Daughter," the male characters try to perfect or protect the central female characters, but the unintended consequences are fatal. In "The Birth-mark," the husband Alymer, an elderly scientist, attempts to remove a birthmark from the cheek of his beautiful young bride, Georgiana, but in doing so, he manages to kill her. To complete the irony, Hawthorne has Georgiana praise her inept husband for his idealism: "My poor Aylmer!" she repeated, with a more than human tenderness. "You have aimed loftily!—you have done nobly! Do not repent, that, with so high and pure a feeling, you have rejected the best that earth could offer. Aylmer—dearest Aylmer—I am dying!" (*Tales and Sketches* 780). Similarly, Dr. Rappacccini poisons his daughter, Beatrice, in an effort to protect her. He secretly inoculates her from worldly dangers by raising her in a garden of poisonous plants whose aromas she inhales. When a would-be lover, Giovanni, learns of her poisonous nature, and his as well, he, too, tries to save them, with an antidote that kills her, as she knew it would. "I would fain have been loved, not feared" (*Tales and Sketches* 1005), she says to Giovanni and her father, as she dies. Some scholars have identified Hawthorne with his male characters and charged him with misogyny; however, the charge seems misplaced since he not only dramatizes the harm men inflict on women in his stories, but also creates an iconic strong woman with *The Scarlet Letter*'s Hester, who successfully resists.

One of Hawthorne's major themes is the danger of loss of sympathy resulting from obsessive projects, both personal and political. A number of his male characters take this tendency to an extreme, becoming like the protagonists in his tales "Wakefield" and "Ethan Brand." Wakefield, "a crafty nincompoop," deserts his wife and family as a mere joke but falls into the habit of observing them from lodgings in the next street for twenty years before returning home:

> As he passes in, we have a parting glimpse of his visage, and recognize the crafty smile, which was the precursor of the little joke, that he has ever since been playing off at his wife's expense. How unmercifully has he quizzed the poor woman!
>
> (*Tales and Sketches* 298)

The much more intelligent character Ethan Brand goes in search of the Unpardonable Sin, "the sin of an intellect that triumphed over the sense of brotherhood with man, and reverence for God," and discovers it at last within himself, because his studies have made him "a cold observer" with a hardened heart. Among his sins, he made a young girl "the subject of a psychological experiment, and wasted, absorbed, and perhaps annihilated her soul in the process" (*Tales and Sketches* 1060). Distraught by what he has done, Brand commits suicide by plunging into a burning lime kiln. In Hawthorne's fiction, those characters who lose their sympathy for their fellow man receive little from the author.

The Scarlet Letter (1850)

The Scarlet Letter combines critiques of the abuse of women, notably Hester Prynne, and of the dangers of hypocrisy. Hawthorne's preface to the novel, titled "The Custom-House," shows the author identifying with Hester as a victim of Puritanical antagonists, in his case blood-thirsty Whigs, in her case seventeenth-century Puritans. In 1846, Hawthorne, through the efforts of a few close friends, won appointment to the office of surveyor in the Custom House at Salem. "The Custom-House," a loosely autobiographical account of his time in that job, features the pains of government service, especially being fired as a result of the "spoils system." Hawthorne's hero, President Andrew Jackson, initiated the system by arguing that the common man could manage the country's business as well as so-called experts and that it was appropriate to appoint members of one's own political party to government posts and boot out those members of the opposing party, no matter how experienced. When the party in power shifted in 1848, with the election of Whig candidate Zachery Taylor to the presidency, Hawthorne was fired.

For a time, he resisted, claiming that because he did not engage in party politics, he should be retained; however, in actuality he had threatened to fire two subordinates who refused to contribute a portion of their bonuses to the Democratic Party. In his preface, written after the romance itself was essentially completed, Hawthorne takes revenge on the Whigs who ousted him by portraying himself as an innocent victim of partisan politics. He also takes the reader into the past step by step through his fictional account of how the manuscript of the story came into his possession—from a previous inspector, who heard it from aged persons, who had known Hester Prynne in her old age. All of this was a fabrication, of course.

Hawthorne's theory of romance, found in "The Custom-House," describes the genre as "a neutral territory, somewhere between the real world and fairyland, where the Actual and the Imaginary may meet, and each imbue itself with the nature of the other" (*CE* 1: 36). Hawthorne peoples his fictional world with actual places, actual historical figures, and actual historical events, yet his characters and their interactions are all products of his imagination. In the preface to his next novel, he explains that his goal is not to portray historical facts, but rather, "the truth of the human heart." In this sense, he was one of the first American writers to create psychological realism, that is, accurate accounts of the workings of the human mind. A host of authors followed him in this vein, notably Henry James and William Faulkner. For Hawthorne, fiction provided a deeper understanding of human behavior than pure history ever could. In an early sketch, he points out that the writings of biographers and historians offer knowledge like that of a "map,—minute, perhaps, and accurate, and available for all necessary purposes,—but cold and naked, and wholly destitute of the mimic charm produced by landscape painting" (*Tales and Sketches* 12). In deciding which persons to represent in his fiction, Hawthorne, unlike contemporary historians, preferred to feature those without power or renown. As Melville discerned, Hawthorne possessed an "unshackled democratic spirit of Christianity in all things" ("Mosses" 527); nevertheless, Hawthorne identified with his more refined fictional characters when they were assailed by their social inferiors, Hester being the most obvious example.

Hawthorne did not intend to write a whole book about Hester and her scarlet letter; he conceived the narrative as one of a series of tales to be brought together as *Tales of My Native Land*, but his editor, James T. Fields, persuaded him to make it a stand-alone work, one now considered a classic of American literature. Some of the less obvious features of *The Scarlet Letter* that deserve attention from readers are first, the richness of the imagery throughout, from the door of the jail at the beginning to the engraved tombstone at the end. Notice also the architectural beauty of the romance as a whole—the use of the three scaffold scenes set at the beginning, middle, and end like three masts on a ship, with each having the four main characters situated in relation to one another in such a way as to suggest the changes taking place in their relationships. There's a centrifugal force at work, bringing them closer and closer together, and this force is a fusion of love and hate, fate and free will, God's law and man's lawlessness. Notice, too, the way Hawthorne not only alternates scenes between the town and the forest, but carefully elaborates upon the values associated with each site, values that can be read as positive or negative, depending on the reader's own political belief system. The wilderness, for example, is credited for making Hester strong, yet it also "taught her much amiss" (*CE* 1: 200). Hawthorne's explicit theme is "be true," but other themes include the cruelty of self-righteousness, the oppression of a male-dominated society, the drabness of a world where beauty and romance and love cannot thrive naturally.

Whereas Melville's early works are filled with action and adventure, Hawthorne's are more slow-moving and descriptive. He is more like a painter than a story-teller. In almost all cases, the external world as he describes it is indicative of his characters' mental and moral states, and the challenge for the reader is to perceive the suggested psychological struggles underway as his narratives unfold. All of the details in his works matter. For example, in chapter 2, "The Recognition," when Arthur Dimmesdale is persuaded to plead with Hester to identify her "fellow-sinner," Hawthorne writes,

> The young pastor's voice was tremulously sweet, rich, deep, and broken. The feeling that it so evidently manifested, rather than the direct purport of the words, caused it to vibrate within all hearts, and brought the listeners into one accord of sympathy. Even the poor baby, at Hester's bosom, was affected by the same influence; for it directed its hitherto vacant gaze towards Mr. Dimmesdale, and held up its little arms, with a half pleased, half plaintive murmur.
>
> (CE 1: 67)

The "recognition" implicit here is the child Pearl's recognition of her father, and the careful reader's recognition of the fellow-sinner's identity.

Again, when the lovers Hester and Arthur meet in the forest after seven years apart, Hester tosses her letter of shame aside, and Hawthorne hints at her sexual arousal by writing:

> There played around her mouth, and beamed out of her eyes, a radiant and tender smile, that seemed gushing from the very heart of womanhood. A crimson flush was glowing on her cheek that had been long so pale. Her sex, her youth, and the whole richness of her beauty, came back from what men call the irrevocable past, and clustered themselves, with her maiden hope, and a happiness before unknown, within the magic circle of this hour. And, as if the gloom of the earth and sky had been but the effluence of these two mortal hearts, it vanished with their sorrow. All at once, as with a sudden smile of heaven, forth burst the sunshine, pouring a very flood into the obscure forest.
>
> (CE 1: 202–203)

The liquid gushing, flushing, blushing, bursting, and pouring in this description, serve to tell the reader how it was that Hester and Arthur created a baby before the novel began. It also indicates that, for Hester, the seven years have not abated her passion for Arthur.

In *The Scarlet Letter*, Hawthorne consistently emphasizes the links between mind and body. The Puritan minister Arthur Dimmesdale pretends to be something he's not, an honorable man, and Hawthorne shows his deceit and hypocrisy eating away at him, sapping his physical and moral strength. By denying his paternity, Arthur loses his integrity, his wholeness, and Hawthorne traces the effects of his hypocrisy upon his body. In chapter 12, "The Minister in a Maze," we see how deceit not only reduces one to confusion, but also dissolves the world and the self.

> To the untrue man, the whole universe is false,—it is impalpable,—it shrinks to nothing within his grasp. And he himself, in so far as he shows himself in a false light, becomes a shadow, or, indeed, ceases to exist.
> (CE 1: 145–146)

This dramatic truth applies not just to those living in seventeenth-century Boston, but also to many readers living in the present. To dissemble takes a toll on the body; whereas integrity allows for a sense of equanimity that relaxes and enhances one's appearance. Chillingworth, Hester's husband, becomes literally darker and more twisted while plying his revenge.

One of Hawthorne's favorite narrative techniques, which he shared with Poe and Melville, was the use of doubling, and in *The Scarlet Letter*, Chillingworth becomes Arthur's double, in the sense that he assumes the role of Arthur's conscience, tormenting him with guilt, just as Poe's William Wilson is tormented. Hester, who refuses to acknowledge the colony's authority over her, maintains her beauty and energy by means of her spirit of independence. The scarlet letter, initially a visual stigma, meant to shame, Hester embraces, as she embraces the child Pearl, who is its embodiment. Her courage thus elevates her above her detractors and serves as an example to all readers, including those stigmatized by words or deed, because of our behavior or appearance, such as, our weight, height, clothes, the way we talk or walk or laugh, because of our race, religion, gender, or age. Because Hester refuses to be shamed, even while accepting her punishment, she maintains her self-respect.

The Scarlet Letter is often taught in high schools; however, it is most suitable for mature readers, though not because it deals with adultery, but because it addresses the question of how to cope with the burden of sin (one of Hawthorne's favorite topics). If a reader has not yet acquired such a burden, the novel can seem too foreign to be engaging, especially since it is set almost four hundred years in the past, among a superstitious and intolerant people, and precious little action occurs in the book, not even the adultery itself. On the other hand, mature readers who have behaved in ways that have violated the moral principles they have tried to live by, can relate and even understand the mental struggles of the main characters, Hester, Arthur, and Chillingworth, all of whom have to deal with their moral failings. The fate of the child Pearl, then, depends on their behavior. When Pearl's father, Arthur, finally confesses his paternity, at the moment of his death, a curse is lifted and Pearl's future becomes bright:

> Pearl kissed his lips. A spell was broken. The great scene of grief, in which the wild infant bore a part, had developed all her sympathies; and as her

tears fell upon her father's cheek, they were the pledge that she would grow up amid human joy and sorrow, nor for ever do battle with the world, but be a woman in it. Towards her mother, too, Pearl's errand as a messenger of anguish was all fulfilled.

(CE 1: 256)

To lighten the gloom that pervades the novel, Hawthorne suggests in the "Conclusion" that Pearl, after inheriting "a very considerable amount of property" from Roger Chillingworth, goes abroad, marries into European nobility, and is "happy, and mindful of her mother."

Hester resolves to stay in Boston, near the spirit of her dead lover, and she dies, "after many, many years," and is buried next to him, "yet with a space between, as if the dust of the two sleepers had no right to mingle" (CE 1: 264). Puritanism thus maintains its unending sway, and, as I have pointed out elsewhere,

> Ultimately, Hawthorne wishes us to discover that the most dangerous persons in the novel are not those characters who conjure up the specter of the devil by following their unruly passions—that is, Chillingworth, Arthur, Hester, Pearl, and Mistress Hibbins—but those who perpetuate a society masking cruelty as righteousness, despotism as justice.

(Reynolds 168)

Hawthorne's sympathies flowed toward his characters, even those who are deeply flawed, and in his *English Notebooks*, he recalls,

> my emotions when I read the last scene of the Scarlet Letter to my wife, just after writing it—tried to read it, rather, for my voice swelled and heaved, as if I were tossed up and down on an ocean, as it subsided after a storm.

(CE 21: 339–340)

Despite his inveterate reserve, Hawthorne possessed, as Melville observed, "boundless sympathy with all forms of being" ("Mosses" 520).

While Hawthorne and his growing family were living in the Berkshires with Melville close by, Hawthorne wrote a children's book, *The Wonder-book for Boys and Girls* (1851), and a romance, *The House of the Seven Gables* (1851). Although *House* has a happy ending (which critics have seen as forced) the romance sets out a powerful critique of the abuse of political power by those who attain high office, like the villain Judge Pyncheon, and control over the weak and vulnerable. It also treats subtly yet harshly those who, like Phoebe Pyncheon, fail to perceive the true nature of these men and their corruption and cruelty. Hawthorne gave Melville an inscribed copy of *House*, when it was published, and Melville, in an April 16, 1851, letter of thanks, reviewed the book, declaring,

> There is a certain tragic phase of humanity which, in our opinion, was never more powerfully embodied than by Hawthorne. We mean the tragicalness of human thought in its own unbiassed, native, and profounder workings. We think that into no recorded mind has the intense feeling of the visable truth ever entered more deeply than into this man's. By visable truth, we mean the apprehension of the absolute condition of present things as they strike the eye of the man who fears them not, though they do their worst to him.
>
> (*Correspondence* 186–187)

Of course, Melville's description of Hawthorne applied more to himself at the time, in the throes of finishing *Moby-Dick*, than it did to his more moderate friend.

During the remaining thirteen years of his life, Hawthorne wrote two more romances, *The Blithedale Romance* (1852), based roughly on his time at Brook Farm, and *The Marble Faun* (1860), set in Italy and focused on three American artists and one young Italian nobleman, who commits a murder that the other three must come to terms with. When Hawthorne returned to Concord, Massachusetts, from seven years abroad in England and Italy, he worked on several other romances, but was unable to complete them. Because he was a pacifist, he struggled to cope with the war fever in Concord and throughout the North, following the South's succession. Two years before his death, he traveled to the war front and wrote a provocative article "Chiefly about War-Matters, by a Peaceable Man" (1862) that earned him vilification from many of his friends and acquaintances.

Melville's youth

Melville, a much more outgoing person than Hawthorne, spent his early life in a Manhattan home with servants, carriages, and other signs of luxury and privilege. He was the third of eight children born to Allan Melville and Maria Gansevoort Melville, both of whom had illustrious genealogies and aristocratic sensibilities. Maria's family had been Dutch patricians, and Allan traced his lineage to Scottish nobility, the lords of Melville and Levin. Melville told Sophia Hawthorne that he and his wife Elizabeth named their son Malcom for it was a family name. In the 1820s, Melville's father imported French fancy goods, but in 1830, when Herman was eleven, his father went bankrupt, and the desperate and impoverished family had to move to Albany, where they depended on the charity of Melville's uncle, Peter Gansevoort, to survive. Several biographers have focused on the moment when Melville and his father left New York City (the rest of the family had gone on ahead). Newton Arvin writes,

> One October night in 1830, in the midst of a violent storm, a middle-aged man and a boy of eleven, Allan Melville and his son Herman, sat waiting

all night at the Cortlandt Street dock for the belated boat to Albany. It was not the first and of course it was not the last of Herman Melville's many embarkations; but there is something in this image—the tempestuous night and the defeated man, with his small son, waiting through the tedious hours for a boat that could only carry them to a painful destination—something touchingly premonitory of much of Melville's life, and especially of his ensuing decade, the vital decade of his teens.

(19–20)

A more recent biography has pointed out that father and son waited out the storm huddled on the boat, but the trauma of the moment remains the same.

A year after the move, Herman was withdrawn from Albany Academy for lack of funds, and three months later, his father died, deep in debt, feverish, and mentally deranged. To help support his family, Herman in his teens worked in a bank, in his older brother's fur cap store in Albany, and on his uncle Thomas's farm in Pittsfield; he also tried unsuccessfully to land a job working on the Erie Canal, and taught for a time at a country school in Greenville, New York, but none of the jobs worked out for him. At the age of nineteen, he signed on as a "boy" on a merchant ship and sailed to Liverpool and back. He then trekked out to the mid-western frontier in Illinois to find work, but found none, just different people and scenes he would incorporate into his writings. In January 1841, he signed on as part of the crew of the whale ship *Acushnet* bound for the South Seas, but after eighteen months at sea, he found conditions unbearable.

> Along with the fearful risks and dangers of the hunt itself, which carried a natural elation with them, there were a thousand things in mere day-to-day life on board a whaler that could only have been galling to a youth like Melville, and have ended by reducing him to rebellious desperation: the cramped, airless, almost lightless filthiness of the forecastle quarters, the dreariness and monotony of the food, the prospect of drawing some trifling wage or no wage at all at the end of a three or four years' voyage, and the association for the most part with the typically brutalized and degraded members of a whaler's crew.
>
> (Arvin 51–52)

Melville and his friend, Toby Greene, jumped ship at the first opportunity in the Marquesan Islands, where he spent several weeks living among a tribe of natives, the Typees. After he left them, he became a beachcomber, was briefly arrested, and made his way to Hawaii where he set pins in a bowling alley, finally signing on a warship, the American frigate USS *United States*, which arrived back in Boston Harbor in 1844. He was twenty-five years old, and he would later tell Hawthorne, "Until I was twenty-five, I had no development at all. From my twenty-fifth year I date my life. Three weeks have scarcely passed, at any time between then and now, that I have not unfolded within myself" (*Correspondence* 193). For Melville, his life began when his intellect became engaged by reading and writing.

The turn to writing

Upon his return to the United States, Melville lived with his family in Lansingburgh, New York, and wrote about his adventures in a best-seller published by John Murray in London under the title *Narrative of a Four Months' Residence Among the Natives of a Valley of the Marquesas Islands*, and by Wiley and Putnam in New York as *Typee: A Peep at Polynesian Life* (1846), as part of their "Library of Choice Reading," which was edited by Evert Duyckinck. This wealthy, well-connected literary gentleman befriended Melville and gave him free access to his large library. Consequently, after his marriage to Elizabeth Shaw and move to New York City, Melville began an exciting project of self-education, becoming a voracious reader. He responded enthusiastically to Shakespeare's plays in a folio edition, and to a number of philosophical and religious works. At the same time, he wrote about his beach-combing adventures in a second best-seller titled *Omoo* (1847), which took missionaries to task for their harsh treatment of native islanders. His growing excitement about abstract and theoretical topics, as well as his interest in the political and social systems of various countries, inspired him to write a massive allegory in his third book, *Mardi* (1849), which few readers could wade through with any sustained interest.

Readers were eager for more light-hearted fare from him, so he quickly wrote what he called two "jobs," *Redburn* (1849) and *White-Jacket* (1850), drawing upon his experiences on a merchant ship and a man-of-war. He went to England to arrange publication of the latter, and the trip inspired him, especially the church services he attended and the plays he saw. He also traveled to France, site of the recent revolution that had led to the overthrow of King Louis Phillippe and the establishment of a provisional republic with the poet-statesman Alphonse de Lamartine at its head. Melville had always had reservations about revolutionary radicalism, for he associated it with atheism, the most intensely negative word in his vocabulary. On the voyage over and during his time in London and Paris, he had long and exciting conversations about metaphysics with George Adler, an animated German-born professor of modern languages at New York University, and later author of *Letters of a Lunatic, A Brief Exposition of my University Life During the Years 1853–54* (1854).

Once back in the United States, Melville started writing a romance about the whale fishery, but when he was part-way through, Duyckinck persuaded him to take a vacation in the Berkshires, where he met Hawthorne. When he made the visit to the Hawthornes' cottage, they found him a delightful guest. For a while they did not know that he was the author of the enthusiastic review of *Mosses*, but they were pleased to discover he was. Sophia Hawthorne described him as "a man with a true warm heart & a soul & an intellect—with life to his finger-tips—earnest, sincere & reverent, very tender & *modest*—And I am not sure that he is not a very great man" (qtd. Melville, *Log* I: 393).

A month after meeting Hawthorne, Melville bought a 160-acre farm in Pittsfield, which he named "Arrowhead," and for the next eighteen months, as he finished *Moby-Dick*, the two men exchanged visits between Pittsfield and Lenox, six miles apart, held long discussions, at times over brandy or champagne, and cigars, and corresponded. Hawthorne's letters from this time have been lost (making the friendship appear one-sided), but Melville's letters survive and show the depth and fervor of the relationship and the deep respect Melville had for Hawthorne. They also reveal the intellectual and emotional excitement that Melville experienced writing his great book.

Moby-Dick (1851)

While writing *Moby-Dick*, Melville displayed tremendous intellectual vitality. The depth and breadth of his thought impelled the book, and reading it tends to exhilarate the mind, enlarge the imagination, and uplift the spirit. During the winter of 1850–1851, he labored intensely, writing in his second-floor study in the Arrowhead farmhouse he had purchased. In a December 1 letter to Duyckinck, he described his days:

> I have a sort of sea-feeling here in the country, now that the ground is all covered with snow. I look out of my window in the morning when I rise as I would out of a port-hole of a ship in the Atlantic. My room seems a ship's cabin; & at nights when I wake up & hear the wind shrieking, I almost fancy there is too much sail on the house, & I had better go on the roof & rig in the chimney.
>
> Do you want to know how I pass my time? My own breakfast over, I go to my workroom & light my fire—then spread my M.S.S. on the table—take one business squint at it, & fall to with a will. At 21/2 P.M. I hear a preconcerted knock at my door, which (by request) continues till I rise & go to the door, which serves to wean me effectively from my writing, however interested I may be. My friends the horse & cow now demand their dinner—& I go & give it to them.
>
> (*Correspondence* 174)

He spent the evenings "in a sort of mesmeric state" with his family gathered around the fireplace downstairs.

As critics have long known, Melville often was not a craftsman. That is, unlike Hawthorne, he did not begin with an architectural plan (like the three scaffold scenes of *The Scarlet Letter*, for example), but rather tried to plot his narratives as he wrote. In *Mardi*, he describes an author named Lombardo who seems much like himself:

> When Lombardo set about his work, he knew not what it would become. He did not build himself in with plans; he wrote right on; and so doing, got deeper and deeper into himself; and like a resolute traveler, plunging

through baffling woods, at last was rewarded for his toils. "In good time," saith he, in his autobiography, "I came out into a serene, sunny, ravishing region; full of sweet scents, singing birds, wild plaints, roguish laughs, prophetic voices. Here we are at last, then," he cried; "I have created the creative."

(595)

When Hawthorne read *Mardi*, he wrote Evert Duykinck that it was

a rich book, with depths here and there that compel a man to swim for his life. It is so good that one scarcely pardons the writer for not having brooded long over it, so as to make it a great deal better.

(CE 16: 362)

With *Moby-Dick*, Melville exerted more control over his plot, but readers have noticed several lapses, such as the disappearance of Ishmael as a character through much of the heart of the book, as Melville takes over as omniscient narrator, reporting information sailor Ishmael could not have been privy to. At these moments, large issues also arise about the nature of human existence. The book has been called a vast symphony, with many motifs and themes woven through it—aesthetic, political, religious, and philosophical. Some of the major interpretations of the novel are as a Shakespearean tragedy using American materials, a rebuttal to the Book of Job, a critique of industrial capitalism, an epic nature myth, an exploration of knowing and being, a study of fate and free will, a satire of Emersonian transcendentalism, a drama of race relations, a critique of tyranny, and a celebration of American democracy.

Ahab and Ishmael dominate the narrative of *Moby-Dick*. Once Ahab emerges from his cabin in chapter 28, he engages his crew, including the younger Ishmael, in the attempt to find and kill the white whale that severed his leg in an earlier voyage. In the course of the hunt, it becomes clear Ahab is not sane. Nor is he humane, though he sees himself as a savior. Ironically, as Ahab seeks justice against Moby Dick and the whale's creator, he abuses his own power, treating his crew as mere tools in his quest. "My one cogged circle fits into all their various wheels, and they revolve" (LoA 971), he says to himself. The result is the death of all, except for Ishmael.

Echoes of *King Lear, Macbeth, Paradise Lost*, and the Bible resound within the plot and language of *Moby-Dick*. These echoes work to elevate Melville's subject, whale hunting, which, at the time was considered a lowly form of butchery, performed by disreputable men, "meanest mariners, and renegades and castaways" (916), Ishmael calls them. In chapters 26 and 27, both titled "Knights and Squires," Melville begins to establish parallels to a Shakespearean tragedy (with Ahab as king, his cabin boy, Pip, as fool, the mates, Starbuck, Stubb, and Flask, as knights, and the harpooners, Queequeg, Tashtego, and Daggoo, as squires). A number of Ahab's speeches take on the cadences of Shakespearean blank verse, as F. O. Matthiessen pointed out long ago.

The opening chapters, all students are happy to find, are quite humorous, with Ishmael in New Bedford coping with the problem of sharing his bed with a head-peddling cannibal, that is, the South Sea Islander Queequeg, with whom he establishes a loving friendship. In chapter 10, "The Bosom Friend," Ishmael even decides to participate, by invitation, in Queequeg's worship of a little black idol named Yojo, following the Golden Rule:

> Now Queequeg is my fellow man. And what do I wish that this Queequeg would do to me? Why, unite with me in my particular Presbyterian form of worship. Consequently, I must unite with him in his; ergo, I must turn idolater. So I kindled the shavings; helped prop up the innocent little idol; offered him burnt biscuit with Queequeg; salaamed before him twice or thrice; kissed his nose; and that done, we undressed and went to bed, at peace with our own consciences and all the world. But we did not go to sleep without some little chat.
>
> (LoA 57)

The homosexual suggestiveness of the relationship is clear to the modern reader, but it is the idolatry that upset Melville's religious contemporaries.

Ahab was even more objectionable. When the captain of the *Pequod* finally emerges on deck, we learn that he was once a devout and high-minded man, but, because of his injury, feels betrayed by the god he once worshipped. His sense of grievance resonates with those readers who have been victims of impersonal forces that have ruined their lives. In other words, Ahab's actions and blasphemy provide a vicarious outlet for the anger and frustration that often wells up inside of persons, as it did for Melville. Ishmael's salvation, both literal and figurative, balances Ahab's downward plunge into madness and death.

For his plot, Melville drew upon the Book of Job. As you may recall, in the King James's version, the book opens by describing Job as "perfect and upright, and one that feared God, and eschewed evil." When Satan comes on the scene, God says to him "Hast thou considered my servant Job, that there is none like him in the earth, a perfect and an upright man, one that feareth God, and escheweth evil?" Satan replies that this is because God has favored Job, which provokes the Lord to say, "Behold, all that he hath is in thy power; only upon himself put not forth thine hand. So Satan went forth from the presence of the Lord." Job subsequently loses his servants, sheep, camels, daughters, sons, and healthy body, which is covered in horrific boils. He is "comforted" by friends who tell him his suffering must be the result of his sinfulness, yet he remains sinless and faithful, though humbled. As Melville interpreted Job's story, God is at fault for allowing the devil to inflict suffering on even the innocent. In chapter 73, "Stubb & Flask kill a Right Whale," the second mate Stubb gives a rendering of "Job," to the third mate, Flask:

> the devil is a curious chap, and a wicked one, I tell ye. Why, they say as how he went a sauntering into the old flag-ship once, switching his tail

about devilish easy and gentlemanlike, and inquiring if the old governor was at home. Well, he was at home, and asked the devil what he wanted. The devil, switching his hoofs, up and says, "I want John." "What for?" says the old governor. "What business is that of yours," says the devil, getting mad,—"I want to use him." "Take him," says the governor—and by the Lord, Flask, if the devil didn't give John the Asiatic cholera before he got through with him ...

(LoA 1141–1142)

Although the writings of both Hawthorne and Melville dwell on unanticipated difficulties, both social and natural, which their characters struggle to understand and control, Melville, much more than Hawthorne, traces human suffering to forces beyond the human realm, that is, to "the old governor," God.

Within *Moby-Dick*, Melville includes a vast amount of material about whales and whale hunting, which serves as ballast to the dramatic adventure story, tying it to the known world, and to the lot of workers. Whaling was a major industry in the US during the first half of the nineteenth century. The whale blubber was stripped from the dead whales and then boiled down into oil onboard the ship in huge copper pots. An expensive commodity, this oil was used for all kinds of lighting, in lamps, streets lights, and lighthouses. In *Moby-Dick,* factories serve as major metaphors, often representing that which is dehumanizing and demonic. The kilns on the deck of the *Pequod* are a key example. In chapter 96, "The Try-Works," the dark night, the fire and smoke from the kilns boiling the whale blubber into oil, the begrimed harpooners stoking the fires, the high wind, the leaping sea all combine to make "the rushing Pequod" seem to Ishmael "the material counterpart of her monomaniac commander's soul" (LoA 1246). Such passages have led some critics to view Ahab as a mad captain of industry, though he shows little interest in the business of whaling. Although Ishmael presents whale hunting as an exciting adventure, he also depicts its wanton destruction of nature. Melville's environmental consciousness has become a recent area of study, and scholars have illuminated the deep respect for nature and its nonhuman inhabitants that the novel reveals, with the possible exception of sharks.

Time and again, Ishmael uses the deceptiveness of natural phenomenon to introduce the problem of knowing, that is, how do we determine the meaning of the world we encounter, within and without. In chapter 58, "Brit," Ishmael uses the sea and land as metaphors to address this problem:

> Consider the subtleness of the sea; how its most dreaded creatures glide under water, unapparent for the most part, and treacherously hidden beneath the loveliest tints of azure. Consider also the devilish brilliance and beauty of many of its most remorseless tribes, as the dainty embellished shape of many species of sharks. Consider, once more, the universal cannibalism of the sea; all whose creatures prey upon each other, carrying on eternal war since the world began. Consider all this; and then turn to this

> green, gentle, and most docile earth; consider them both, the sea and the land; and do you not find a strange analogy to something in yourself?
>
> (LoA 1087)

As the narrative of *Moby-Dick* moves forward, the white whale himself becomes the foremost physical object difficult to understand. Before the voyage, Ishmael imagines him as a mythic creature, "one grand hooded phantom, like a snow hill in the air" (800). The pragmatic first mate Starbuck calls him "a dumb brute" (967), provoking Ahab to exclaim:

> All visible objects, man, are but as pasteboard masks. But in each event—in the living act, the undoubted deed—there, some unknown but still reasoning thing puts forth the mouldings of its features from behind the unreasoning mask. How can the prisoner reach outside except by thrusting through the wall?
>
> (LoA 967)

For Ahab, life imprisons us in a world of flesh and blood and bones, yet to encounter the builder of this prison, which often includes instruments of torture, we have to escape it.

Multiple interpretations have been offered of the white whale. For some he is a mere animal. For others, he indeed acts as an agent of a higher power. To still others he symbolizes the gigantic forces of Nature, with a capital N, that must be treated with respect. And to others he represents Fate, in the sense that life, especially Ahab's life, resembles a Greek tragedy, in which character and Fate are inseparable. Ahab claims that his path to the future is "laid with iron rails, whereon my soul is grooved to run" (972); he sees himself as a train, a mindless machine without the ability to alter course. But, of course, he is making excuses for his monomania. The English Captain Boomer, who appears in chapter 100, also lost a limb, an arm, to the white whale and is philosophical about it, which gives the lie to Ahab's claim.

Yet, Moby Dick the whale can also be seen as death, the fate that comes to us all, in different guises. If so, Ahab's assertion about thrusting through the wall becomes more probing and profound. At times, Melville seems to be using Ahab and whiteness to address questions such as what lies beyond death; why do we exist? Who created us? Where is our creator and who created him or her? In the famous chapter 42, "The Whiteness of the Whale," Melville tries to articulate the difficulty of interpreting what lies beyond human understanding, as represented by whiteness:

> Is it that by its indefiniteness it shadows forth the heartless voids and immensities of the universe, and thus stabs us from behind with the thought of annihilation, when beholding the white depths of the milky way? Or is it, that as in essence whiteness is not so much a color as the visible absence of color, and at the same time the concrete of all colors; is

it for these reasons that there is such a dumb blankness, full of meaning, in a wide landscape of snows—a colorless, all-color of atheism from which we shrink?

(LoA 1001)

Whereas Ishmael exudes humility in the face of the incomprehensible, his captain responds with defiance.

Ahab is portrayed as a radical Transcendentalist, someone who believes, like Emerson, that certain natural facts are symbols of certain spiritual facts; however, for Ahab these spiritual facts are malign. As he explains to the first mate Starbuck, he sees in the white whale "outrageous strength, with an inscrutable malice sinewing it. That inscrutable thing is chiefly what I hate; and be the white whale agent, or be the white whale principal, I will wreak that hate upon him" (967). In chapter 119, "The Candles," Ahab taunts his god by claiming, "I know that of me, which thou knowest not of thyself, oh, thou omnipotent. There is some unsuffusing thing beyond thee, thou clear spirit, to whom all thy eternity is but time, all thy creativeness mechanical" (1334). Ahab imagines himself a Promethean figure, defying the gods or God on behalf of man. He is also Lucifer challenging God's authority over him (Melville admired Milton almost as much as he did Shakespeare and Hawthorne). In two of the most arresting sentences in *Moby-Dick*, Ishmael explains what the whale represents to Ahab:

> All that most maddens and torments; all that stirs up the lees of things; all truth with malice in it; all that cracks the sinews and cakes the brain; all the subtle demonisms of life and thought; all evil, to crazy Ahab, were visibly personified, and made practically assailable in Moby Dick. He piled upon the whale's white hump the sum of all the general rage and hate felt by his whole race from Adam down; and then, as if his chest had been a mortar, he burst his hot heart's shell upon it.
>
> (LoA 989)

And so, Ahab's purpose appears heroic, yet his behavior is insane.

As Ishmael explains, "There is a wisdom that is woe; but there is a woe that is madness" (1248). Wisdom consists in acknowledging the darkness in the world, but not letting it become all you can see. At the end of "The Try-Works" chapter, Melville uses a striking metaphor to convey this point:

> And there is a Catskill eagle in some souls that can alike dive down into the blackest gorges, and soar out of them again and become invisible in the sunny spaces. And even if he for ever flies within the gorge, that gorge is in the mountains; so that even in his lowest swoop the mountain eagle is still higher than other birds upon the plain, even though they soar.
>
> (LoA 1248)

Ishmael, of course, is that eagle able to fly out of the gorges, whereas Ahab cannot; nevertheless, Ahab deserves credit, Melville implies, for being superior to those who never dive into the darkness.

Throughout *Moby-Dick*, Melville obviously uses the colors black and white as moral signifiers; however, at times, whiteness takes on racial connotations as well, and critics have noticed that when Ahab presides over a Black Mass on the deck of the *Pequod* in "The Quarter-Deck" chapter, the dark-skinned harpooners eagerly participate. These include Daggoo (an African), Tashtego (a Native American), and Queequeg (a South Sea Islander), not to mention Fedallah (a South Asian), who is Ahab's secret harpooner in the hold of the ship. Given this grouping, the harpooners seem enlisted in revenge against a white antagonist, representing, perhaps, the imperialism and aggression of the white race. Melville becomes almost explicit about this political theme in his "Fast Fish and Loose Fish" chapter, which explains how whalers claim possession by sticking poles in whale carcasses as they chase other whales:

> What was America in 1492 but a Loose-Fish, in which Columbus struck the Spanish standard by way of waifing it for his royal master and mistress? What was Poland to the Czar? What Greece to the Turk? What India to England? What at last will Mexico be to the United States? All Loose-Fish.
> (LoA 1219)

Throughout his works, including *Moby-Dick*, Melville expresses concern for the subjugated and oppressed, and he criticizes the imperial drive, that is, the claiming of resources while ignoring indigenous rights.

One of the most dramatic violent events on the *Pequod* occurs in chapter 40, "Forecastle-Midnight," which begins with singing, dancing, and shouting by drunken sailors from different places and races, but descends into a knife fight between Daggoo and a Spanish sailor who taunts him, saying, "harpooner, thy race is the undeniable dark side of mankind—devilish dark at that" (980). The fight is stopped by a tremendous storm that hits the ship, and Pip, the little black cabin boy prays, "Oh, thou big white God aloft there somewhere in yon darkness, have mercy on this small black boy down here; preserve him from all men that have no bowels to feel fear!" (982). In an illuminating essay, Walter E. Bezanson cites "Ahab's enlistment of a worldwide primitivism for his wild quest" and summarizes "Forecastle-Midnight" by observing, "Race conflict runs deep" (54); however, it is important to note the responsible party for the brawl. As it gets underway, a sailor calls for fair play and a ring, and in reply an old Manx sailor responds, "Ready formed. There! The ringed horizon. In that ring Cain struck Abel. Sweet work, right work! No? Why then, God, mad'st thou the ring?" (981).

Ahab's monomaniacal revenge, along with alcohol, natural depravity, and racial animosity, evoke violence among the crew, yet Melville balances this by developing the theme of democratic brotherhood. He celebrates the sailors as the "kingly commons" and Ishmael makes the case for the dignity of his fellow man:

> But this august dignity I treat of, is not the dignity of kings and robes, but that abounding dignity which has no robed investiture. Thou shalt see it shining in the arm that wields a pick or drives a spike; that democratic dignity which, on all hands, radiates without end from God; Himself! The great God absolute! The centre and circumference of all democracy! His Omnipresence, our divine equality.
>
> (LoA 916)

Early and late, the Ishmael-Queequeq relationship exemplifies the democracy that runs counter to the tyranny that Ahab practices and to animosity among the crew. In the early chapters the two sailors become a cozy, loving pair, sharing a bed in the chapter "The Honeymoon." Later, Ishmael is saved by a coffin turned lifebuoy with Queequeg's tattoos, representing "a complete theory of the heavens and the earth" (1307), carved into its lid.

For one brief moment before the final fatal three-day chase of the white whale, Ahab reveals his own repressed humanity by recalling his wife and child and shedding a tear at the memory, but he soon declares himself fated by God to pursue his course, asking how "can this one small heart beat; this one small brain think thoughts; unless God does that beating, does that thinking, does that living, and not I." Such union of self with God, which the Transcendentalists thought made the world more perfect, for Ahab justifies his violent actions. As he says to his first mate Starbuck, "Look! See yon Albicore! Who put it into him to chase and fang that flying-fish? Where do murderers go, Man! Who's to doom, when the judge himself is dragged to the bar?" (1375).

The final chapters of *Moby-Dick* contain thrilling descriptions of the chase and the attempt to harpoon Moby Dick, who destroys boats, sailors, and the *Pequod* itself, along with its captain who is hanged and drowned by the line attached to the harpoon he throws into the whale. The three chase chapters constitute one of the most realistic and exciting conclusions one could hope for in such an epic adventure story. Before he dies, Ahab has his moment of catharsis as he exclaims, "Oh, lonely death on lonely life! Oh, now I feel my topmost greatness lies in my topmost grief" (1406).

After the *Pequod* sinks beneath the waves, and "the great shroud of the sea rolled on as it rolled five thousand years ago" (1407), Melville lets Ishmael have the last word in an "Epilogue," headed by a quote from "Job": "And I only am escaped alone to tell thee." Ishmael recalls,

> Buoyed by that coffin, for almost one whole day and night, I floated on a soft and dirge-like main. The unharming sharks, they glided by as if with padlocks on their mouths; the savage sea-hawks sailed with sheathed beaks. On the second day, a sail drew near, nearer, and picked me up at last.
>
> (LoA 1408)

This pastoral fantasy, then, tempers the realistic violence that precedes it.

Career shift

Melville finished writing his book in August 1851 in New York City, where he had made arrangements to have it printed at his own expense, so he could give the plates to publishers of his choosing, one in the United States, the other in England. His English publisher, Bentley, did not receive the "Epilogue" or the dedication to Hawthorne before going to press, and also used an earlier title, *The Whale*, rather than the final one Melville chose: *Moby-Dick; or The Whale*. Reviews of the book were mixed, and one cause of negative responses was Ishmael's religious openness, such as his willingness to join Queequeg in his idol worship. Melville's friend Duyckinck in a review objected to the book's "piratical running down of creeds and opinions," which "is out of place and uncomfortable," adding, "We do not like to see what, under any view, must be to the world the most sacred associations of life violated and defaced" (612).

As noted earlier, when Melville gave a copy of *Moby-Dick* to Hawthorne, he confessed that he had "written a wicked book" but felt "spotless as the lamb." Hawthorne's letter of thanks inspired Melville to declare that it made him feel as if "your heart beat in my ribs and mine in yours, and both in God's." "A sense of unspeakable security is in me this moment," he added, "on account of your having understood the book ... Knowing you persuades me more than the Bible of our immortality" (*Correspondence* 212–213). Hawthorne's "joy-giving" letter in response to the gift of *Moby-Dick* made Melville ecstatic for several reasons. While he was finishing the book, he lamented to Hawthorne, "What I feel most moved to write, that is banned,—it will not pay. Yet, altogether, write the *other* way I cannot. So the product is a final hash, and all my books are botches" (*Correspondence* 191). At some level, however, he surely knew he had completed an extraordinary work of art, not a botch, and he had gifted it to one person with sufficient genius to appreciate it.

Because of his indebtedness and the weak sales of *Moby-Dick*, Melville, though in an exhausted and overwrought state of mind, began writing the novel *Pierre*, which he called "a rural bowl of milk," but featured incest, murder, and a destructive quest for truth on the part of his immature would-be-author protagonist Pierre. The book became a commercial failure and caused Melville's family to worry about his mental health. In the early 1850s, he turned to writing anonymous short stories and novellas for two major periodicals, *Harper's* and *Putnam's*, which addressed contemporary issues, such as urbanization, the exploitation of workers, racism, and slavery. Melville's writings at this time tended to be opaque and resistant to interpretation, which has led to voluminous critical commentary about them.

In brief, his story "Bartleby, the Scrivener: A Story of Wall-Street" (1853) deals with the law profession, and the title character, a human Xerox machine—that is, a copyist—finally declares to his employer he would "prefer not to" undertake his duties anymore. The story has befuddled readers for some time, and the lawyer who must deal with Bartleby becomes befuddled as well. It has been interpreted as a retelling of Christ's sacrifice, an allegory of the relation between God and Man, a portrait of absolute negation and despair, a study of mental illness, a critique of business society, and so on. Students often declare that the lawyer should "just fire the guy," yet the response runs counter to the author's exclamation at the end, "Ah, Bartleby! Ah, Humanity!" The story has numerous layers, and on one of these, Bartleby deserves our deepest sympathy.

The same multiplicity inheres in *Benito Cereno* (1855), Melville's retelling of an account of an actual slave revolt at sea. The reader is forced to unravel a mystery, that is, what has happened on the Spanish Captain Cereno's disabled ship, but the reader's understanding is impeded by a limited point of view, that of the American Captain Delano, a genial racist, trying to help Cereno and his crew. Ambiguity, deception, illusion and delusion color everything gray, rather than black and white. A key question is whether Babo, the leader of the revolt, is a heroic black liberator, or evil personified, or neither. Readers must fill in his story, for it is not provided, and he remains significantly mute at the end. He is hanged, his body burned, and his head fixed on a pole in the Plaza of Lima, Peru.

Two of Melville's stories form a diptych, paired like photographs in adjoining frames. "The Paradise of Bachelors and Tartarus of Maids" (1855) seems to critique the excesses of bachelor life in London and the oppression of factory women in the mills of New England. The latter has also been read as an allegory of the female reproductive system and the toll it takes on women who must cope with their relentless menstrual cycles and with childbirth itself. The narrator travels to a paper mill on Black, his horse, and finds there pale young women folding blank paper in a factory situated near a boiling Blood river. When Melville wrote these stories, by the way, he lived in a house with numerous females—including his wife, his mother, three sisters, and two female servants. His two daughters were also born during these years.

After collecting his stories in a volume titled *The Piazza Tales* (1856), Melville wrote his most cynical piece of fiction, *The Confidence Man* (1857), set on a Mississippi riverboat, in which the characters prove to be either knaves or fools. One appears to be the devil, in many disguises, and readers struggle to tell who is telling the truth and who is not. Two characters are based on Emerson and Thoreau. The former appears as "The Mystic" Mark Winsom and the latter as "his practical disciple Egbert," both of whom subscribe to a philosophy that argues against helping friends in need. Melville also brings Poe into the scene as a crazy beggar, with "raven curls," trying to sell "a rhapsodical tract" he has written, but Winsom (Emerson) gives him the cold shoulder and declares, "I never patronize scoundrels." Some scholars find the book the most intricate and sophisticated work Melville ever wrote. Contemporary readers did not buy it.

To relieve Melville's growing depression, his father-in-law, Lemuel Shaw (Chief Justice of the Massachusetts Supreme Court), gave him funds for a ten-month trip to the Middle East to recover his health and spirits. On the way,

Melville stopped in Liverpool to see Hawthorne, who was the American consul there at the time. He and Hawthorne walked on the sand beside the Atlantic, and Hawthorne recorded in his journal,

> Melville, as he always does, began to reason of Providence and futurity, and of everything that lies beyond human ken, and informed me that he had "pretty much made up his mind to be annihilated"; but still he does not seem to rest in that anticipation … He can neither believe, nor be comfortable in his unbelief; and he is too honest and courageous not to try to do one or the other. If he were a religious man, he would be one of the most truly religious and reverential; he has a very high and noble nature, and better worth immortality than most of us.
>
> (*CE* 22: 163)

During the Civil War, Melville took up poetry in earnest, relying on newspaper accounts of battles and casualties to keep abreast of the war and visiting the battlefields in Virginia accompanied by his brother Allan. He enlisted in the Pittsfield militia and supported the Union effort; however, he also sympathized with Southern civilians victimized by the war, and he admired evidence of Southern bravery. In the Supplement he wrote to his collection of poems titled *Battle Pieces* (1866), he argued for moderation in the treatment of the defeated South, a position that Frederick Douglass and other black leaders vigorously opposed, for they knew that reconciliation would mean continued duress for black people in the South and the imposition of the white power structure in new forms. As the scholar Caroline L. Karcher has pointed out, the failure of Reconstruction proved Douglass right and Melville's sympathy misplaced.

Melville spent the last decades of his life in obscurity, as a deputy inspector of customs on the docks of New York City. These were dark days for him, made worse by the apparent suicide of his son Malcom at age eighteen, and the death of his other son Stanwix at age thirty-five, in a brothel in San Francisco. Melville himself struggled with alcohol and depression, and apparently engaged in spousal abuse. In 1867 his wife's relatives hatched a plot to kidnap her to get her away from Herman, but she stayed with him and their marriage seems to have improved. As Melville's biographer Andrew Delbanco has put it, "in their later years, a settled tenderness took hold between Herman and Lizzie" (289). Most of Melville's later work, published privately in small volumes, was poetry, including a long religious poem titled *Clarel* (1876), about a pilgrimage to the Holy Land by a group of diverse characters. His novella *Billy Budd* began as a poem but captured his narrative interest so strongly that he kept expanding and revising it.

The *Billy Budd* manuscript, in various stages, was unfinished when Melville died in 1891, but it has been edited several times so as to be read as a coherent, yet problematic study of the ways innocence can suffer at the hands of depraved individuals and oppressive systems of authority. The obvious political conflict at the heart of the book concerns the rights of man versus the need to maintain law and order, especially in time of war. Melville set the piece in 1797, during the French Revolutionary Wars, when France and England were engaged in a struggle for dominance on sea and land. The title character is falsely accused of mutiny, and while knowing him to be innocent, the captain argues that he must be hanged to maintain order on the ship, for he has accidentally killed his false accuser, Claggart, the master-at-arms, chief policeman on the ship. The reader must struggle to determine whether the captain's sacrifice of the young Christ-like sailor is just or not, and Melville complicates the work in a number of ways, most notably by relating the three main characters to Christ, Satan, and God the Father. At the end, Billy apparently forgives Captain Vere by shouting out, "God bless Captain Vere!" (1426), but whether this is another instance of Melville's irony remains debatable. In fact, critics have been analyzing and judging Vere's actions for many years. One persuasive argument put forth is that since Melville's own harsh discipline contributed to the death of his son Malcolm, the ending may be a fantasy of forgiveness that Melville created to soothe his own conscience.

The novella has also been contextualized by reference to the turbulent 1880s in the United States, when laborers and agents of factory owners were warring with each other in the streets of many cities including New York and Chicago. Stirred by the French Revolution of 1871, workers joined unions and staged protests and strikes to gain living wages and safer working conditions. Owners of various industries employed private police as well as public police forces to break up strikes. In Chicago, violence broke out leading to the hanging of four convicted anarchists. The argument made for their hanging was that though they may have been innocent, they must die as examples to quell the mob violence of the workers. Human rights versus law and order was the issue. Thomas Paine's radical *The Rights of Man* (1791) and Edmund Burke's conservative *Reflections on the Revolution in France* (1790) influenced Melville's story and continue to express the main two perspectives on such conflicts.

Almost all the writings of Hawthorne and Melville maintain their relevance to the human condition, yet Hawthorne emphasized the ways we treat one another, whereas Melville emphasized the creator's role in making humans suffer and behave as they do, like sharks at times on the hunt for resources. In *Billy Budd*, there is a brief throw-away metaphor that's pregnant with meaning. As Melville describes the villain Claggart's evil nature, he asks "what recourse is left to it but to recoil upon itself and, like the scorpion, *for which the Creator alone is responsible*, act out to the end the part allotted it" (1385) (italics added).

Robert K. Martin has provided the most thorough study to date of the homoerotic elements in Melville's works, focusing on the conflict between a democratic eros expressed in male friendship and "a hierarchical eros expressed in social forms of male power" (4). In *Billy Budd*, there is a strong homoerotic subtext in the tension between Claggart and Billy, whereas in *Moby-Dick* and "The Paradise of Bachelors," it is even more obvious, not to mention its presence in the letters Melville sent to Hawthorne. These letters have convinced some readers that the two men were sexually attracted to one another, but if this is the case, which seems likely, nothing lasting seems to have come of it. Hawthorne left the Berkshires and his friend in November 1851, not because of any homosexual proposition, as one biographer has speculated, but because he felt out of sorts living in a small rented house and dealing with a troublesome landlord, Caroline Sturgis Tappan.

Though Melville visited Hawthorne in Concord, in 1852, they saw one another again only twice, in Liverpool before and after Melville's 1856 trip to the Middle East. Although the two men drifted apart, Melville's poem "Monody," written after Hawthorne's death in 1864, suggests the strong effect the man may have had upon him. It reads, in part,

> To have known him, to have loved him
>   After loneness long;
> And then to be estranged in life,
>   And neither in the wrong;
> And now for death to set his seal—
>   Ease me, a little ease, my song!
> By wintry hills his hermit-mound
>   The sheeted snow-drifts drape,
> And houseless there the snow-bird flits
>   Beneath the fir-trees' crape:
> Glazed now with ice the cloistral vine
>   That hid the shyest grape.
>   (*Poems*, 221)

Conclusion

Even though a voluminous amount of criticism has been written about Hawthorne and Melville, the issues they raise within their work, which would reward further study, are legion, including ethnicity, sentimentalism, emerging technologies, disability, the sensational, textuality, mass culture, and queerness. Recent studies of both authors have begun to probe the transnational perspectives one can take on their writings, and the roles that race, empire, and gender play in their thought. Relations between races, and between men and animals, the human and nonhuman, provide another rich area of study for not only the works of Melville, but those of Hawthorne as well. In other words, their current high standing within the canon of the American Renaissance seems likely to persist for scholars and teachers of their works.

Suggestions for further reading

Berthoff, Warner. *The Example of Melville*. Princeton: Princeton University Press, 1962.

Bezanson, Walter E. "Moby-Dick: Work of Art." *Moby-Dick Centennial Essays*. Eds. Tyrus Hillway and Luther S. Mansfield. Dallas: Southern Methodist University Press, 1953. 30–58.

Delbanco, Andrew. *Melville: His World and Work*. New York: Knopf, 2005.
Elbert, Monika, Ed. *Hawthorne in Context*. New York: Cambridge University Press, 2018.
Greven, David. *The Fragility of Manhood: Hawthorne, Freud, and the Politics of Gender*. Columbus: Ohio State University Press, 2012.
Millington, Richard H., Ed. *The Cambridge Companion to Nathaniel Hawthorne*. New York: Cambridge University Press, 2004.
Reynolds, Larry J., Ed. *Historical Guide to Nathaniel Hawthorne*. New York: Oxford University Press, 2001.
Sanborn, Geoffrey. *The Value of Melville*. New York: Cambridge UP, 2018.

References

Arvin, Newton. *Herman Melville: A Critical Biography*. New York: Viking, 1950.
Bezanson, Walter E. "Moby-Dick: Work of Art." *Moby-Dick Centennial Essays*. Eds. Tyrus Hillway and Luther S. Mansfield. Dallas: Southern Methodist University Press, 1953. 30–58.
Delbanco, Andrew. *Melville: His World and Work*. New York: Knopf, 2005.
Duyckinck, Evert A. "Notice of Moby-Dick." 1851. Rpt. "[A Friend Does His Christian Duty]." In *Moby-Dick; or, The Whale*. By Herman Melville. Eds. Hershel Parker and Harrison Hayford. A Norton Critical Edition. Second Edition. New York: Norton, 2002. 610–613.
Emerson, Ralph Waldo. *The Journals and Miscellaneous Notebooks of Ralph Waldo Emerson*. Ed. William H. Gilman, Ralph H. Orth, et al. 16 vols. Cambridge, MA: Belknap Press of Harvard University Press, 1960–1982. Abbreviated JMN.
Fuller, Margaret. "'The Impulses of Human Nature': Margaret Fuller's Journal from June through October 1844." Eds. Martha L. Berg and Alice de V. Perry. *Massachusetts Historical Society Proceedings* 102 (1990): 38–126.
Hawthorne, Nathaniel. *The Centenary Edition of the Works of Nathaniel Hawthorne*. Ed. William Charvat et al. 23 vols. Columbus: Ohio State University Press, 1962–1997. Abbreviated CE and volume number.
Hawthorne, Nathaniel. *Tales and Sketches*. New York: Library of America, 1982.
Karcher, Carolyn L. "White Fratricide, Black Liberation: Melville, Douglass, and Civil War Memory." In *Frederick Douglass & Herman Melville: Essays in Relation*. Eds. Robert S. Levine and Samuel Otter. Chapel Hill: University of North Carolina Press, 2008. 349–368.
Lathrop, Rose Hawthorne. *Memories of Hawthorne*. 1897. New York: AMS Press, 1969.
Martin, Robert K. *Hero, Captain, and Stranger: Male Friendship, Social Critique, and Literary Form in the Sea Novels of Herman Melville*. Chapel Hill: University of North Carolina Press, 1986.
Melville, Herman. *Correspondence*. Ed. Lynn Horth. Evanston: Northwestern University Press and Newberry Library, 1993.
Melville, Herman. "Hawthorne and His Mosses: By a Virginian Spending July in Vermont." *Moby-Dick*. Eds. Hershel Parker and Harrison Hayford. Norton Critical Edition. Second Edition. New York: Norton, 2002. 517–532.
Melville, Herman. *Mardi: And a Voyage Thither*. Eds. Harrison Hayford, Hershel Parker, and G. Thomas Tanselle. Evanston: Northwestern University Press, 1970.

Melville, Herman. *The Melville Log: A Documentary Life of Herman Melville, 1819–1891.* Ed. Jay Leyda. 2 vols. New York: Harcourt, Brace, 1951.

Melville, Herman. *Poems of Herman Melville.* Ed. Douglas Robillard. New Haven: College & University Press, 1976.

Melville, Herman. *Redburn, White-Jacket, Moby-Dick.* New York: Library of America, 1983. Abbreviated LoA.

Mitchell, Thomas R. *Hawthorne's Fuller Mystery.* Amherst: University of Massachusetts Press, 1998.

Reynolds, Larry J. *Devils and Rebels: The Making of Hawthorne's Damned Politics.* Ann Arbor: University of Michigan Press, 2008.

5 Douglass, Stowe, Jacobs, and anti-slavery

Frederick Douglass's *Narrative of the Life of Frederick Douglass, an American Slave, Written by Himself* (1845) has emerged as a key text in the American Renaissance, as has Harriet Beecher Stowe's *Uncle Tom's Cabin; or, Life Among the Lowly* (1852) and Harriet Jacobs's *Incidents in the Life of a Slave Girl* (1861). Despite their initial success, these works were not highly regarded by literary historians before the Civil Rights movement of the 1960s brought issues of race to the fore on college campuses and scholars turned to these works for their powerful arguments against slavery. The narratives of Douglass (1818–1895) and Jacobs (1813–1897) are autobiographical, and draw upon their actual experiences as slaves. Stowe (1811–1896), a middle-class white woman, used what she knew and learned about slavery to create a popular sentimental novel that, while fictional, evoked massive sympathy for slaves and widespread antipathy to slavery.

All three books reveal, in compelling prose, the physical and psychological horrors of slavery, and by design they contributed to the growing US opposition to slavery, which began in the late eighteenth century and grew in intensity in the nineteenth century, as editors, journalists, and public lecturers joined fugitive slaves in the call for its abolishment. While this may seem counterintuitive now, abolitionists, as they were called, were initially regarded as dangerous fanatics, especially those calling for immediate emancipation. Their critics feared that their writings and lectures were stirring up horrific racial violence like that which occurred during the Haitian Revolution of 1791–1804 and Nat Turner's slave rebellion of 1831. The literature of anti-slavery arose within hemispheric and transnational contexts, and the violent upheavals in Europe and the Americas provided inspiration to anti-slavery writers prior to the Civil War.

Haiti and Toussaint Louverture

The Haitian Revolution, which began in the French colony of Saint-Domingue, exerted a powerful emotional influence on views of race relations in the United States. The Revolution became notorious for the bloodshed and cruelty suffered by non-combatants, especially unarmed women and children. Prior to the

DOI: 10.4324/9781315751627-5

Revolution, Saint-Domingue was the richest colony in the French empire, producing sugar and coffee using slave labor. Half the enslaved people were survivors of the horrific Middle Passage, and they had been subjected to tortures, mutilations, and terror at the hands of the plantation owners. The Revolution began with a series of nocturnal meetings among slave leaders in the summer of 1791, and on the night of August 22, a massive insurrection began as the slaves killed, and in some cases tortured, every white person they could find. For abolitionists, the horrors of the Revolution served as an example of what a slaveholder could expect if he did not free his slaves. Over the course of ten years, countless plantations were destroyed and chaos prevailed as slaves, free men of color, the French, the Spanish, and the British fought for dominance on the island of Hispaniola and used all means to attain it. Historians estimate that during the course of the Revolution some 300,000 persons were killed, including 100,000 of the 500,000 enslaved black people and 25,000 of the 40,000 white colonists.

Out of the chaos, a well-educated former slave named Toussaint Louverture rose to leadership. According to most accounts, he did not participate in the massacre of whites in the initial revolt, but he emerged as a brilliant military commander and astute politician. He organized the slaves and fought with the Spanish, then switched his allegiance to the French and fought against the Spanish and the British, driving the latter from the island. Claiming loyalty to France but asserting his independent authority, Toussaint conquered Spanish Santo Domingo in the east, put down an uprising of free men of color in the west and the south, and took control of all of Hispaniola in 1801, restoring peace and order. Napoleon, outraged and determined to re-establish slavery in the French West Indies, sent an army of 20,000 men to Haiti, forcing Toussaint to surrender.

After he signed a peace treaty, Toussaint was betrayed, bound, transported to France, and died in a dungeon there in 1803. With the help of yellow fever, Toussaint's successor, Jean-Jacques Dessalines, drove the French from the island, massacred all remaining whites, completed the Revolution, and established the new nation of Haiti in 1804. As C. L. R. James famously declared, this was

> the only successful slave revolt in history, and the odds it had to overcome is evidence of the magnitude of the interests that were involved. The transformation of slaves, trembling in hundreds before a single white man, into a people able to organize themselves and defeat the most powerful European nations of their day, is one of the great epics of revolutionary struggle and achievement.
>
> (*The Black Jacobins* ix)

Nat Turner's insurrection

Toussaint would become a role model for former slaves such as Frederick Douglass, who also idolized the slave leader Nat Turner. The inspiration for Turner's insurrection, which occurred in Southampton County, Virginia, during the summer of 1831, came not primarily from Haiti but the Bible, particularly the visions and voices it evoked. Turner's *Confessions* (1831) were transcribed by local lawyer Thomas Gray and contain much that seems added by Gray; however, Turner's own distinctive voice often emerges, for example, when he declares,

> I had a vision—and I saw white spirits and black spirits engaged in battle, and the sun was darkened—the thunder rolled in the Heavens, and blood flowed in streams—and I heard a voice saying, "Such is your luck, such you are called to see, and let it come rough or smooth, you must surely bare [sic] it."
>
> (Turner 44–45)

In the early morning hours of August 22, 1831 (the anniversary of the Haitian Revolution), Turner and his band of seven black men, armed with crude weapons, began breaking into local houses, killing every white man, woman, and child they could find. During the next two days, as the rebels moved along, they recruited followers, some seventy in all, mostly enslaved black men, and they killed at least fifty-seven white people. They were soon confronted, chased down, and arrested by groups of white militias.

In the days that followed, countless black people were tortured and killed in retaliation. Seventeen rebels were executed and the rest were transported out of the state of Virginia. Turner hid out for two months but was discovered, arrested, tried, and hanged on November 11, 1831. The leading abolitionist William Lloyd Garrison, editor of the anti-slavery newspaper the *Liberator*, insisted that slave insurrections such as Turner's were morally wrong and ineffectual, yet he extended understanding and sympathy to slaves who did revolt. In a piece written two months before Turner's execution, Garrison condemned the "white butchers" who "are slaying their victims in a most ferocious manner, and exhibiting a cannibal thirst for human blood. They have not the excuse of the infuriated slaves—ignorance and a deprivation of liberty" (*Liberator*, September 17, 1831: 151). Harriet Jacobs, in her *Incidents in the Life of a Slave Girl* (1861), gives an eye-witness account of the immediate effects of Turner's rebellion on her small North Carolina town of Edenton, some seventy miles away. "It was a grand opportunity for the low whites," she writes, "who had no negroes of their own to scourge." These men, "like a pack of hungry wolves," terrorized the black people of the area and slaves:

> Every where men, women, and children were whipped till the blood stood in puddles at their feet. Some received five hundred lashes; others were tied hands and feet, and tortured with a bucking paddle, which blisters the skin terribly. The dwellings of the colored people ... were robbed of clothing and every thing else the marauders thought worth carrying away. All day long these unfeeling wretches went round, like a troop of demons, terrifying and tormenting the helpless ... Towards evening the

turbulence increased. The soldiers, stimulated by drink, committed still greater cruelties. Shrieks and shouts continually rent the air. Not daring to go to the door, I peeped under the window curtain. I saw a mob dragging along a number of colored people, each white man, with his musket upraised, threatening instant death if they did not stop their shrieks.

(54–56)

Turner's rebellion had positive as well as negative effects on the struggle to end slavery. As Eric Sundquist has pointed out, in the aftermath of the rebellion, "the Virginia House of Delegates undertook the most serious debate in its history on the question of slave emancipation" ("Slavery" 9–10). Although opposition in the South prevailed, Turner became a heroic figure in the eyes of Douglass, Stowe, and other Northern abolitionists. Douglass in a speech in 1848 asserted that Turner endeavored "to gain his own liberty, and that of his enslaved brethren, by the self-same means which the Revolutionary fathers employed" (*FDP*, 2: 131). Stowe, in 1865, near the end of the Civil War, declared, "The prophetic visions of Nat Turner, who saw the leaves drop blood and the land darkened, have been fulfilled. The work of justice which he predicted is being executed to the utmost" ("The Chimney-Corner" 115). In her novel *Dred: A Tale of the Great Dismal Swamp* (1856), she created a title character partly based on Turner, and in an appendix included extracts from Turner's *Confessions*. *Dred*, as Lawrence Buell observes, responds to the growing violence of the late 1850s and allows its title character to make a powerful case for seeking righteous vengeance against white oppressors.

Colonization

Turner's rebellion, with its horrific features, injected a sense of urgency into the problem of slavery in the United States, which no one seemed to know how to solve. An early solution, put forth by the American Colonization Society (ACS), founded in 1816, was to establish colonies where freed slaves and other black people could emigrate. The ACS was made up of humanitarians and racists; the former wished to relieve the suffering and oppression of "Negroes," and the latter wanted to rid the country of what they considered a dangerous and degraded race. The first and largest colony the ACS founded was Liberia, an African territory 130 miles long and 40 miles wide, bounded on the west by the Atlantic Ocean. It was acquired in December, 1821, from the reluctant King Peter of Africa, by agents for the Society who pointed a loaded pistol at his head and threatened to kill him.

The first emigrants, who chose to go, or were coerced, struggled with malaria and hostile natives, but Nat Turner's slave uprising caused a surge in emigration, and by 1832, more than 1,500 persons had been transported, on 22 expeditions. By the mid-1830s, the Colonization movement lost steam due to opposition from abolitionists and free black Americans. Although a number of free and freed black people, who believed they would always suffer from racism in the United States, chose to emigrate, others, including Douglass, argued strenuously that the United States was just as much their country as any white person's. They had no desire to be "sent back" to Africa, a place they did not know. As Douglass put it in a piece in his *North Star* paper in 1848,

> For two hundred and twenty-eight years has the colored man toiled over the soil of America, under a burning sun and a driver's lash—plowing, planting, reaping, that white men might roll in ease, their hands unhardened by labor, and their brows unmoistened by the water of genial toil, and now ... the mean and cowardly oppressor is mediating plans to expel the colored man entirely from the country. Shame upon the guilty wretches that dare propose, and all that countenance such as a proposition. We live here—have lived here—have a right to live here, and mean to live here.
>
> (qtd. Ammons 227)

Stowe, unlike Douglass, supported Colonization during the 1840s, and at the end of *Uncle Tom's Cabin*, has her heroic character George Harris declare, "As a Christian patriot, as a teacher of Christianity, I go to *my country*,—my chosen, my glorious Africa!" (395). In her own words, Stowe then addresses her Christian readers, asking them to help educate freed slaves and fugitives "until they have attained to somewhat of a moral and intellectual maturity, and then assist them in their passage to those shores, where they may put in practice the lessons they have learned in America" (405). She would later change her mind about Colonization, perhaps due to the opposition her advocacy received from black writers, including Douglass. Although Stowe regarded black people with an ingrained condescension, she was willing to alter her racist views when challenged by black individuals she admired.

Abolition

In addition to the colonization movement, another solution to the slavery issue, suggested by some in the US, was the British model set out by the Slave Emancipation Act of 1833, which granted all slaves in the British Empire their freedom after serving as apprentices for ten years; however, the cost of compensation, £20,000,000 (some three trillion dollars in today's money) paid to West Indies plantation owners for their "loss of property," made the scheme seem impractical for the United States, with its millions of slaves. Liberal clergymen in the North initially argued that perhaps extending culture and civilization to Southerners might persuade them to end slavery, yet this, too, proved too sanguine, in both senses of the term. In an 1845 speech, Ralph Waldo Emerson declared,

> Elevate, enlighten, civilize the semi-barbarous nations of South Carolina, Georgia, Alabama—take away from their debauched society the Bowie-

> knife, the rum-bowl, the dice-box, and the stews—take out the brute, and infuse a drop of civility and generosity, and you touch those selfish lords with thought and gentleness.
>
> (*AW* 38)

Such condescension only added to Southern anger about anti-slavery rhetoric and publications.

The most prominent, and provocative, approach to ending slavery in the antebellum period was the immediate and unqualified abolition advocated by William Lloyd Garrison and Frederick Douglass. In the 1830s, Garrison's editorials and speeches featured fiery biblical rhetoric, causing many whites in the North and South to consider him fanatical and dangerous. In his newspaper, the *Liberator*, Garrison warned that if "the glorious day of universal emancipation" did not arrive,

> woe to the safety of this people! … A cry of horror, a cry of revenge, will go up to heaven in the darkness of midnight, and re-echo from every cloud. Blood will flow like water—the blood of guilty men, and of innocent women and children. Then will be heard lamentations and weeping, such as will blot out the remembrance of the horrors of St. Domingo.
>
> ("Dangers of the Nation" 59)

Although members of the Massachusetts Anti-Slavery Society under Garrison's leadership in the 1830s practiced nonresistance and discouraged slave revolts, their bloodthirsty rhetoric provoked mobs that attacked their speakers as well as mobs that attacked free black people. In the wake of Nat Turner's slave rebellion, a bounty was put on Garrison's head in the South, and in Boston, in 1835, he was attacked by an anti-abolitionist mob who dragged him through the streets with a rope around his neck, before he was rescued.

A number of black leaders in Baltimore and elsewhere argued that the kind of moral suasion Garrison was relying on to end of slavery would prove ineffective. For them, actual violence and warfare seemed the only way slavery would ever end. In 1829, David Walker, a black activist living in Boston, published his *Appeal, in Four Articles* directed toward slaves in the South, asking them

> had you not rather be killed than to be a slave to a tyrant, who takes the life of your mother, wife, and dear little children? Look upon your mother, wife and children, and answer God Almighty; and believe this, that it is no more harm for you to kill a man who is trying to kill you, than it is for you to take a drink of water when thirsty.
>
> (28)

The *Appeal* was widely distributed, and there is evidence that Turner may have been influenced by Walker (Hinks xli.).

Throughout the 1830s and 1840s, Garrison's abolitionist movement gained adherents, and a number of heroic individuals put their lives at risk by speaking out publicly against slavery. The Southern, white Grimké sisters, Sarah and Angelina, traveled throughout the North, giving abolitionist lectures, incurring the wrath of many men, who felt public speaking unsuitable for women. The Grimkés inspired the formation of female anti-slavery societies, including one in Concord, Massachusetts, which included Lidian Emerson and Thoreau's mother and sisters. Angelina also wrote an "Appeal to the Christian Women of the South" (1836) to encourage Southern women to help end slavery, but the appeal fell on deaf ears. Race hatred merged with the hatred of abolitionists, and stereotypes of "Negroes" as savage and demonic fueled riots directed at both in the North. In 1838 when Angelina spoke to a racially mixed crowd in Pennsylvania Hall in Philadelphia, a mob formed to yell and throw bricks at the building. Grimké was able to survive the protest, but the next day, the mob burned the building down.

In 1837 Elijah Lovejoy, a white newspaper editor, who argued against slavery, was killed by an angry mob in Alton, Illinois, who wrecked his press and threw it into the Mississippi River. That same year a mob in Cincinnati destroyed the press of James G. Birney, publisher of an anti-slavery paper. They threw his press into the Ohio River and unable to find Birney, destroyed the homes of a number of black families. Harriet Beecher Stowe, two months from delivering twins, witnessed her brother Henry join the effort to disperse the Cincinnati mob and expressed the desire to defend Birney and his newspaper: "If I were a man," she wrote, "I would go, for one, and take good care of at least one window" (qtd. Hendrick 106). After learning of the murder of Lovejoy, John Brown, perhaps the most famous and violent antagonist of slavery, committed his life to fighting against it. (He and his sons participated in the violence of "Bleeding Kansas" in the mid-1850s, and after his failed raid on the federal arsenal at Harpers Ferry in 1859, he was hanged.) Both Douglass and Harriet Jacobs regarded Brown as a heroic martyr.

Douglass as abolitionist

Like a number of other ex-slave authors, Douglass gained celebrity as a speaker before he became a writer. As Philip Gould has pointed out, "the abolitionist lecture circuit was an important development shaping the style and content of the antebellum slave narrative" (19). Douglass benefited from several unique opportunities to acquire the skills needed to excel at writing and speaking. He was born in 1818 on the eastern shore of Maryland, the son of the slave Harriet Bailey and an unknown white man, probably his mother's master. He was raised by his grandmother and lived on the plantation of Edward Lloyd until he was sent to Baltimore at age eight to live with the prosperous family of Hugh Auld, a shipbuilder. With help from Hugh's wife, Sophia, he learned to read, and he practiced writing in secret on his own at night. As he tells in his *Narrative*, during his first stay in Baltimore, he heard about the abolitionists, and they gave him hope that others were working to free him and other slaves:

> After a patient waiting, I got one of our city papers, containing an account of the number of petitions from the north, praying for the abolition of slavery in the District of Columbia, and of the slave trade between the States. From this time I understood the words *abolition* and *abolitionist*, and always drew near when that word was spoken, expecting to hear something of importance to myself and fellow-slaves.
>
> (*Autobiographies* 43)

At age fifteen, he was sent back to his new owner in Talbert County, Thomas Auld, Hugh's brother, who found himself unable to manage the defiant teenager. Auld turned him over to Edward Covey, a slave breaker, who failed to subdue Douglass, and after a failed escape, he was returned to the Aulds in Baltimore. In 1838, at age twenty, Douglass, with help from his fiancé Anna Murray, finally fled Maryland and made his way to Massachusetts and freedom. There he worked as a day laborer in New Bedford and became a preacher in the African Methodist Episcopal Zion church. When he spoke at an anti-slavery meeting in 1841, Garrison heard him and invited him to attend the Massachusetts Anti-slavery Convention on Nantucket, where Douglass delivered three impressive speeches and was hired as a lecturer by Garrison's struggling American Anti-Slavery Society. The Society had split and lost members in 1840, due to its support of women speakers and its unwillingness to engage in party politics. (Garrison called the US Constitution, with its Fugitive Slave Law, a "covenant with death and agreement with hell.")

During 1841–1843 Douglass traveled throughout New England, New York and the Midwest, becoming more and more effective at drawing crowds, all the while maintaining Garrison's emphasis on moral suasion, rather than force, as the means to end slavery. In August 1843, he attended the National Convention of Colored Citizens, held in Buffalo, New York, and heard the radical black minister Henry Highland Garnet give his infamous speech, "Call to Rebellion," addressed to slaves. "Brethren, arise, arise!" Garnet declared:

> Strike for your lives and liberties. Now is the day and the hour. Let every slave throughout the land do this and the days of slavery are numbered. You cannot be more oppressed than you have been—you cannot suffer greater cruelties than you have already. *Rather die freemen than live to be slaves.* Remember that you are 4 millions!
>
> ("Call to Rebellion" 36)

Douglass felt that Garnet's speech did not accord with Christ's directive to turn the other cheek, but a month later, he began to change his mind.

When speaking in Pendleton, Indiana, he was attacked by an anti-abolitionist mob and fought back, picking up a board to strike out at his attackers, before they pummeled him to the ground, and beat him severely. Douglass's right hand was broken in this assault and never healed properly. According to Philip Foner, Douglass "never forgot the experience. Three years later he wrote to a friend that it still 'haunted his dreams'" (Douglass, *Life and Writings* 1: 57).

In the months that followed the mob scene in Pendleton, Douglass's rhetoric understandably became angrier and more bellicose. In a letter written late in his life, he recalled, "I was a Non-Resistant til I got to fighting with a mob at Pendleton, Ind: in 1843 ... fell never to rise again, and yet I cannot feel I did wrong" (qtd. Goldstein 64). In February 1844 Nathaniel P. Rogers, editor of *Herald of Freedom*, described one of Douglass's "volcanic" speeches, given in Concord, New Hampshire:

> It was the storm of insurrection—and I could not but think, as he stalked to and fro on the platform, roused up like the Numidian Lion—how that terrible voice of his would ring through the pine glades of the South, in the day of her visitation—calling the insurgents to battle and striking terror to the hearts of the dismayed and despairing mastery. He reminded me of Toussaint among the plantations of Haiti ... He was not up as a speaker—performing. He was an insurgent slave taking hold on the right of speech, and charging on his tyrants the bondage of his race.
> (qtd. *Frederick Douglass Papers* 1: 26–27)

As the scholar Robert Levine has shown, Douglass was inspired by the Haitian revolutionaries of 1791–1804 ("Frederick Douglass, War, Haiti" 1865).

In 1844, Douglass joined with Emerson and other speakers in Concord, Massachusetts to celebrate the tenth anniversary of the emancipation of the slaves in the British West Indies. The speakers praised the British and castigated US politicians for not following their example. Emerson went so far as to declare, "the arrival in the world of such men as Toussaint, and the Haytian heroes, or of the leaders of their race in Barbadoes and Jamaica, outweighs in good omen all the English and American humanity" (*AW* 31). In his journal, Emerson had written "it seems to me that the arrival of such men as Toussaint if he is pure blood, or of Douglas [sic] if he is pure blood, outweighs all the English & American humanity" (*JMN* 9: 125). Emerson recognized and admired Douglass's black revolutionary spirit. In the months following Douglass's "volcanic" speech in New Hampshire, he wrote his *Narrative*, published in May 1845, and the defiance running through that book probably gained intensity from the violence he had recently encountered as an anti-slavery activist.

Narrative of the Life of Frederick Douglass (1845)

Douglass's *Narrative* is a riveting account of his life as a slave, and reveals how intelligent, courageous, and skilled as a reader and writer he was. The book is meant, of course, to advance the abolitionist cause, and Douglass provides a first-hand account of the pain and suffering that slaves endure at the hands of cruel masters and their agents. He begins with a sensational scene he witnessed as a boy, the whipping of his Aunt Hester by his master:

> I have often been awakened at the dawn of day by the most heart-rending shrieks of an own aunt of mine, whom he used to tie up to a joist, and

whip upon her naked back till she was literally covered with blood. No words, no tears, no prayers, from his gory victim, seemed to move his iron heart from its bloody purpose. The louder she screamed, the harder he whipped and where the blood ran fastest, there he whipped longest. He would whip her to make her scream, and whip her to make her hush, and not until overcome by fatigue, would he cease to swing the blood-clotted cowskin.

(*Autobiographies* 18)

Such horrific violence engages the reader and sets out the most affecting evil of slavery that Douglass witnessed personally; however, the scene shares elements of the sexualized violence of Gothic fiction and has led some scholars to question the *Narrative's* gender politics. Saidiya V. Hartman, who has studied scenes of subjection in slave narratives, asks, "Is the act of 'witnessing' a kind of looking no less entangled with the wielding of power and the extraction of enjoyment?" (22), and Deborah E. McDowell has argued that "Douglass's repetition of the sexualized scene of whipping projects him into a voyeuristic relation to the violence against slave women, which he watches, and thus he enters into a symbolic complicity with the sexual crime he witnesses" (178).

Whether this charge is valid has become a matter of critical debate. Douglass's admirers point out that he is bringing to light the actual atrocities that the slave-owning South tried to deny occurred. As for his desire to wield power, Douglass, as his *Narrative* makes clear, sought to claim a manhood that racists and slaveowners had insisted black males, slave or free, did not possess. For this reason, among others, he emphasizes his physical and moral superiority to his white oppressors, and he makes a two-hour fight with the slave-breaker Covey the dramatic turning point of his life as a slave. As a number of scholars have discussed, violence and manhood become linked as he describes his transformation from slave to man. After the fight scene, Douglass asserts,

It rekindled the few expiring embers of freedom, and revived within me a sense of my own manhood ... He only can understand the deep satisfaction which I experienced, who has himself repelled by force the bloody arm of slavery. I felt as I never felt before. It was a glorious resurrection, from the tomb of slavery, to the heaven of freedom. My long-crushed spirit rose, cowardice departed, bold defiance took its place, and I now resolved that however long I might remain a slave in form, the day had passed forever when I could be a slave in fact.

(*Autobiographies* 65)

Douglass follows this passage with a warning, "the white man who expected to succeed in whipping, must also succeed in killing me" (65). Such an assertion provided a counterpoint to his recent publicized beating in Pendleton.

Although Douglass conflates physical strength with manhood, his resurrection from slavery also depended upon his learning to read and write. As the

Narrative points out, he was taught to read as a young slave in Baltimore, at first by his mistress Sophia Auld, who turned against him after her husband, Hugh Auld, forbade it. Douglass dwells on the irony that at first, when Sophia Auld was teaching him, he did not realize what power he was gaining until Hugh Auld declared, "It would forever unfit him to be a slave":

> These words sank deep into my heart, stirred up sentiments within that lay slumbering, and called into existence an entirely new train of thought. It was a new and special revelation, explaining dark and mysterious things, with which my youthful understanding had struggled, but struggled in vain. I now understood what had been to me a most perplexing difficulty—to wit, the white man's power to enslave the black man. It was a grand achievement, and I prized it highly. From that moment, I understood the pathway from slavery to freedom.
>
> (*Autobiographies* 37–38)

Literacy became the foundation for Douglass's rise in the world from slave to celebrated writer, teacher, and lecturer. As the *Narrative* reveals, as a slave, he acquired expertise in the use of figurative language and other rhetorical techniques, helped in part by his study of Caleb Bingham's *The Columbian Orator* (1797), a collection of patriotic speeches for young schoolboys, which Douglass studied and memorized. Later, while working for a Mr. Freeland, he teaches a group of other slaves to read at a Sabbath school, until it is violently broken up by a group of white men "all calling themselves Christians! Humble followers of the Lord Jesus Christ!" (*Autobiographies* 71).

Throughout his *Narrative* and especially in his "Appendix," Douglass critiques so-called Christians in the South. As he puts it, "I love the pure, peaceable, and impartial Christianity of Christ: I therefore hate the corrupt, slaveholding, women-whipping, cradle-plundering, partial and hypocritical Christianity of this land" (*Autobiographies* 97). It was such animus that provoked white ministers and churches throughout the country to shun abolitionists such as Douglass, Garrison, and eventually even Emerson. Black churches, however, welcomed them. After his successful escape to freedom, using a pass he wrote himself, Douglass in New Bedford became a part-time preacher. He also labored.

> There was no work too hard—none too dirty. I was ready to saw wood, shovel coal, carry the hod, sweep the chimney, or roll oil casks,—all of which I did for nearly three years in New Bedford, before I became known to the anti-slavery world.
>
> (*Autobiographies* 95)

The point he is making is that while a slave reluctantly labors for a master, a free man willingly works for himself and his family.

Unfortunately, during his three years working as a speaker for Garrison's American Anti-Slavery Society, Douglass received only about half the pay of his white colleagues. Racism was prevalent in the North, even among abolitionists. When the Boston Anti-Slavery Society published his *Narrative* in 1845, it included introductory letters from Garrison and Wendell Phillips, a white Boston lawyer known for his eloquent abolitionist speeches. This introductory frame, or "white envelope" as it has been called, meant to recommend the unknown author to the reader, has encouraged modern scholars to notice issues of control, mediation, and exploitation of a black author, and these issues have also arisen with regard to Jacobs's narrative and Stowe's *Uncle Tom's Cabin*.

Douglass's book, decidedly his own production, is both an autobiography and a carefully constructed work of art. The rhetorical address to the ships on the Chesapeake Bay, supposedly voiced when he was a boy, seems clearly a set piece written long after the fact:

> You are loosed from your moorings, and are free; I am fast in my chains, and am a slave! You move merrily before the gentle gale, and I sadly before the bloody whip! You are freedom's swift-winged angels, that fly round the world; I am confined in bands of iron! O that I were free! Oh, that I were on one of your gallant decks, and under your protecting wing! Alas! Betwixt me and you, the turbid waters roll. Go on, go on. O that I could also go! Could I but swim! If I could fly! O, why was I born a man, of whom to make a brute!
>
> (*Autobiographies* 59)

In addition to inserting such set pieces into the *Narrative*, Douglass shaped it with omissions as well. For example, the fight scene with Covey is described in such a way as to emphasize the courage of Douglass as a sixteen-year-old slave. When Douglass later retold this account in his second autobiography, *My Bondage and My Freedom* (1855), he recorded the presence and assistance of the two other slaves, Bill and Caroline, who disobey Covey's orders and help him. "We were all in open rebellion, that morning," Douglass acknowledges, and Caroline received "several sharp blows" (*Autobiographies* 285) from Covey as a result. The scholar Robert Levine has argued that this shift in emphasis by Douglass reveals his new desire in the 1850s to be identified not as a heroic individual, as in his *Narrative*, but as "a black freedom fighter who has joined hands with his black compatriots" (*Lives* 163).

Scholars have also pointed out that women in addition to Caroline feature more prominently in the later autobiographies. Douglass's mother, for example, only briefly mentioned in the *Narrative,* appears in later works visiting her son and protecting him from Aunt Katy, a cook who is mistreating him: "That night I learned the fact," he writes, "that I was not only a child but somebody's child" (*Autobiographies* 155). Despite Douglass's addition of others to his accounts of his life, his first wife Anna Murray, a free black woman who provided funds for his successful escape, barely appears in any of them. The two were married in New York in 1838, and Anna, who was illiterate all her life, took care of their five children while Douglass traveled on his many lecture tours in the US and abroad. After Anna died in 1882, Douglass married Helen Pitts, a much younger white clerk in his office, to the dismay of prominent black admirers. He responded by joking that his first wife "was the color of my mother, and the second, the color of my father" (*Life and Writings* 4: 116). Black leaders, however, charged that he had shown contempt for the women of his own race.

Douglass's relations with women were at times complicated. In 1848 when the first women's rights convention was held in Seneca Falls, New York, the organizers presented a "Statement of Sentiments" declaring, "We hold these truths to be self-evident; that all men and women are created equal." Douglass attended that convention and was the only man to speak in favor of Elizabeth Cady Stanton's resolution for women's suffrage. He and Stanton became long-term friends, and only found themselves at odds with each other after the Civil War, when they were working for political legislation, Douglass on behalf of the Fifteenth Amendment that would grant suffrage to black males, Stanton on behalf of an amendment that would grant suffrage to all women. Douglass withheld his support for Stanton's efforts, because he believed they could hurt his own effort, and she in turn expressed some racist comments about black males. The Fifteenth Amendment passed, of course, but it would take until 1920 for the Nineteenth Amendment to be ratified, granting women the right to vote. The rift between Douglass and Stanton lasted until the 1880s, when he was again invited to speak at major women's rights meetings (see Levine *Lives* 297–298).

Independence

After the publication of his *Narrative,* which became a best seller on its appearance, selling some 20,000 to 30,000 copies within five years of its publication, Douglass's reputation grew, as did his assumption of leadership among black and white admirers. As a lecturer, he became known for eloquence, humor, and biting satire. After he parted from Garrison and the Massachusetts Anti-Slavery Society, the number and variety of the topics he spoke about soared. Racism throughout the North as well as slavery in the South were the two main ills he addressed, convinced they were sins upon the nation. Garrison had asked him to focus on his life as a slave in his lectures before audiences at the Anti-Slavery Society meetings, which he eventually resented. As he recalled in *My Bondage and My Freedom,* "'Tell your story, Frederick,' would whisper my then revered friend, William Lloyd Garrison, as I stepped upon the platform. I could not always obey, for I was now reading and thinking" (*Autobiographies* 367). Finally, he chose to resist, by setting out on his own.

His spirit of independence was enhanced in part by the international fame that came his way after the publication of his *Narrative* and the reception he received while traveling in England, Scotland, and Ireland during 1845–1847. The trip was necessary, because with the appearance of his book, those in the South could identify him as a fugitive and try to capture him. The lecture tour, which drew large crowds and positive press coverage, gave him the idea to become editor of his own newspaper. He came back to the United States a free man because a group of anti-slavery Britons purchased his freedom. They also provided him with funds to start his own newspaper *The North Star* in Rochester, New York, away from Garrison in Boston and the *Liberator*. He did not tell Garrison of his plans beforehand, nor did he ask him for advice. When Garrison found out, he wrote to his wife, "such conduct grieves me to the heart" (qtd. McFeely 149). The two consequently quarreled, and Garrison attacked Douglass's ingratitude in the *Liberator* and spread gossip about Douglass's alleged adultery with his friend and business manager, Julia Griffiths, a white English woman who lived in the same house with Douglass and his wife.

Douglass's split with Garrison included political, as well as personal causes, for after moving to Rochester, New York in 1848, and starting his own paper, Douglass became friends with Gerrit Smith, a wealthy New York landowner, heavily engaged in politics, and Douglass arrived at the conclusion that the Constitution, despite its literal support of slavery, contained an argument on behalf of liberty, and was, at heart, an anti-slavery instrument. On July 5, 1852, he gave the now-famous speech "What to the Slave Is the Fourth of July," where he not only emphasizes the irony of asking him to join in the celebration of liberty, but also critiques the assumption that the Constitution supported slavery:

> Fellow-citizens! there is no matter in respect to which, the people of the North have allowed themselves to be so ruinously imposed upon, as that of the pro-slavery character of the Constitution. In *that* instrument I hold there is neither warrant, license, nor sanction of the hateful thing; but, interpreted as it *ought* to be interpreted, the Constitution is a GLORIOUS LIBERTY DOCUMENT. Read its preamble, consider its purposes. Is slavery among them? Is it at the gateway? or is it in the temple? it is neither.
>
> (143–144)

Garrison, who would burn the Constitution on stage at the end of some speeches, was enraged at Douglass's change of position with regard to political engagement and charged him in the *Liberator* with "apostasy," "defamation," and "treachery." Harriet Beecher Stowe sought to mediate between the two with some success, asking Garrison, "Where is this work of excommunication to end? Is there but one true anti-slavery church and all others infidels?" (qtd. McFeely 178). As William S. McFeely has observed, Douglass "would never acknowledge a break with Garrison, but neither would he accept what he now regarded as a dead-end approach to ridding the country of slavery" (177). Eventually, however, the two men renewed their friendship, but not before Douglass in *My Bondage* identified Garrison as racist and oppressive.

Douglass and John Brown

As Douglass became more politically involved, he also became more aligned with those willing to be aggressive on behalf of social justice. In 1848, he applauded the French revolutionaries who had overthrown King Louis Phillippe, established a provisional government, and abolished slavery in the French West Indies. In 1848, Douglass also began a friendship with the radical white abolitionist John Brown, and listened to his plans to lead an insurrection of slaves in the South and establish an independent black colony in the Appalachia mountains. Although Brown killed Southern settlers in Kansas in cold blood, Douglass credited him with making Kansas a free state. And after Brown's unsuccessful raid on Harpers Ferry, which led to his hanging, Douglass praised him time and again in his lectures, crediting him with starting the Civil War that led to emancipation.

> Until this blow was struck, the prospect of freedom was dim, shadowy and uncertain. The irrepressible conflict was one of words, votes and compromises. When John Brown stretched forth his arm the sky was cleared. The time for compromises was gone ... and the clash of arms was at hand.
>
> ("John Brown" 66)

Brown had asked Douglass to join him in the raid on the federal arsenal at Harpers Ferry, and Douglass provides a dramatic account of their meeting in his third autobiography, *Life and Times of Frederick Douglass* (1893). They met at night at Brown's request, in a deserted stone quarry on the outskirts of Philadelphia. Brown was a wanted man for his exploits in Kansas, and he came to the meeting armed. Douglass, who felt he was on a dangerous mission, brought with him a free black friend, Shields Green, and they listened to Brown tell of his plans. "Come with me Douglass," Brown said. "I will defend you with my life. I want you for a special purpose. When I strike, the bees will begin to swarm, and I shall want you to help hive them" (*Autobiographies* 760). Douglass told Brown that he was going into a steel trap, and Brown replied that he would take hostages, if needed, in order to get out of the town. Astonished, Douglass warned that "Virginia would blow him and his hostages sky-high, rather than that he should hold Harper's Ferry an hour" (*Autobiographies* 759). Douglass understood Virginians better than Brown. The raid proved a military disaster. Ten of Brown's men were killed, including two of his sons, plus three townsmen, two slaves, one free black man, one slaveholder, and one marine. Five of Brown's men were captured and executed, including Shields Green, who, unlike Douglass, was moved to join Brown. The state of Virginia tried Brown for treason and hanged him on December 2, 1859, but not before he wrote a number of eloquent public letters defending his actions.

Effects of fugitive slave law

Tensions between the North and the South had been growing for years before the unsuccessful raid on Harpers Ferry convinced the southern states that they needed to form militias and prepare for war. In 1850, a compromise bill was passed in the US Congress in order to prevent warfare between the two sections, but what it did mostly was terrorize fugitive slaves, outrage New Englanders, and invigorate the abolitionist movement. The major provisions of the Compromise were that California would enter the union as a free state, the slave trade in Washington DC would be abolished, and the Fugitive Slave Law, already implicit in the Constitution, would be made explicit and harsher. Anyone who refused to assist in the capture of a run-away slave when asked would be subject to a $1000 fine and 6 months in prison. The Law thus made everyone, even those opposed to slavery, complicit in maintaining slavery with all of its well-known abominations. In his private journal, Emerson fumed, "I will not obey it, by God" (*JMN* 11: 412). Thoreau, too, threatened in his journal to light the fuse of a bomb under the capitol building and blow it up. "Rather than thus consent to establish Hell upon earth—to be a party to this establishment—I would touch a match to blow up earth & hell together. I will not accept life in America or on this planet on such terms" (*Journal* 8: 165–166). Friends of Emerson and Thoreau formed a vigilance committee to be on the lookout for slave catchers and to harass them while protecting the fugitives they sought.

In her autobiography, Harriet Jacobs describes the horrifying effect of the Fugitive Slave Law on runaway slaves living in the North:

> Many a poor washer-woman, who, by hard labor, had made herself a comfortable home, was obliged to sacrifice her furniture, bid a hurried farewell to friends, and seek her fortune among strangers in Canada. Many a wife discovered a secret she had never known before—that her husband was a fugitive, and must leave her to insure his own safety. Worse still, many a husband discovered that his wife had fled from slavery years ago, and as "the child follows the condition of its mother," the children of his love were liable to be seized and carried into slavery. Every where, in those humble homes, there was consternation and anguish. But what cared the legislators of the "dominant race" for the blood they were crushing out of trampled hearts?
>
> (148)

Jacobs herself lived in a state of anxiety with her children until making her way to the New England countryside sheltered by the wife of an unnamed senator.

Uncle Tom's Cabin (1852)

In 1850 Harriet Beecher Stowe was living in Brunswick, Maine, with her family, including her husband Calvin, who taught at Bowdoin College. When the Fugitive Slave Law was passed, Stowe was outraged and her sister-in-law encouraged her to use her literary skills to attack the new law and slavery itself. Stowe later recalled, "My heart was bursting with the anguish excited by the cruelty and injustice our nation was showing to the slave, and praying God to let me do a little and to cause my cry for them to be heard" (qtd. C. E. Stowe 149). In June of 1851 she began publishing *Uncle Tom's Cabin* serially in the *National Era*, and the next year she published it as a book in two volumes, and it became an immediate best-seller.

Stowe had grown up in Litchfield, Connecticut, the seventh of nine children. Her father, Lyman Beecher, a well-known evangelical minister, remarried a year after Stowe's mother, Roxane Foote Beecher, died when Harriet was five years old. Stowe attended the Hartford Female Seminary, run by her sister Catharine Beecher, and then at age twenty-one moved with her family to Cincinnati, Ohio, where her father was appointed president of the Lane Theological Seminary. In Cincinnati, Stowe published short stories and essays for magazines and newspapers, as well as a geography book for children and a collection of sketches. In 1836, she married Calvin Stowe, a professor at the Seminary, and during the first seven years of her marriage, she bore five children, and then spent fifteen months at a water cure in Vermont to recover from physical and emotional exhaustion. The cure involved eating a meager diet, drinking lots of water, being wrapped in dripping sheets, and resting.

After her return to Cincinnati, in 1848, Stowe had a sixth child, Samuel Charles (Charley), who died an agonizing death from cholera, and the experience left her with a compassion for those slave mothers separated from their children. As she explained in a letter about Charley:

> It was at his dying bed and at his grave that I learned what a poor slave mother may feel when her child is torn away from her ... There were circumstances about his death of such peculiar bitterness, of what seemed almost cruel suffering that I felt that I could never be consoled for it unless this crushing of my own heart might enable me to work out some great good to others.
>
> ("Letter to the Abolitionist" 444)

It was while living in Cincinnati that Stowe became sensitized to the plight of slaves and fugitives, with whom she and her family sympathized. Although Ohio was a free state, most of its citizens supported slavery and were fiercely anti-abolitionist. When she made a visit to Kentucky in the spring of 1833, she was shocked by the sight of a slave auction.

The Ohio River, separating Ohio and Kentucky, provided the setting for one of the most spectacular and thrilling escape scenes in American literature. In Chapter VII of *Uncle Tom's Cabin*, the young slave mother Eliza flees from slave-catchers, with her little boy, Harry, in her arms, crossing the frigid river on the ice flows, risking death by doing so. Stowe writes,

> Right on behind they came; and, nerved with strength such as God gives only to the desperate, with one wild cry and flying leap, she vaulted sheer over the turbid current by the shore, on to the raft of ice beyond. It was a

desperate leap—impossible to anything but madness and despair ... The huge green fragment of ice on which she alighted pitched and creaked as her weight came on it, but she staid there not a moment. With wild cries and desperate energy she leaped to another and still another cake;—stumbling—leaping—slipping—springing upwards again! Her shoes are gone—her stockings cut from her feet—while blood marked every step; but she saw nothing, felt nothing, till dimly, as in a dream, she saw the Ohio side, and a man helping her up the bank.

(54–55)

As Stowe's biographer Joan D. Hendrick points out, with reference to the River Jordan and the River Styx, "Eliza's flight across the river draws its power not only from its dramatic, visual character, but from the intensity of maternal feeling Stowe brought to it and the layers of Christian and pre-Christian myth that the imagery plumbed" (213).

Eliza's flight north forms one of the two main plots Stowe uses in her narrative. The book begins in Kentucky, on the farm of Arthur Shelby, who sells little Harry and Uncle Tom to a slave trader in order to get out of debt. While Eliza and Harry flee north to Canada, along with Eliza's husband George Harris, also a fugitive, who joins them on the way, Tom is taken south to New Orleans, where he lives two years as the slave of Augustin St. Clare before being sold, after St. Clare's death, to despicable Simon Legree and taken to a Gothic plantation deep in rural Louisiana, where he is beaten to death protecting fellow slaves.

Stowe uses George Harris and Uncle Tom to emphasize the two ways, physical and spiritual, that slaves had any chance of rising above the horrors of slavery. As Eliza, Harry, and George make their way north, pursued by slave hunters, kind-hearted Quakers assist them, and George, unlike Uncle Tom, shows himself willing to fight and kill in defense of his family and their freedom:

> "I will attack no man," said George. "All I ask of this country is to be let alone, and I will go out peaceably; but,"—he paused, and his brow darkened and his face worked,—"I've had a sister sold in that New Orleans market. I know what they are sold for; and am I going to stand by and see them take my wife and sell her, when God has given me a pair of strong arms to defend her? No; God help me! I'll fight to the last breath, before they shall take my wife and son. Can you blame me?"
>
> (172)

Making a stand on the top of a rock cliff, George shoots one of the slave hunters, Tom Loker, which allows George and his family to escape capture. The Quakers nurse Loker to health and almost convert him. Meanwhile Eliza, Harry, and George cross over in disguise to Canada by way of Lake Erie and enjoy their freedom, eventually becoming missionaries to Africa.

Uncle Tom, because of his Christian beliefs, does not resist his enslavement, absorbing punishment to avoid giving it. In New Orleans, he is treated well by St. Clare and forms a deep bond with the angelic child Eva, St. Clare's daughter. Together they read the Bible and discuss its teachings. As Eva dies a lingering death from illness, she makes her father promise he will free his slaves, and Stowe endows the death scene with all the emotion she felt at her son Charley's death. When Eva passes "from death unto life," Stowe writes,

> Farewell, beloved child! The bright, eternal doors have closed after thee; we shall see thy sweet face no more. O, woe for them who watched thy entrance into heaven, when they shall wake and find only the cold gray sky of daily life, and thou gone forever!
>
> (270)

Although Stowe's pious sentimentality may strike today's readers as unrealistic and cloying, it exerted a strong emotional impact on its thousands of contemporary readers.

Stowe's description of Uncle Tom's death is equally affecting, and he, too, converts others as he dies. Although St. Clare promised Eva he would give Tom and all his slaves their freedom, he dies an accidental death before doing so, and his heartless wife sells Tom to the cruel Legree, a New Englander by birth. Stowe, before she began the novel, imagined the martyrdom of Tom, who saves others through his suffering, though not Legree. Stowe, according to her son's biography, heard the words of Jesus about helping others:

> It seemed as if the crucified, but now risen and glorified Christ, were speaking to her through the poor black man, cut and bleeding under the blows of the slave whip ... That Sunday afternoon she went to her room, locked the door, and wrote out, substantially as it appears in the published editions, the chapter called "The Death of Uncle Tom."
>
> (C. E. Stowe 145)

In the chapter, Tom behaves heroically in protecting a fifteen-year old slave named Emmeline and Legree's enslaved mistress Cassy, but he is beaten to death for doing so. As he dies, he forgives Legree and the two brutal slaves, Sambo and Quimbo, who have whipped him to the point of death:

> "I forgive ye, with all my heart!" said Tom, faintly.
> "O, Tom! Do tell us who is *Jesus*, anyhow?" Said Sambo;—"Jesus, that's been a standin' by you so, all this night!—Who is he?"
> The word roused the failing, fainting spirit. He poured forth a few energetic sentences of that wondrous One,—his life, his death, his everlasting presence, and power to save.
> They wept,—those two savage men.

> "Why didn't I never hear this before?" said Sambo; "but I do believe!—I can't help it! Lord Jesus, have mercy on us!"
>
> "Poor critters!" said Tom, "I'd be willing to bar' all I have, if it'll only bring ye to Christ! O, Lord! Give me these two more souls, I pray!"
>
> That prayer was answered!
>
> (377–378)

The conversion of non-believers within the novel receives emphasis equal to the horrors of slavery. In the Eliza and George narrative, however, righteous violence, rather than self-sacrifice, becomes the effective means of liberation, and Stowe anticipates the change of perspective she, along with Douglass and others, would acquire as the Civil War approached.

White Southerners, of course, claimed that Stowe misrepresented the institution of slavery and had filled her book with fictions that had no counterpart in reality. Her follow-up book, *A Key to "Uncle Tom's Cabin"* (1853), proved them wrong with its factual documentation; however, it is true that she had no first-hand knowledge of slavery, other than the glimpses she obtained in Cincinnati, and on her one and only visit to Kentucky. Yet, she read about the lives of slaves, especially the narratives of Henry Bibb and Joseph Henson. In fact, she borrowed from both of them.

She also queried Frederick Douglass, asking him for details of life under slavery. Douglass was cordial, praised her novel, and for a time believed she would fund his plan to create an industrial school for black youth; however, when she returned from a celebrated trip to Great Britain and Europe in 1853, she had changed her mind. In his *Life and Times of Frederick Douglass* (1892), Douglass laments,

> I have never been able to see any force in the reasons for this change. It is enough, however, to say that they were sufficient for her, and that she no doubt acted conscientiously, though her change of purpose ... placed me in an awkward position before the colored people of this country, as well as to friends abroad.
>
> (*Autobiographies* 733)

Despite his disappointment about Stowe's failure to follow through on support for the industrial college, Douglass maintained his admiration for *Uncle Tom's Cabin*, calling it "a work of marvelous depth and power," adding, "Nothing could have better suited the moral and humane requirements of the hour. Its effect was amazing, instantaneous, and universal" (*Autobiographies* 726).

Over the course of the twentieth century, Stowe's novel lost favor among many readers because its racialism became more and more apparent. As Cindy Weinstein has pointed out, *Uncle Tom's Cabin* has been "a lightning rod for debates about race in US literature" (9). Tom's Christlike pacifism combined with his passivity has led a number of later commentators to detest him. "Uncle Tom" is now an epithet bestowed on black men who do the bidding of whites without standing up for themselves or others of their race. Stowe's argument at the end of the book on behalf of Colonization, that is, sending black people to Africa, also reveals a latent racism, prevalent throughout antebellum white society. In the twentieth century, the eminent black writer James Baldwin, in a famous critique, declared that Stowe "was not so much a novelist as an impassioned pamphleteer," whose sentimentality was devoted to a cause, rather than actual human beings. Baldwin writes,

> Sentimentality, the ostentatious parading of excessive and spurious emotion, is the mark of dishonesty, the inability to feel; the wet eyes of the sentimentalist betray his aversion to experience, his fear of life, his arid heart; and it is always, therefore, the signal of secret and violent inhumanity, the mask of cruelty.
> (496)

Despite such criticisms, *Uncle Tom's Cabin* had a tremendous influence in American culture, selling a million copies and inspiring countless stage plays throughout the nineteenth century. Supposedly Lincoln greeted Stowe during a visit to the White House as "the little woman who brought on the war." In a brilliant defense of the value of Stowe's book, the scholar Jane P. Tompkins argues that *Uncle Tom's Cabin* gains its power by dramatizing "a pervasive cultural myth," that is, that "the highest human calling is to give one's life for another" (545). She points out that while it is difficult for modern readers to take seriously "a novel that insists on religious conversion as the necessary precondition for sweeping social change," Stowe and her readers indeed took it seriously (549). Thanks in large part to Tompkins's defense of the novel, *Uncle Tom's Cabin* has gained a place in the American literary canon. It still evokes strong negative reactions due to its pervasive racism, but it has gained recognition for the sincerity of its emphasis on love and sacrifice, the cultural and political work it performed, and its centrality to current discussions about race relations, race theory, and the definition of literary greatness.

Incidents in the Life of a Slave Girl (1861)

One black woman affected strongly by *Uncle Tom's Cabin* was Harriet Jacobs, a fugitive slave, who felt inspired to write her own autobiographical narrative, *Incidents in the Life of a Slave Girl* (1861), using the pseudonym Linda Brent. Jacobs asked Stowe for help in this effort, but did not receive it. Readers for some time suspected the book was fiction, written by the prominent abolitionist Lydia Maria Child, whose name appeared on the title page as editor; however, in 1981, the scholar Jean Fagan Yellin demonstrated conclusively that the book was autobiography and that Jacobs, not Child, was its author. In a letter to Jacobs, Child explained,

> I have very little occasion to alter the language, which is wonderfully good, for one whose opportunities for education have been so limited. The events are interesting, and well told; the remarks are also good, and to

the purpose. But I am copying a great deal of it, for the purpose of transposing sentences and pages, so as to bring the story into continuous *order*, and the remarks into *appropriate* places.

(193)

Jacobs's fascinating and difficult life matches the story of Linda Brent. Born a slave in Edenton, North Carolina, Jacobs describes the psychological abuse suffered by women in slavery, occasioned by sexual harassment, rape, concubinage, miscegenation, and separation from one's children. At one point Jacobs explicitly declares, "Slavery is terrible for men; but it is far more terrible for women. Superadded to the burden common to all, *they* have wrongs, and sufferings, and mortifications peculiarly their own" (64). Throughout her book, Jacobs emphasizes that her desire for freedom was matched by her desire to protect her children and create a safe home for them.

Jacobs was born a slave but "never knew it till six years of happy childhood had passed away" (9). She was the daughter of the slaves Delilah Horniblow and Daniel Jacobs, a carpenter. She had one brother, John S., who became a prominent abolitionist speaker after running away and settling in Boston. (In his mid-thirties, he and Douglass lectured together in the towns and villages around Rochester, New York.) When Jacobs was six years old, her mother died, and she became the slave of Margaret Horniblow, who died when Jacobs was twelve. Instead of willing Jacobs her freedom, she left her to her three-year-old niece, the daughter of Dr. James Norcom, the villain of Jacobs's narrative, where he appears as Dr. Flint. Because the will was witnessed by Norcom, but not signed by Margaret Horniblow, Jacobs's biographer, Jean Fagan Yellin, has posed the question, "was it Dr. Norcom himself, who seized the opportunity to control his sister-in-law's bright young slave girl?" (15). Jacobs was unaware of this possibility and felt betrayed by her mistress, whom she regarded as a mother. In *Incidents*, she writes,

> As a child, I loved my mistress; and, looking back on the happy days I spent with her, I try to think with less bitterness of this act of injustice. While I was with her, she taught me to read and spell; and for this privilege, which so rarely falls to the lot of a slave, I bless her memory.
>
> (11)

In *Incidents*, we do not learn the sexual specifics of Dr. Flint's harassment, because in the interests of not offending her readers, Jacobs discusses it in generalities. We do learn that he cuts off all of Linda's hair, strikes her, throws her down the stairs at one point, and threatens to kill her at another. His lecherous advances, moreover, are devious, threatening, relentless, and psychologically damaging. Jacobs writes,

> No pen can give an adequate description of the all-pervading corruption produced by slavery. The slave girl is reared in an atmosphere of

licentiousness and fear. The lash and the foul talk of her master and his sons are her teachers. When she is fourteen or fifteen, her owner, or his sons, or the overseer, or perhaps all of them, begin to bribe her with presents. If these fail to accomplish their purpose, she is whipped or starved into submission to their will ... But resistance is hopeless.

(44)

Norcom apparently made a practice of raping his young female slaves, and according to Jacobs, fathered at least eleven slave children. Perhaps the most surprising revelation in *Incidents* is that Norcom's wife, who knew of her husband's horrid behavior, blamed not him but his victims, subjecting Jacobs to verbal abuse and jealous rage. The doctor's plan to force Jacobs to become his concubine by building a cottage for her four miles out of town precipitated her decision at age fifteen to begin a sexual relationship with Samuel Tredwell Sawyer, an unmarried white attorney and later US congressman, who courted her with sympathy and flattery. Jacobs felt ashamed of this five-year liaison, which outraged Norcom, and resulted in two children, Joseph and Louisa. Jacobs's beloved grandmother, Molly Horniblow, was very judgmental and angry when she learned about Jacobs's first pregnancy and only reluctantly took pity on her. "She did not say, 'I forgive you;'" Jacobs writes, "but she looked at me lovingly, with her eyes full of tears. She laid her old hand gently on my head, and murmured, 'Poor child! Poor child!'" (49).

After Jacobs refused Norcom's ultimatum to become his concubine and sever relations with Sawyer, she was punished by being sent to work on Norcom's son's plantation some six miles out of town. While there, she learned of the plan to make her and her children stay there permanently and decided she had to flee and hide. "My plan," Jacobs writes,

was to conceal myself at the house of a friend, and remain there a few weeks till the search was over. My hope was that the doctor would get discouraged, and, for fear of losing my value, and also of subsequently finding my children among the missing, he would consent to sell us; and I knew somebody would buy us.

(75)

The "somebody" was her lover, who did manage to buy the children and also her brother, but not Jacobs, who continued in hiding to be near her children, first in an upstairs room of a kind white woman in the town, and then in the small garret of her grandmother's house.

For seven years, she lived in that space, nine feet long, seven feet wide and only three-feet high at its peak. She suffered from little light, stifling air, rats, mice, insects, and intense cold in the winter and heat in the summer. She was often ill for weeks, and without the ability to stand, she lost the use of her legs. She movingly recalls her despair during one long illness:

> Dark thoughts passed through my mind as I lay there day after day. I tried to be thankful for my little cell, dismal as it was, and even to love it, as part of the price I had paid for the redemption of my children. Sometimes I thought God was a compassionate Father, who would forgive my sins for the sake of my sufferings. At other times, it seemed to me there was no justice or mercy in the divine government. I asked why the curse of slavery was permitted to exist, and why I had been so persecuted and wronged from youth upward. These things took the shape of mystery, which is to this day not so clear to my soul as I trust it will be hereafter.
>
> (98)

Despite these sufferings, she remained close to her children and could often see and hear what transpired on the street below, and she used this information to manipulate Norcom with bogus letters and to frustrate his search for her. Eventually, she descended at times into a storeroom, until one day when an untrustworthy slave apparently saw her and Jacobs knew she must flee.

Jacobs never told the details of her escape to the North, but apparently her uncle and a friend persuaded a white boat captain to take her to Philadelphia. By then, her daughter had been sent to Sawyer's relatives on Long Island, and her grandmother was able to send Jacobs's son north to New York City and then Boston, where he reunited with his uncle and mother. Like Frederick Douglass, Jacobs does not give the names of those friends in the North who assisted her in her escape, but she does name the Reverend Jeremiah Durham, who greeted her upon her arrival in Philadelphia and put her up at his house before helping her make her way to New York City. In a moment of candor, Jacobs told the good reverend about her children and sexual history, which evoked his reply "don't answer every body so openly. It might give some heartless people a pretext for treating you with contempt." Jacobs writes, "That word *contempt* burned me like coals of fire. I replied, 'God alone knows how I have suffered; and He, I trust, will forgive me.'" She goes on to relate that his words "made an indelible impression upon me. They brought up great shadows from the mournful past" (127).

Jacobs's shame about her sexual history prevented her from telling her life's story to others in the North after her escape. In *Incidents* she introduces it with a wrenching plea to her readers:

> O, ye happy women, whose purity has been sheltered from childhood, who have been free to choose the objects of your affection, whose homes are protected by law, do not judge the poor desolate slave girl too severely! If slavery had been abolished, I, also, could have married the man of my choice; I could have had a home shielded by the laws; and I should have been spared the painful task of confessing what I am now about to relate; but all my prospects had been blighted by slavery. I wanted to keep myself pure; and, under the most adverse circumstances, I tried hard to preserve my self-respect; but I was struggling alone in the powerful grasp of the demon Slavery; and the monster proved too strong for me. I felt as

if I was forsaken by God and man; as if all my efforts must be frustrated; and I became reckless in my despair.

(46)

Jacobs declares that "it seems less degrading to give one's self, than to submit to compulsion," but she does not realize, as readers do now, that rape is not comparable to having consensual sexual relations. It's about power and domination. Thus, even if the young Jacobs had been unsuccessful in warding off the advances of Dr. Norcom, the sin would have been his and his alone. Even abolitionists failed to understand this, and often spoke of slavery as "that harlot." Emerson in his essay "American Civilization" (1862) calls the South that country "where the position of the white woman is injuriously affected by the outlawry of the black woman" (168).

Blaming the victim in cases of rape remains a serious injustice throughout the world even today, and in the antebellum US, it was common practice to blame black female slaves for being raped and bearing mixed-race children. The so-called "mulatto" population of the South grew exponentially before the Civil War, and, as Nancy Bentley has shown,

> Biracial characters were made the symbols of an inescapable history of Southern guilt. And the miscegenation crimes of the slavocracy were not sins of sexual violation only; the scandal of race "confusion" was an odious crime in itself, and white writers often had their characters express this confusion as a painful lived experience.
>
> (504)

Jacobs's mother and father were both of mixed race, and her own two children were very light-skinned and could have passed for white but chose not to. With help from a friend, Jacobs found work in the North as a nurse to the child of N. P. Willis and his wife, Mary. Willis, a well-known and well-off writer and editor was Fanny Fern's brother, whom she satirized as the egotistical and hard-hearted dandy Hyacinth in *Ruth Hall*. On his travels Willis visited Virginia slave plantations and wrote about negro happiness and the beauties of slavery as an institution. He did not know that Jacobs was a fugitive slave, or that while working in his home she would direct fierce irony at a gentleman like him who found slavery a beautiful patriarchal institution. In *Incidents*, writing as Linda Brent, she asks,

> What does *he* know of the half-starved wretches toiling from dawn till dark on the plantations? Of mothers shrieking for their children, torn from their arms by slave traders? Of young girls dragged down into moral filth? Of pools of blood around the whipping post? Of hounds trained to tear human flesh? Of men screwed into cotton gins to die? The slaveholder showed him none of these things, and the slaves dared not tell of them if he had asked them.
>
> (62)

Fortunately, Willis's first wife, Mary Stace Willis, who died in 1845, and his second wife, Cornelia Grinnell Willis, held anti-slavery views, and helped Jacobs and her children avoid capture by slave-hunters. Cornelia Willis (Mrs. Bruce in *Incidents*) even purchased Jacobs and her children, and at the end of her book, Jacobs bestows on her the word "friend," adding that for her, "the word is sacred" (156).

A key feature of Jacobs's narrative is her recognition of the large number of friends and family that helped her during her ordeal as a slave. Her grandmother was primary, of course, but her brother and uncles, too, were essential. An unnamed female friend in Edenton concealed her at her house; a good friend named Peter in the book risked his life to help her escape; and a black housemaid named Betty hid her under the floorboards of her kitchen. She also blesses the white members of the community who came to her aid, and in this sense her narrative differs from Douglass's, for even those whites who first help him, such as Sophia Auld in Baltimore, turn out to act cruelly toward him. Jacobs's first mistress teaches her to read and write; an elderly white woman buys and frees her grandmother; a white slave-owner visiting the North recognizes her fugitive uncle and helps him travel safely to New York. "That man was a miracle" (24), Jacobs writes. A friendly white woman in Edenton hides her upstairs in her house; and a white boat captain and white sailors care for her and another runaway as they take them to Philadelphia. "Be it said to the honor of this captain," Jacobs writes, "Southerner as he was, that if Fanny and I had been white ladies, and our passage lawfully engaged, he could not have treated us more respectfully" (125). Once in the North, she is surprised at the "prejudice against color" she encounters, but with the Mrs. Willises and abolitionist friends in Boston and Rochester, she makes dear white friends, especially the Quaker Amy Post, who encourages her to write a story of her life.

Of course, there were several Northern women who did not assist Jacobs, the leading one being Harriet Beecher Stowe. Jacobs deeply admired Stowe, but when both Amy Post and Cornelia Willis wrote to Stowe on Jacobs's behalf, mentioning her life story and her desire to visit and secure some advice in writing about it, Stowe asked for verification that the story was true and said, if it were, "she would incorporate it into *The Key to Uncle Tom's Cabin*, which she was rushing to complete before sailing to England" (Yellin 121). Willis and Jacobs both wrote several more times saying Jacobs would be happy to supply Stowe with any facts she needed, but that she wished to publish her story herself. Stowe did not answer any of these letters, which offended Jacobs. She labored some six more years, working on her book alone, at night, with no assistance and bouts of illness. When she completed her manuscript and took it to the Boston publishers Phillips and Samson, they agreed to publish it if she could acquire a preface by Stowe. Jacobs approached Stowe again and received a rejection. When another publisher, Thayer and Eldridge, agreed to publish the book if the well-known author and activist L. Maria Child would write a preface, Jacobs met with Child, who enthusiastically agreed.

As a number of critics have pointed out, the theme of motherhood is prominent in *Incidents* and one source of its appeal for female readers. Time and again Linda expresses the love she had for her children and her desire to create a home where they could be safe and free. One of her greatest disappointments is that her son Benjamin joins his Uncle William in California and then Australia, and she's parted from him. Yet, one of her greatest joys is having Ellen, her daughter, as her companion and seeing her gain an education. Jacobs ends her narrative on a subdued note, which distinguishes it and bears witness to its sincerity:

> Reader, my story ends with freedom; not in the usual way, with marriage. I and my children are now free! ... The dream of my life is not yet realized. I do not sit with my children in a home of my own. I still long for a hearthstone of my own, however humble. I wish it for my children's sake far more than for my own. But God so orders circumstances as to keep me with my friend Mrs. Bruce. Love, duty, gratitude, also bind me to her side. It is a privilege to serve her who pities my oppressed people, and who has bestowed the inestimable boon of freedom on me and my children.
>
> (156)

Although Jacobs wanted to end her book with a tribute to John Brown, her editor Child, a fervent supporter of Brown, persuaded her that it would be more fitting (and less offensive to readers, no doubt) to conclude with "the death of your grandmother" (qtd. Yellin 141). As a consequence, Jacobs's last lines recall "gloomy recollections" that come with "tender memories of my good old grandmother, like light, fleecy clouds floating over a dark and troubled sea" (156).

Conclusion

Although Douglass, Stowe, and Jacobs all contributed to the anti-slavery movement that led to emancipation, only Douglass and Stowe achieved financial success during their lifetimes. After writing *Uncle Tom's Cabin*, Stowe wrote her second anti-slavery novel, *Dred* (1856), and then a series of popular stories and novels centered upon life in New England. She made three trips to Europe, where she was lavished with praise, and she settled in a Gothic Revival mansion in Hartford, Connecticut, where she died in 1896. Douglass recruited black soldiers for the celebrated African American 54th Massachusetts regiment during the Civil War and was appointed Marshall of the District of Columbia in 1877 and served as United States Minster to Haiti in 1889–1891. In 1892 he published the revised *Life and Times of Frederick Douglass* focused on his eminent public career, spoke out against lynching in 1894, and died in Washington DC in 1895.

Jacobs's efforts on behalf of "her people" left her with minimal physical and financial resources. During and after the Civil War she spoke out on behalf of former slaves. In 1862, she published a letter titled "Life among the Contrabands" in the *Liberator*. Contrabands were slaves who escaped to the North during the Civil War and were kept together as stolen "property." Jacobs's letter reported on the terrible conditions in the contraband camps, where men, women, and children were huddled together, hungry, naked, and sick. Jacobs also gave a powerful speech to black soldiers that challenged the racism they faced from Lincoln and others in the North. In 1863, she started the Jacobs Free School for poor black children in Alexandria, Virginia, and after moving to Savannah, Georgia, she worked raising money for a home for orphans and old people. In 1871, she finally met Stowe through mutual friends, and Stowe presented her with a signed copy of *Uncle Tom's Cabin*. During the final years of her life, she witnessed the failure of Reconstruction, and the failure of those in the North and the South to protect the rights of former slaves like herself. She tried keeping several boarding houses, but could not make them pay, and she ended up being a housekeeper in Cambridge, until she got sick. Although she subsequently died in poverty and obscurity in 1897, her unique and compelling autobiography has gained recognition as a classic work of American literature.

Suggestions for further reading

Dayan, Joan. *Haiti, History, and the Gods*. Berkeley: University of California Press, 1995.

Foster, Frances Smith. *Witnessing Slavery: The Development of Ante-Bellum Slave Narratives*. Westport, CT: Greenwood, 1979.

Gossett, Thomas F. *Uncle Tom's Cabin and American Culture*. Dallas: Southern Methodist University Press, 1985.

Levine, Robert S. *The Lives of Frederick Douglass*. Cambridge, MA: Harvard University Press, 2016.

Sanchez-Eppler, Karen. *Touching Liberty: Abolition, Feminism and the Politics of the Body*. Berkeley: University of California Press, 1993.

Sundquist, Eric J. *To Wake the Nations: Race in the Making of American Literature*. Cambridge, MA: Harvard University Press, 1993.

Uncle Tom's Cabin and American Culture: A Multi-Media Archive. http://utc.iath.virginia.edu/index2f.html

References

Ammons, Elizabeth. "Freeing the Slaves and Banishing the Blacks: Racism, Empire, and Africa." *Harriet Beecher Stowe's Uncle Tom's Cabin: A Casebook*. Ed. Elizabeth Ammons. New York: Oxford University Press, 2007. 227–246.

Baldwin, "Everybody's Protest Novel." 1955. Rpt. *Uncle Tom's Cabin by Harriet Beecher Stowe*. Ed. Elizabeth Ammons. Second Edition. A Norton Critical Edition. New York: Norton, 2010. 532–539.

Bentley, Nancy. "White Slaves: The Mulatto Hero in Antebellum Fiction." *American Literature* 65 (September 1993): 501–522.

Buell, Lawrence. "Harriet Beecher Stowe and the Dream of the Great American Novel." *The Cambridge Companion to Harriet Beecher Stowe*. Ed. Cindy Weinstein. Cambridge: Cambridge University Press, 2004. 190–202.

Child, Lydia Maria. "Letters to Harriet Jacobs." In *Incidents in the Life of a Slave Girl*. Eds. Nellie Y. McKay and Frances Smith Foster. Norton Critical Edition. New York: Norton, 2001. 193–195.

Douglass, Frederick. *Autobiographies: Narrative of the Life of Frederick Douglass, an American Slave; My Bondage and My Freedom; Life and Times of Frederick Douglass*. New York: Library of America, 1994.

Douglass, Frederick. *The Frederick Douglass Papers. Ser. 1, Speeches, Debates, and Interviews*. 5 vols. Ed. John W. Blassingame et al. New Haven: Yale University Press, 1979–1992.

Douglass, Frederick. "John Brown: An Address at the Fourteenth Anniversary of Storer College." In Benjamin Quarles. *Allies for Freedom and Blacks on John Brown*. Cambridge, MA: Da Capo, 2001. 54–66.

Douglass, Frederick. *The Life and Writings of Frederick Douglass*. 5 vols. Ed. Philip S. Foner. New York: International Publishers, 1950–1975.

Douglass, Frederick. "What to the Slave Is the Fourth of July." 1852. *Narrative of the Life of Frederick Douglass, An American Slave*. Ed. Ira Dworkin. New York: Penguin Books, 2014. 119–147.

Emerson, Ralph Waldo. *Emerson's Antislavery Writings*. Eds. Len Gougeon and Joel Myerson. New Haven: Yale University Press, 1995. Abbreviated AW.

Emerson, Ralph Waldo. *The Journals and Miscellaneous Notebooks of Ralph Waldo Emerson*. Ed. William H. Gilman, Ralph H. Orth, et al. 16 vols. Cambridge, MA: Belknap Press of Harvard University Press, 1960–1982. Abbreviated JMN.

Garnet, Henry Highland. "Call to Rebellion." In *Words That Changed America*. Ed. Alex Barnett. n.l.: Lyons Press, 2003. 33–36.

Garrison, William Lloyd. "The Dangers of the Nation." 1832. In *Selections from the Writings and Speeches of William Lloyd Garrison*. 1852. Rpt. New York: Negro Universities Press, 1968. 44–61.

Goldstein, Leslie Friedman. "Violence as an Instrument for Social Change: The Views of Frederick Douglass (1817–1895)." *Journal of Negro History* 61 (January 1976): 61–72.

Gould, Philip. "The Rise, Development, and Circulation of the Slave Narrative." In *The Cambridge Companion to the African American Slave Narrative*. Ed Audrey Fisch. New York: Cambridge University Press, 2007. 11–27.

Hartman, Saidiya V. *Scenes of Subjection: Terror, Slavery, and Self-Making in Nineteenth-Century America*. New York: Oxford University Press, 1997.

Hendrick, Joan D. *Harriet Beecher Stowe: A Life*. New York: Oxford University Press, 1994.

Hinks, Peter P. "Introduction." In *David Walker's Appeal to the Coloured Citizens of the World*. Ed. Peter P. Hinks. University Park: The Pennsylvania State University Press, 2000.

Jacobs, Harriet. *Incidents in the Life of a Slave Girl*. Eds. Nellie Y. McKay and Frances Smith Foster. Norton Critical Edition. New York: Norton, 2001.

James, C. L. R. *The Black Jacobins: Toussaint L'Ouverture and the San Domingo Revolution*. Second Edition Revised. New York: Random House, 1963.

Levine, Robert S. "Frederick Douglass, War, Haiti." *PMLA* 124 (October 2009): 1864–1868.

Levine, Robert S. *The Lives of Frederick Douglass*. Cambridge, MA: Harvard University Press, 2016.

McDowell, Deborah E. "In the First Place: Making Frederick Douglass and the Afro-American Narrative Tradition." In *Narrative of the Life of Frederick Douglass, An American Slave, Written by Himself*. Ed. William L. Andrews. Norton Critical Edition. New York: Norton, 1997. 172–183.

McFeely, William S. *Frederick Douglass*. New York: Norton, 1991.

Stowe, Charles Edward. *Harriet Beecher Stowe: The Story of Her Life*. Boston: Houghton Mifflin, 1911.

Stowe, Harriet Beecher. "Letter to the Abolitionist Eliza Cabot Follen." (December 16, 1852.) Rpt. *Uncle Tom's Cabin*. Ed. Elizabeth Ammons. Second Edition. Norton Critical Edition. New York: Norton, 2010. 444–446.

Stowe, Harriet Beecher. "The Chimney-Corner." *Atlantic Monthly* 15 (January 1865): 110–115.

Stowe, Harriet Beecher. *Uncle Tom's Cabin*. Ed. Elizabeth Ammons. Second Edition. Norton Critical Edition. New York: Norton, 2010.

Sundquist, Eric J. "Slavery, Revolution, and the American Renaissance." In *The American Renaissance Reconsidered*. Eds. Walter Benn Michaels and Donald E. Pease. Baltimore: Johns Hopkins University Press, 1985. 1–33.

Thoreau, Henry David. *Journal Vol. 8*. 1854. Ed. Sandra Harbert Petrulionis. Princeton: Princeton University Press, 2002.

Tompkins, Jane P. "Sentimental Power: *Uncle Tom's Cabin* and the Politics of Literary History." 1978. Rpt. *Uncle Tom's Cabin by Harriet Beecher Stowe*. Ed. Elizabeth Ammons. Second Edition. Norton Critical Edition. New York: Norton, 2010. 539–561.

Turner, Nat. *The Confessions of Nat Turner*. Ed. Kenneth S. Greenberg. Second Edition. Boston: Bedford/St Martin's, 2017.

Walker, David. *Appeal to the Coloured Citizens of the World*. Ed. Peter P. Hinks. 1829. Rpt. University Park: The Pennsylvania State University Press, 2000.

Weinstein, Cindy. "Introduction." *The Cambridge Companion to Harriet Beecher Stowe*. Ed. Cindy Weinstein. Cambridge: Cambridge University Press, 2004. 1–14.

Yellin, Jean Fagan. *Harriet Jacobs: A Life*. New York: Basic Books, 2004.

6 Whitman, Dickinson, and the Civil War

Although Poe, Emerson, and Melville all made significant contributions to the poetry of the American Renaissance, Walt Whitman (1819–1892) and Emily Dickinson (1830–1886) stand out as two of the nineteenth century's most original and accomplished poets. Each was strikingly innovative in his and her own way. Whitman pioneered what is now called free verse, a poetry without regular meter and rhyme. He drew upon examples of prose-poetry by others, most notably James Macpherson's *The Poems of Ossian* (mentioned in Chapter 3), but Whitman dealt with subject matter that was new, shockingly new, for it featured celebrations of the common man and the human body, male and female, as well as acts of love, handled metaphorically.

Dickinson was original in her verse as well, using unique language and structure to create dazzling descriptions of external phenomena and psychological states of being. She forsook conventional punctuation, such as commas and periods, substituting dashes throughout her lines. She also altered the meter of her lines to create special effects, and she experimented with her rhymes for the same reason, using exact rhymes, off rhymes, and no rhymes. Dickinson liked to use nouns for verbs and verbs for nouns, and she chose every word carefully, claiming that for several years her dictionary (or "Lexicon," as she called it) was her only companion (*Letters* 2: 404). She, like Whitman, introduced erotic imagery into her poems, though not with his specificity.

Both poets drew upon the British Romantic tradition, but Whitman went "afoot with his vision," as he put it, and wrote of all regions of the United States, and catalogued all sorts of individuals, occupations, and activities. Dickinson, eleven years younger than he, wrote intense private poetry, dealing with moments of revelation, of vision, that transported her. She once told a friend,

> If I read a book [and] it makes my whole body so cold no fire ever can warm me, I know *that* is poetry. If I feel physically as if the top of my head were taken off, I know *that* is poetry. These are the only ways I know it. Is there any other way?
>
> (*Letters* 2: 473–474)

DOI: 10.4324/9781315751627-6

Whitman aspired to become America's national bard, as his Preface to the first edition of *Leaves of Grass* (1855) clearly shows, but only near the end of his life did this recognition occur. Dickinson, by all accounts, wished to gain recognition as a poet, but it only came after her death.

Whitman as an adult circulated within the rowdy urban life of Brooklyn and Manhattan, while Dickinson lived far inland in sedate and conservative Amherst, Massachusetts. Both poets shared an affinity for ecstatic experience, but their methods of describing it varied widely. Whitman's free verse had few models and overflowed with loose lines and seemingly spontaneous thoughts and feelings. Dickinson's poems are characterized by their tight syntax, unusual metaphors, and ironic wit. She drew upon the poetry of seventeenth-century metaphysical poets such as John Donne, as well as the Bible, Shakespeare, Keats, and Elizabeth Barrett Browning. Dickinson and Whitman were both influenced by Emerson—not necessarily by his poetry, which tended to be rather conventional in form and content, but his emphasis on a transcendental approach to natural phenomena. For Dickinson, such phenomena included sunsets, thunder, bees, birds, wind, the aurora borealis, and of course, grass. The objects that inspired Whitman were myriad, but grass, birds, and the sea stand out.

Whitman was expansive in his ever-growing *Leaves of Grass* (published in seven editions during his lifetime), but Dickinson was reductive, in the best sense, writing short lyric poems, few of which were published in her lifetime. Some she enclosed in letters to friends, but copies of more than eight hundred were found by her sister wrapped together in small packets (called fascicles) in Dickinson's dresser drawer after her death. Beginning about 1858, she had copied these poems on high-quality, unlined stationery, folded them in sheets, and sewed groups of them together.

In several of her poems, she describes her poetry as "attar" (perfume), arrived at by "expression," literally a process of mechanically pressing plants such as flowers to squeeze out their aromatic essence. Here is one of those poems:

> Essential Oils—are wrung—
> The Attar from the Rose
> Be not expressed by Suns—alone—
> It is the gift of Screws—
>
> The General Rose—decay—
> But this—in Lady's Drawer
> Make Summer—When the Lady lie
> In Ceaseless Rosemary—
> (FP 772)

The "this" in the second stanza refers to the poem itself, which indeed makes "Summer," for the reader, after the lady (Dickinson?) has passed away. "Summer," and "Noon" were two of Dickinson's most weighty and positive metaphors. Sprigs of rosemary, by the way, were placed on coffins as traditional emblems of remembrance.

This ritual of remembrance figures into some of Whitman's poems as well, in ways that illustrate his expansiveness compared with Dickinson's compression. For example, in his great elegy, or poem of lamentation, for Lincoln, titled "When Lilacs Last in the Dooryard Bloom'd" (1865), the poet places a sprig of lilac on Lincoln's coffin, and adds,

> All over bouquets of roses,
> O death, I cover you over with roses and early lilies,
> But mostly and now the lilac that blooms the first,
> Copious I break, I break the sprigs from the bushes,
> With loaded arms I come, pouring for you,
> For you and the coffins all of you O death.
>
> (461)

This poem, like Dickinson's, itself serves as a token of remembrance, and Whitman extends his elegy to include not just Lincoln, who goes unnamed in the poem, but all the young men who died during the Civil War. (Lilacs, by the way, have heart-shaped leaves and are appropriate symbols of love.)

Personal and private

One of Dickinson's most valued correspondents was Thomas Wentworth Higginson—Unitarian minister, author, editor, abolitionist, and leader of the first black regiment to serve in the Civil War. In one of her first letters to Higginson, she wrote, "You speak of Mr. Whitman—I never read his Book—but was told that he was disgraceful—" (*Letters* 2: 404). Given Dickinson's playfulness and love of irony, there is reason to question this assertion. Because Whitman published "Bardic Symbols" (1860) in the *Atlantic*, which Higginson helped edit and Dickinson read, it is probable she was familiar with Whitman's poetry. He would not have known about hers, however. Only about eleven of her poems appeared in print during her lifetime, out of some eighteen hundred that she wrote, and those were published anonymously. The exact total is uncertain, because she wrote different versions of some poems, and she often wrote what can be considered poetry within her letters and even on envelopes and scraps of paper. Images of her poems in manuscript can be seen at www.edickinson.org.

Dickinson did not choose to remain a private poet, but her domestic circumstances and reclusive personality conspired to delay her public recognition. She was the second of three children born to Edward Dickinson and Emily Norcross Dickinson of Amherst, and she lived almost all her adult life in her spacious family home called "The Homestead," with brief visits to Boston, Philadelphia, and Washington DC. From ages ten to seventeen, she attended the Amherst Academy and then went to the Mount Holyoke Female Seminary for a year. She was close to her older brother Austin and her younger sister Lavinia ("Vinnie"), but she did not share her poetry with them, nor with her parents. Like most of those living in Amherst, Dickinson's family were church-going Calvinists, skeptical of the liberal developments taking place in Boston (not to mention Concord). During her year at Mount Holyoke, Dickinson was categorized as one "without hope" of becoming a Christian. Supposedly when the headmistress asked the students to stand if they wanted to accept Christ as their savior, Emily remained seated. "'They thought it queer I didn't rise,'" she told a classmate, "adding with a twinkle in her eye, 'I thought a lie would be queerer'" (qtd. Leyda 1: 136).

She stopped going to church with her family at the age of thirty, and yet she used the meter and rhyme of the Protestant hymnal for most of her poems. In several poems, she expressed her religious independence, most defiantly in one that begins

> I'm ceded—I've stopped being Theirs—
> The name They dropped upon my face
> With water, in the country church
> Is finished using, now,
> And They can put it with my Dolls,
> My childhood, and the string of spools,
> I've finished threading—too—
> (FP 353)

In Dickinson's poems addressing God, she often attributes to him traits she associated with her father, Edward Dickinson, who was a pillar of rectitude in the Amherst community She told a correspondent, "My father seems to me often the oldest and oddest sort of a foreigner. Sometimes I say something and he stares in a curious sort of bewilderment, though I speak a thought quite as old as his daughter" (Sewall, *Lyman Letters* 70). Edward Dickinson served in the state legislature and then the United States Congress, and for thirty-seven years as treasurer of Amherst College (which his father, Samuel, helped found to counter the liberal Unitarianism at Harvard). When Dickinson was twenty, she wrote her brother,

> Father was *thoughtful* enough to spend last evening with us *socially* & as he seemed rather dull, I endeavoured to entertain him by reading spicey passages from Fern leaves [Fanny Fern's columns], where upon he brightened up sufficiently to correct me as I went along.
> (Bingham 312–313)

Supposedly Dickinson's father bought books for her but begged her not to read them, "because he fears they joggle the Mind" (*Letters* 2: 404). He did not allow novels in the house, but she and her brother smuggled some in. "Father is too busy with his Briefs—to notice what we do" (*Letters* 2: 404), she famously said, and after his death, she observed, "His Heart was pure and terrible and I think no other like it exists" (*Letters* 2: 528).

Dickinson's mother was domestic, quiet, and loving. Emily's sister Vinnie said, "She was so fond of every bird & flower & so full of pity for every grief" (qtd. Sewall, *Life* 89). Obviously, Dickinson acquired positive traits from her mother, but in 1862, she told Higginson, "My mother does not care for thought" (*Letters* 2: 404). After her mother became debilitated by a severe stroke in 1875, Dickinson cared for her until she died in 1883, and during this time their relationship improved. "We were never intimate Mother and Children while she was our Mother—but Mines in the same Ground meet by tunneling and when she became our Child, the Affection came—" (*Letters* 3: 754–755).

Although Dickinson never married, she seems to have fallen in love several times. During 1848–1849, when she was in her late teens, she became close to a law student in her father's office, Benjamin Franklin Newton, who was nine years older than she. He praised her poetry and gave her Emerson's *Poems* (1847) to read, but did not court her. After his death in 1853, Dickinson wrote, "Mr. Newton became to me a gentle, yet grave Preceptor, teaching me what to read, what authors to admire, what was most grand or beautiful in nature, and that sublimer lesson, a faith in things unseen, and in a life again, nobler, and much more blessed—" (*Letters* 1: 282). In her early twenties, Dickinson developed a romantic crush on her good friend Susan Huntington Gilbert. In 1852, while Susan was away, Dickinson wrote to her:

> Is there any room there for me, or shall I wander away all homeless and alone? Thank you for loving me, darling, and *will* you "love me more if ever you come home"?—it is enough, dear Susie, I know I shall be satisfied. But what can I do towards you?—*dearer you cannot* be, for I love you so already, that it almost breaks my heart—perhaps I can love you *anew*, every day of my life, every morning and evening—Oh if you will let me, how happy I shall be!
>
> (*Letters* 1: 177)

Dickinson's brother Austin also fell in love with Susan, and the two married in 1856. The newlyweds moved into a house next door called the Evergreens, built for them by Edward Dickinson.

Emily wrote Susan hundreds of letters and poems, filled with expressions of love and desire, and Susan seems to have appreciated Emily as a dear friend, a loving sister-in-law, and an accomplished poet. Whether the two women ever enjoyed a same-sex physical relationship has been debated for some time. At the very least, Dickinson seems to have imagined they did, with a poem such as this:

> Her face was in a bed of hair,
> Like flowers in a plot—
> Her hand was whiter than the sperm
> That feeds the sacred light.
> Her tongue more tender than the tune
> That totters in the leaves—
> Who hears may be incredulous,
> Who witnesses, believes.
>
> (FP 1755)

Scholars have debated whether it would matter one way or another if they did or did not have a physical relationship, but surely it would matter, in the sense that the background knowledge one brings to literature affects one's understanding of it.

Dickinson herself found poetic inspiration in both intense pleasure and crippling pain. Her poems such as "Wild Nights! Wild Nights!" (FP 269) and "I Taste a Liquor Never Brewed" (FP 207) treat moments of intense joy, which help balance her poems about pain and despair, which she, or her persona, claims to value for the awareness they bring. "A Wounded deer leaps highest" (FP 181) and "I like a look of Agony" (FP 241) are perhaps the most well-known expressions of this. The second reads:

> I like a look of Agony,
> Because I know it's true—
> Men do not sham Convulsion,
> Nor simulate, a Throe—
>
> The eyes glaze once—and that is Death—
> Impossible to feign
> The Beads upon the Forehead
> By homely Anguish strung.

The word "homely" in the last line means simple or modest, and "homely Anguish" extends the pleasure/pain paradox Dickinson sets out with her shocking opening line.

Although her external life consisted of time spent in her garden, her conservatory, the kitchen (she baked award-winning bread), and her second-story bedroom, her inner life was intense and, at times, highly dramatic. As Jane Wald has pointed out, Dickinson's lived experience in her home reveals much about her literary intentions, in particular, her desire for refinement, precision, and revelation. Her niece Martha Dickinson Bianchi recalled Dickinson's poetics of baking:

> Her [cooking] utensils were private, those exquisite moulds from which her wine-jelly slipped trembling without a blemish in pattern of a rose or sheaf of wheat; and the round bread pans she used to ensure crust in baking her father's "daily bread" for which he asked each morning at Family Prayers. An imaginary line was drawn about all her "properties" which seemed to protect them against alien fingers—lent a difference in taste to the results she produced. She was rather precieuse about it—using silver to stir with and glass to measure by.
>
> (Bianchi 15)

Dickinson brought the same intensity, care, and originality to the making of her poems.

As Richard B. Sewall has pointed out, "She saw words as infinitely powerful to heal or to kill. She gloried in them as they sit 'princelike among their peers on the page'" (*Life* 569). The following poem humorously describes her process:

> Shall I take thee, the Poet said
> To the propounded word?
> Be stationed with the Candidates
> Till I have finer tried—
>
> The Poet searched Philology
> And when about to ring
> For the suspended Candidate
> There came unsummoned in—
>
> That portion of the Vision
> The Word applied to fill
> Not unto nomination
> The Cherubim reveal—
>   (FB 1243)

The "Candidates" here are the potential words marshalled forward in an elaborate ceremony of artistic choice. "Cherubim," as you may know, are angelic creatures, so in this poem it appears they escort the chosen Word, or "portion," into the poem as a revelation, just as the poet is about to choose another.

Many of the poems Dickinson wrote in the early 1860s, when she was in her thirties, are expressions of psychic pain, which seems related to an unspecified crisis in her life. No one knows for sure what caused it, but it corresponded to a surge in her production of poems, from some 88 in 1861 to 227 in 1862, and 295 in 1863, including some of her greatest poems, including "There's a certain Slant of light" (FP 320), "I felt a Funeral, in my Brain" (FP 340), and "After great pain, a formal feeling comes" (FP 372). Dickinson found new and powerful ways of expressing psychic distress, and readers have attested to the accuracy of her accounts. A number of possible causes of this distress, put forth by biographers, include anxiety about her religious apostasy, her failure to gain recognition as a poet, worry about her eye trouble, reports of Civil War deaths, and, most likely, a frustrated love affair.

As for the poet's love interest, the Reverend Charles Wadsworth, a married minister seventeen years older than she, has been identified as the most likely candidate. In 1855, Dickinson spent two weeks in Philadelphia where she met and got to know Wadsworth, who apparently recognized a kindred spirit in Dickinson. As a youth, Wadsworth had gained the reputation as a prodigy, writing romantic poems in the manner of Lord Byron, filled with gloom and worldly woe. After he gave up poetry and turned to the ministry, he became famous for his moving sermons. "Judging from contemporary reports, Wadsworth's deep bass tones, reserved emotional power, and luminous language, combined with his original exposition of Old School Presbyterian thought, produced an unforgettable effect" (Habegger 330). Though known for his reclusiveness (he avoided his parishioners and fellow pastors), he felt drawn to Dickinson and she to him. They exchanged letters, and he visited her in Amherst in 1860. She later recalled,

> once when he seemed almost overpowered by a spasm of gloom, I said 'You are troubled.' Shivering as he spoke, 'My Life is full of dark secrets,' he said. He never spoke of himself, and encroachment I know would have slain him.
> (*Letters* 3: 744–745)

In 1862, Wadsworth left Philadelphia to become minister of the Calvary Presbyterian Church in San Francisco, and his departure seems to have affected Dickinson acutely.

Her series of letters to an unnamed "Master" written in 1861 have also been linked to Wadsworth. As Sewall has observed, "what is new about the letters is their sustained revelation of the intensity, depth, and power of her love and the agony of its frustration" (*Life* 513). The longest one begins:

> MASTER.
> If you saw a bullet hit a Bird—and he told you he was'nt shot—you might weep at his courtesy, but you would certainly doubt his word.
> One drop more from the gash that stains your Daisy's bosom—then would you *believe?* Thomas' faith in Anatomy, was stronger than his faith in faith. God made me—Master—I did'nt be—myself. I dont know how it was done. He built the heart in me—Bye and bye it outgrew me—
> (*Letters* 2: 373)

It was also at this time that Dickinson gradually withdrew from society and dressed all in white, like a bride. In an 1862 poem, she declares that although she is not legally married, she thinks of herself so:

> Title divine—is mine!
> The Wife—without the Sign!
> Acute Degree—conferred on me—
> Empress of Calvary!
> (FP 194)

The reclusiveness Dickinson assumed in the early 1860s added distinctiveness to her life and increased the distance between herself and her Amherst neighbors, with whom she had little in common. In several of her poems, she satirizes them, as in "What Soft—Cherubic Creatures— / These Gentlewomen are— / One would as soon assault a Plush— / Or violate a Star—" (FP 675) (a "plush" was a rich piece of fabric, often covering a cushion). She knew how brilliant she was and revealed an impatience with slow-wittedness, which some biographers believe contributed to her withdrawal.

At one point during a visit from Higginson, she asked,

> How do most people live without any thoughts. There are many people in the world (you must have noticed them in the street). How do they live. How do they get strength to put on their clothes in the morning.
>
> (*Letters* 2: 474)

The twentieth-century poet Adrienne Rich observes, "I have a notion that genius knows itself; that Dickinson chose her seclusion, knowing she was exceptional and knowing what she needed" (158). Class consciousness may also have informed her behavior. The scholar Betsy Erkkila has argued,

> Although Dickinson's acts of self-enclosure were at least in part a means of protecting her artistic creation, they were also class acts, manifesting her desire to define herself against and distinguish herself from the potentially polluting incursions of the democratic multitude.
>
> (7)

In a number of her poems, Dickinson assumes the role of a proud elitist, as in the following, which may be read as self-satirical:

> The Soul selects her own Society—
> Then—shuts the Door—
> To her divine Majority—
> Present no more—
>
> Unmoved—she notes the Chariots—pausing—
> At her low Gate—
> Unmoved—an Emperor be kneeling
> Upon her Mat—
>
> I've known her—from an ample nation—
> Choose One—
> Then—close the Valves of her attention—
> Like Stone—
>
> (FP 409)

One acquaintance Dickinson chose and even entertained as a visitor in her home was Thomas Wentworth Higginson, who reported to his wife from Amherst, "I never was with any one who drained my nerve power so much. Without touching her, she drew from me. I am glad not to live near her" (*Letters* 2: 474).

Dickinson and Higginson

Dickinson's correspondence with Higginson began in 1862, when she sent four poems and a request for his opinion in response to his *Atlantic* article "Advice to a Young Contributor." In her letter, she adopts the persona of a little girl (although in her 30s at the time), needing advice from an accomplished older man, a "preceptor"; however, she later refused to alter her style of writing, or accept his "surgery," as she called it.

> Mr Higginson,
> Are you too deeply occupied to say if my Verse is alive?
> The Mind is so near itself—it cannot see, distinctly—and I have none to ask—
> Should you think it breathed—and had you the leisure to tell me, I should feel quick gratitude—
> If I make the mistake—that you dared to tell me—would give me sincerer honor—toward you—
> I enclose my name—asking you, if you please—Sir—to tell me what is true?
> That you will not betray me—it is needless to ask—since Honor is it's own pawn—
>
> (*Letters* 2: 403)

Although Higginson discouraged Dickinson from seeking publication, he entered a twenty-four-year correspondence with her, during which she sent him more than a hundred of her poems, obviously hoping to please him, yet resistant to his suggestions to change her style, which he called "spasmodic," "uncontrolled," and "wayward."

In one letter to Higginson, she enclosed a poem "I cannot dance upon my Toes" (FP 381), which appears on one level to agree with his criticism of her skill as a poet, yet ironically shows how clever she is: She writes,

> I cannot dance upon my Toes—
> No Man instructed me—
> But oftentimes, among my mind,
> A Glee possesseth me,
>
> That had I Ballet knowledge—
> Would put itself abroad
> In Pirouette to blanch a Troupe—
> Or lay a Prima, mad,
>
> And though I had no Gown of Gauze—
> No Ringlet, to my Hair,
> Nor hopped to Audiences—like Birds
> One Claw upon the air—
>
> Nor tossed my shape in Eider Balls
> Nor rolled on wheels of snow
> Till I was out of sight, in sound,
> The House encore me so—

Notice the jarring meter and rhymes in the first two stanzas, but then the skill with which she actually hops in the third stanza ("like Birds"), using a spondee (two stressed syllables), and then speeds up, leaps and twirls in the final stanza using numerous "s" sounds (10 of them) to suggest the whoosh of her dance.

Although Dickinson may have been ironic in her dealings with Higginson, it is also possible she sincerely wished to gain his help and approval. She sent nearly forty poems in thirty letters to another editor, her good friend Samuel Bowles of the *Springfield Republican*, who published several of them anonymously. She also wrote numerous poems about fame and carefully assembled her packets of poems for someone to find after her death, all of which attests to her ambition. Along with her sense of otherness, she expressed confidence in her own abilities. One of her poems addresses her belief that though more popular poets have come before her, her day or "summer" will come:

> I shall keep singing!
> Birds will pass me
> On their way to Yellower Climes—
> Each—with a Robin's expectation—
> I—with my Redbreast—
> And my Rhymes—
>
> Late—when I take my place in summer—
> But—I shall bring a fuller tune—
> Vespers—are sweeter than Matins—Signor—
> (FP 270)

Dickinson's "vespers," her evening songs, indeed took their place in American literary history beginning at the end of the nineteenth century, and they have been gaining a larger audience with each passing year.

Visitations

Dickinson had a good sense of humor and an affinity for puns, riddles, and provocative declarations. One of her most hilarious poems describes the visit of a spider to her privy and perhaps her bottom:

> Alone and in a Circumstance
> Reluctant to be told
> A spider on my reticence
> Assiduously crawled
>
> And so much more at Home than I
> Immediately grew
> I felt myself a visitor
> And hurriedly withdrew.
> (FP 1174)

The pun contained in "Assiduously" is especially wicked.

Her easiest riddle poems include "A narrow Fellow in the Grass" (FP 1096) (snake) and "I like to see it lap the Miles—" (FP 383) (train), while "A Route of Evanescence" (FP 1489), would be one of the most difficult. It reads,

> A Route of Evanescence
> With a revolving Wheel—
> A Resonance of Emerald—
> A Rush of Cochineal—
> And every Blossom on the Bush
> Adjusts its tumbled Head—
> The mail from Tunis, probably,
> An easy Morning's Ride—

Many students guess this is a sunset, but Dickinson, in a letter, gave it the title "A Humming Bird." To make it from Tunis near the Mediterranean Sea to New England in a morning suggests how fast the little bird could fly. Such riddles, along with many of her nature poems, have been called "visitations," for they seem to capture some fleeting moment of experience that the mind can sense yet not comprehend, at least at first. That is, even though many of her poems seem impenetrable, the struggle to understand them is part of her goal. In this sense, she is like Emerson, who often refused to go from A to B to C, but instead offered A and C, forcing the reader to provide the intellectual spark needed to connect the two poles of thought.

It has been suggested, given Dickinson's love of words, that at times external reality disappears into language within her poems, making style itself more insistent than meaning. In this way, she would anticipate some writers and artists of twentieth-century modernism. More likely, however, she wanted to communicate with prospective readers, but on her own terms, in her own way. In her role as poet, Dickinson sought to reveal truths she had discovered, and she justified the difficulty of her poems with the following well-known declaration:

> Tell all the truth but tell it slant—
> Success in Circuit lies
> Too bright for our infirm Delight
> The Truth's superb surprise
> As Lightning to the Children eased
> With explanation kind
> The Truth must dazzle gradually
> Or every man be blind—
> (FP1263)

Ironically, this poem is one of her most direct and clear.

For Dickinson, her means for pursuing the challenge to comprehend what lies beyond the material world were metaphorical; for Emerson, symbolical.

That is, whereas he argues that natural facts are symbols of particular spiritual facts, which the divinity within us allows us to perceive, for Dickinson, natural facts remain Other, just as God does, and serve to remind us of the boundaries imposed on individual human existence. Her poem "The Rat is the concisest Tenant" (FP 1369), suggests this, as it ends "Hate cannot harm / A Foe so reticent— / Neither Decree prohibit him—Lawful as Equilibrium." In other words, the rat has natural rights humans cannot suspend. Her snake poem, "A narrow Fellow in the Grass" (FP 1096), establishes the same otherness with its ending: "I … never met this Fellow / Attended, or alone / Without a tighter breathing / And Zero at the Bone—."

Circumference

In typically enigmatic fashion, Dickinson told Higginson "—My Business is Circumference—" (*Letters* 2: 412), and scholars have discussed this assertion at length. On the one hand, a circumference encloses a totality, a world of one's making, and this seems to be the point of poems such as "My Faith is larger than the Hills" (FP 489) and "The Brain—is wider than the Sky—" (FP 598); however, to have business with "Circumference" can also mean exploring boundaries, not just creating them. Time and again, Dickinson addresses that which lies beyond normal human understanding, and any number of her poems show her probing human consciousness, using words and her imagination to articulate liminal experiences. Death, of course, marks the boundary between life on this earth and whatever lies beyond human existence, and her more famous poems indeed are fantasies about dying (from her bedroom window she watched funeral processions). The best include "Because I could not stop for death" (FP 479), "I heard a Fly buzz—when I died" (FP 591), and "I felt a Funeral, in my Brain" (FP 340). The concluding stanza of the latter captures this liminality:

> And then a Plank in Reason, broke,
> And I dropped down, and down—
> And hit a world, at every plunge,
> And Finished knowing—then—

The last line can be read as complete or incomplete, depending upon whether "knowing" is read as a noun or verb form.

Some readers, of course, find such poems morbid, or just uninteresting, but Dickinson, unmarried, without dependents, living in her parents' house, possessed the resources, leisure, and skill to travel imaginatively to places few others have. Alone in her room, with her major work being thinking and writing, consciousness itself became a fascination for her and death a boundary she sought to go beyond, or rather, to explore imaginatively to see where it would lead. David Porter has described this project as probing beyond the last tick-tock of human existence. He writes,

> Dickinson scanned these dark holes in psychic space with various canny metaphors, but death was the allegory always at hand, for death killed time and introduced the terrifyingly drained interval between experiences and the "most profound experiment appointed unto Men."
>
> (11)

If one has ever, like Melville, felt the terrors of oblivion, of nothingness, of total aloneness, then Dickinson's project offers an odd reassurance or sympathy. The same is true of her piercing poems about despair.

Dickinson rejected many of the tenets of Calvinist theology, especially the concept of original sin and the arbitrary separation of mankind into the elect and the damned. Yet, by moving away from the religious orthodoxy of her immediate community, she found herself not only free from an established set of beliefs, but also uncertain about what she did believe. In an 1882 letter to Judge Otis Lord, she wrote, "On subjects of which we know nothing, … we both believe, and disbelieve a hundred times an Hour, which keeps Believing nimble" (*Letters* 3: 728). As Patrick J. Keane reminds us, "To wrestle with God, even at times to denounce him, is still to have a relationship, however stormy" (2). Often Dickinson used humor to address the relationship, but it could slip into annoyance, as in the following hide-and-seek poem:

> I know that He exists.
> Somewhere—in Silence—
> He has hid his rare life
> From our gross eyes.
>
> 'Tis an instant's play.
> 'Tis a fond Ambush—
> Just to make Bliss
> Earn her own surprise!
>
> But—should the play
> Prove piercing earnest—
> Should the glee—glaze—
> In Death's—stiff—stare—
>
> Would not the fun
> Look too expensive!
> Would not the jest—
> Have crawled too far!
>   (FP 365)

One can almost hear echoes of Poe's lines here that "the play is the tragedy, 'Man,' / And its hero the Conqueror Worm." Although one does not care to imagine the body rotting in the grave, being eaten by worms, Dickinson and Poe went there.

Far more consoling is her famous poem "Because I Could not Stop for Death" (FP 479), where Death as a gentleman caller escorts the poet past stages of life to the graveyard. Yet even here uncertainty reigns, for the ride had just begun:

> Since then—'tis Centuries—and yet
> Feels shorter than the Day
> I first surmised the Horses' Heads
> Were toward Eternity—

Though dead, the speaker tells the reader nothing about Eternity itself, other than the disappearance of time within it. Try as she might, Dickinson could not imagine a convincing life after death without resorting to conventional thought, which she resisted.

Whitman's youth

Whitman, a far more sanguine and explicit poet than Dickinson, was the second of eight surviving children, a number of whom suffered from mental and behavioral issues, including insanity and alcoholism. He was born on rural Long Island, but the family moved to Brooklyn when he was four. Whitman's father was an unsuccessful carpenter and builder, and after his death in 1855, Whitman's mother relied upon Walt for emotional and financial support. In the semi-autobiographical poem "There was a Child Went Forth," Whitman seems to describe his own parents:

> The mother at home quietly placing the dishes on the supper-table,
> The mother with mild words, clean her cap and gown, a wholesome odor falling off her person and clothes as she walks by:
> The father, strong, selfsufficient, manly, mean, angered, unjust,
> The blow, the quick loud word, the tight bargain, the crafty lure, ...
> These became part of that child who went forth every day, and who now goes and will always go forth every day ...
>
> (LoA 139)

Whitman chose not to help his father build houses, but worked as a teacher instead. He himself acquired only a fifth-grade public education, having quit school at eleven to help his family financially. Like Melville, Whitman was essentially self-taught and became a voracious reader. As a teenager, he read Walter Scott's poetry, Shakespeare, Ossian, Homer, Dante, ancient Hindu poems, and especially the Old and New Testaments. The Bible was a major influence on him, and he later adopted many biblical rhetorical devices in *Leaves of Grass*, such as catalogs, parallel clauses at the beginning of lines, and prophetic statements without subordination or qualification. He came to think of himself as a modern-day prophet, and in his Preface to the first edition of *Leaves*, he self-identifies as the "greatest poet": "He is a seer ... he is individual ... he is complete in himself ... the others are as good as he, only he sees it, and they do not" (LoA 10).

Whitman's father and mother were not regular church-goers, but they admired Quaker customs and ideas. Walt was drawn to Quakerism, with its emphasis upon egalitarianism and the "inner light," but he would eventually absorb the ideas of a multitude of religions, claiming to transcend them all. In "Song of Myself" (1855), he declares "My faith is the greatest of faiths and the least of faiths, / Enclosing worship ancient and modern and all between ancient and modern." He then presents himself as a collector of world religions:

> Taking myself the exact dimensions of Jehovah and laying them away,
> Lithographing Kronos and Zeus his son, and Hercules his grandson,
> Buying drafts of Osiris and Isis and Belus and Brahma and Adonai,
> In my portfolio placing Manito loose, and Allah on a leaf, and the crucifix engraved,
> With Odin, and the hideous-faced Mexitli, and all idols and images,
> Honestly taking them all for what they are worth, and not a cent more ...
> (LoA 73–74)

One should not take Whitman's claim to comprehensive knowledge of world religions too seriously. Dogma interested him little. His main interest was celebrating himself and the beauty of the world around him.

During his youth, Whitman spent summers on rural Long Island, which was sparsely settled. In the prose *Specimen Days* (1882), he lovingly recalls the farms, light houses, seashore, fishermen, seagulls, and natural beauty of the island. He also recalls the rustle of the ocean waves, the saline smell, bathing in the sea and afterward racing up and down on the sand reciting passages from Homer and Shakespeare. Later, in his poetry, he would draw upon the rhythms of the sea, that is, the regular irregularity of the waves, and the way they provide a hypnotic rhythm, suggestive of profound themes. One of his most beautiful poems "Out of the Cradle Endlessly Rocking" depicts the sea as a lover (or "some old crone") whispering to the young boy the secret word "death," which leads to the speaker's birth as a poet, at least within the poem: "My own songs awaked from that hour, / And with them the key, the word up from the waves, / The word of the sweetest song and all songs ..." (LoA 393–394). Time and again, Whitman, like Emerson, envisioned creation and death as linked events in an ongoing process to be celebrated, not feared or lamented. In section 6 of "Song of Myself," Whitman asserts,

> there is really no death,
> And if ever there was it led forward life, and does not wait at the end to arrest it,
> And ceas'd the moment life appeared.
> All goes onward and outward ... nothing collapses,
> And to die is different from what any one supposed, and luckier.
> (LoA 32)

Whitman's evocative poem "Crossing Brooklyn Ferry" captures a similar sense of an ongoing continuous present. Although Whitman spent his youth on

Long Island and Brooklyn, he visited Manhattan theaters as a teenager, crossing the East River on a ferry many times. In the poem, the literal crossing of the East River from Manhattan to Brooklyn merges with the crossing of day into night (the original title was "Sun-Down Poem"), of the present and future, of matter and spirit, and ultimately of poet and reader, which can be startling:

> Closer yet I approach you,
> What thought you have of me now, I had as much of you—
>   I laid in my stores in advance,
> I consider'd long and seriously of you before you were born.
>
> Who was to know what should come home to me?
> Who knows but I am enjoying this?
> Who knows, for all the distance, but I am as good as looking at you now,
>   for all you cannot see me?
>
> (LoA 311–312)

The "dumb, beautiful ministers," at the end of the poem are all those palpable things that surround poet and reader, namely, sea birds, summer sky, water, ships, flags, fires, shadows, and so on. All become numinous, filled with an indwelling spirit that makes time and space converge.

Whitman, like the Transcendentalists, was an idealist, a man who perceived the divine, often through communion with nature. Like Thoreau, he loved the material world, especially its almost indescribable beauty. For him, the transcendental experience, which was also mystical, combined the material world with that which was spiritual. As he said with regard to a field of grain, "How shall my eye separate the beauty of the blossoming buckwheat field from the stalks and heads of tangible matter? How shall I know what the life is except as I see it in the flesh?" (qtd. Matthiesen 525). For Whitman, the divine was not just to be found in nature, however, as Thoreau believed. Human beings as well for Whitman shone with divinity. As he says in section 48 of "Song of Myself," "Be not curious about God, ... I see something of God each hour of the twenty-four, and each moment then, / In the faces of men and women I see God, and in my face in the glass" (LoA 85).

Whitman's moments of transcendence in his poetry arrive not through asceticism or mortification of the body, but rather, through emersion in the senses, especially that of touch. Section 5 of "Song of Myself," for example, describes the transcendental experience as a sexual union between body and soul, and the result is not a flight into the abstract "All," but rather, a renewed appreciation of the smallest natural fact:

> I mind how once we lay in June, such a transparent summer morning,
> You settled your head athwart my hips and gently turned over upon me,
> And parted the shirt from my bosom-bone, and plunged your tongue to
>   my barestript heart,
> And reached till you felt my beard, and reached till you held my feet.

Swiftly arose and spread around me the peace and joy and knowledge that pass all the art and argument of the earth;
And I know that the hand of God is the elderhand of my own,
And I know that the spirit of God is the eldest brother of my own,
And that all the men ever born are also my brothers ... and the women my sisters and lovers,
And that a kelson of the creation is love;
And limitless are leaves stiff or drooping in the fields,
And brown ants in the little wells beneath them,
And mossy scabs of the wormfence, and heaped stones, and elder and mullen and pokeweed.

(LoA 30–31)

Whitman's poetry celebrates the human body, male and female, and what other people of his day found obscene, such as human genitalia, bodily functions, and sexual intercourse. A "procreative urge" impels his poetry, and there's an orgasmic quality in many of his lines, some featuring fairly vivid moments of ejaculation, using metaphors of filaments. Late in life, he explained to a young friend, Horace Traubel, who recorded their conversations, "I think Swendenborg was right when he said there was a close connection—a very close connection—between the state we call religious ecstasy and the desire to copulate. I find it confirmed in all my experience" (qtd. Reynolds 268). Emanuel Swedenborg was an eighteenth-century Swedish scientist and mystic, whose writings exerted a strong influence on the American transcendental movement. He was the primary source of Emerson's ideas about the correspondence between natural and spiritual facts.

The long foreground

At age twenty-one, Whitman gave up teaching in country schools on Long Island and moved to New York City, where in the early 1840s, he worked as a printer, journalist, and editor. He wrote sensational short stories, conventional poems, journalistic essays, and the temperance novel *Franklin Evans* (1842). In 1845 he moved back to Brooklyn where he worked building houses, and edited the Brooklyn *Daily Eagle* for almost two years. In February, 1848, he traveled by train, stagecoach, and steamboat to New Orleans with his brother Jeff and worked for four months on the *New Orleans Daily Crescent* before returning to New York by way of the Mississippi, the Great Lakes, and the Hudson River. The trip enhanced his growing first-hand knowledge of the diversity of the American people and features of the American landscape, both essential to his goal of becoming the country's national poet. In 1852 he also published the serialized novel *Life and Adventures of Jack Engle*, discovered in 2017 by graduate student Zachary Turpin. None of this work gives an indication of the originality and brilliance that would appear in *Leaves of Grass*. It tends to be lurid, violent, and horrific, more akin to Poe, yet without his craft and irony.

A number of scholars have tried to account for the miraculous appearance of the first edition of *Leaves of Grass* in 1855, which represented a startling departure from Whitman's previous work. They have put forward such causes as a New Orleans love affair, the reading of Emerson's essays, a mystical experience, unsatisfied homosexual desires, and the turbulent politics of the day; however, no one knows for sure the particular inspiration for Whitman's revolutionary new poetry. It is clear, however, that he did become more politically engaged at the beginning of the 1850s. He was especially moved by the excitement surrounding the European Revolutions of 1848 and the passage of the Compromise of 1850 with its hated Fugitive Slave Act.

Soon after arriving in New Orleans and starting work on the *New Orleans Crescent* newspaper, he learned about the recent revolution in France, when workers and students overthrew King Louis Philipe and established a provisional government with the poet Alphonse de Lamartine at its head. Soon a wave of upheavals broke out across Europe as absolutist governments fell. As Paul Zweig has said,

> It was one of the few times in Whitman's life when he was in the right place to share the excitement of a great event. New Orleans swarmed with European refugees who were delirious with joy at the news from across the ocean.
>
> (74)

Whitman's elation at the savage, justified vengeance of these events, he recalled in his poem "Resurgemus," which begins:

> Suddenly, out of its sta[l]e and drowsy [l]air of slaves,
> Like lightning Europe le'pt forth,
> Sombre, superb and terrible,
> As Ahimoth, brother of Death.
>
> God, 'twas delicious!
> That brief, tight, glorious grip
> Upon the throats of kings.
>
> (*Early Poems* 38)

"Resurgemus" was the last of a four-poem cluster Whitman published in the *New-York Tribune* in March and June of 1850, and it was the first of his poems that he would include, without its title, in the first edition of *Leaves of Grass*. The other three poems of the cluster, which he did not select for *Leaves*, express his outrage at those politicians, especially Daniel Webster, who supported the Compromise of 1850.

With "Resurgemus," Whitman first began to create the revolutionary new poetry that would become distinctively his own. In it one sees the characteristically rhythmical lines without regular meter or rhyme yet controlled by selected poetic devices, including the parallelisms, repetitions, and rhythms of the King James Bible. The title translates as "We will rise again," and refers to the Italian *risorgimento* and the young men recently shot and hanged for attempting to overthrow the Pope and establish republican government throughout Italy. It echoes Margaret Fuller's last dispatches from Italy to the *Tribune*, and as it works to cheer up the oppressed and to horrify their oppressors, it introduces the themes of liberty and rebirth, using the metaphor of grass to do so:

> Not a grave of the murdered for freedom but grows seed for freedom ... in its turn to bear seed,
> Which the winds carry afar and re-sow, and the rains and the snows nourish.
>
> (LoA 134)

He would repeat this image in "Song of Myself," where grass becomes "the beautiful hair of graves" which transpires "from the breasts of young men" (LoA 31).

Despite his arguments on behalf of freedom in Europe and "free soil" in the Western United States, Whitman at times revealed an ambivalence about Southern slavery. Both Brooklyn and New York City had many Southern sympathizers, who were hostile toward the reform movements coming out of New England, especially abolitionism. Whitman's family while living on Long Island had owned slaves, and he himself said some rather derogatory things about black people.

In the early editions of *Leaves of Grass* (1855, 1856, 1860–1861), he expresses sympathy toward slaves, even identifying with them. In section 10 of "Song of Myself," the poet speaker tends to a runaway slave, and in section 33 he declares, "I am the hounded slave ... I wince at the bite of dogs, / Hell and despair are upon me" (LoA 65). In the following three editions of *Leaves of Grass* (1867, 1871, 1881), however, slavery fades as an issue. As Ed Folson has pointed out, Whitman in his notebook declared, "I am the poet of slaves and of the master of slaves," and his Civil War poetry does not identify slavery as a major issue. Like Lincoln, he saw preservation of the Union as the most important goal of the War (Folson 50, 56). After the War, Whitman opposed black suffrage, writing in an 1874 essay,

> As if we had not strained the voting and digestive caliber of American Democracy to the utmost for the last fifty years with the millions of ignorant foreigners, we have now infused a powerful percentage of blacks, with about as much intellect and caliber (in the mass) as so many baboons.
>
> (qtd. Folson 81)

Late in life, Whitman expressed admiration for the black troops who fought for the Union, but he maintained his opposition to assimilation and equal rights.

Leaves of Grass

When Whitman self-published the first edition of *Leaves of Grass* in 1855, he shattered many poetic conventions. The slender book of ninety-five pages included a ten-page preface and twelve untitled poems that resembled prose, not conventional poetry. Whitman's name did not appear on the book's title page; instead, a frontispiece featured an engraved photograph of him in jeans and open work shirt, wearing a cocked hat and posed with his hand on his hip. Midway in the first poem, he identifies himself as

> Walt Whitman, an American, one of the roughs, a kosmos,
> Disorderly fleshy and sensual ... eating drinking and breeding
> No sentimentalist ... no stander above men and women or
>   apart from them ... no more modest than immodest.
>
> (LoA 50)

Whitman, in person, as opposed to "Walt," the robust speaker in "Song of Myself," was a rather shy and gloomy individual, according to his biographers, and he spent many hours just watching, listening, and absorbing the sights and sounds on rural Long Island and busy Manhattan. In fact, it is his power of observation that gives his poems such precise descriptions, which he then imbues with exceptional compassion and love. One of the joys of reading the early Whitman is being introduced to the idealized America and Americans he imagined and felt so ardent about. He was obviously most attracted to working-class people, like himself, rather than those with money or status. President Lincoln later was an exception, in part because Whitman knew of Lincoln's modest background and folksy speech and manner. During the Civil War, Whitman, living in Washington DC, described Lincoln to several friends:

> He has a face like a Hoosier Michael Angelo, so awful ugly it becomes beautiful, with its strange mouth, its deep cut, criss-cross lines, and its doughnut complexion.—My notion is too, that underneath his outside smutched mannerism, and stories from third-class barrooms (it is his humor), Mr. Lincoln keeps a fountain of first-class practical telling wisdom.
>
> (*Civil War* 63–64)

Whitman maintained a lifelong interest in the human voice and human speech. He composed orally, as his recollection of reciting Homer and Shakespeare suggests, and as a youth he dreamed of becoming a successful orator and joining the likes of Daniel Webster, Emerson, and Lincoln himself. Whitman even wrote a number of lectures and advertised his availability as a speaker, but the plan did not work out. Apparently, his voice, though strong, did not project well. The columnist Fanny Fern described it in conversation as "high—deep—and clear, as a clarion note ... Such a voice is a gift as rare as it is priceless" (qtd.

Warren 162). Whitman's poetry relies upon the cadences of human speech and is easily read aloud, as it should be for greatest effect.

Music

Music, like oratory and the sea, exerted a major influence upon his poetry, particularly the Italian opera, which he at first disdained, but then came to love. Keep in mind that Whitman called his poems songs, and his writing singing. During the early 1850s, he spent many nights at the opera in New York City. He was an ardent fan of the Italian tenor Allesandro Bettini, who probably appears as the "tenor large and fresh as the creation" in section 26 of "Song of Myself." The performances of the contralto Marietta Alboni, also thrilled him to his core, as other lines from the section show:

> I hear the train'd soprano … . she convulses me like the
>   climax of my love-grip;
> The orchestra whirls me wider than Uranus flies,
> It wrenches such unnamable ardors from my breast,
> It throbs me to gulps of the farthest down horror … .
> (LoA 54)

He later titled a poem "To a Certain Cantatrice" and called it a "gift" to Alboni. He writes that he had been reserving it for some hero, speaker, or general, adding, "But I see that what I was reserving belongs to you just as much as to any" (LoA 173).

Two of his finest poems, "When Lilacs Last in the Dooryard Bloom'd," and "Out of the Cradle Endlessly Rocking," feature birds— a hermit thrush and a mockingbird, respectively—who become his operatic soloists, expressing deep feelings of loss. In the two poems, you can see the operatic devices, alternating recitative (talking moments) and arias (emotional solos). He also uses the operatic crescendo (gradually increasing sound), fortissima (very loud) and diminuendo (gradually decreasing). The end of section 14 of "Lilacs," for example, illustrates the waves of sound and emotion of the hermit thrush's aria, conveyed by italics, imagery, and variations of line length:

> *The night in silence under many a star,*
> *The ocean shore and the husky whispering wave whose voice I know,*
> *And the soul turning to thee O vast and well-veil'd death,*
> *And the body gratefully nestling close to thee.*
>
> *Over the tree-tops I float thee a song,*
> *Over the rising and sinking waves, over the myriad fields and the prairies wide,*
> *Over the dense-pack'd cities all and the teeming wharves and ways,*
> *I float this carol with joy, with joy to thee O death.*
> (LoA 465)

Whitman was sometimes criticized for lack of intellectual depth because of his tendency to privilege emotion over reason, yet he defended the evocative "Out of the Cradle" from the charge of meaninglessness in an anonymous review he wrote, in which he explained,

> the purport of this wild and plaintive song, well-enveloped, and eluding definition, is positive and unquestionably, like the effect of music. This piece will bear reading many times.—perhaps indeed only comes forth, as from recesses, by many repetitions.
>
> (qtd. Mayhan 113)

There is little consensus about which edition of *Leaves of Grass* is the best. Whitman kept revising his poems and adding to his book throughout his life. Whitman himself declared that he wanted the last edition of the seven, the 1892 "Death-bed Edition," "to absolutely supersede all previous ones" (qtd. Kaplan 51). This edition is a reprint of the 1881–1882 edition with "annexes." Nevertheless, the first edition of 1855 is considered the most bold and innovative by many scholars. The first appearance of the untitled poem now generally known as "Song of Myself," with its emphasis on freedom, equality, and sensual joy is regarded as a classic. Throughout the poem, Whitman's subject seems to be himself, but his techniques of identifying with all men and women and speaking as an inspired seer, help him cross the conceptual border dividing the self and others, the body and soul, life and death. The poem insists that the soul is not more than the body, that God is everywhere, in every person and everything, that all is immortal and death is not to be feared, and that nothing is greater than the self. The sources of Whitman's eclectic religion have been traced to Greek pantheism and various Eastern religions, yet the celebration of the body seems to have arisen from Whitman's own personality and sexual makeup.

Emerson's influence

Like the Transcendentalists, Whitman privileged spiritual vision over logical argument. In the Preface to the second edition of *Leaves* (1856), he echoed Emerson by declaring, "the expression of the American poet is to be transcendent and new." By all accounts, including his own, he was influenced by Emerson, whom he called "Master." He declared, "I was simmering, simmering, simmering; Emerson brought me to a boil" (Trowbridge 166). Several times, however, when asked directly, he declared that Emerson had no influence on his poetry. Such inconsistency calls to mind his declaration in "Song of Myself": "Do I contradict myself? / Very well then … I contradict myself; / I am large. I contain multitudes" (87). Whatever the degree of Emerson's influence, Whitman clearly became the original American bard Emerson called for in a lecture "The Poetry of the Times," which Whitman covered in 1842 for a New York newspaper called the *Aurora*. Whitman reported, "the lecture was one of the richest and most beautiful compositions, both for its matter and style, we have ever heard anywhere, at any time" (qtd. Allen 401).

Emerson's lecture was published as the essay "The Poet" (1844), and includes the following appeal:

> I look in vain for the poet whom I describe. We do not, with sufficient plainness, or sufficient profoundness, address ourselves to life, nor dare we chaunt our own times and social circumstance ... Our logrolling, our stumps and their politics, our fisheries, our Negroes, and Indians, our boasts, and our repudiations, the wrath of rogues, and the pusillanimity of honest men, the northern trade, the southern planting, the western clearing, Oregon, and Texas, are yet unsung. Yet America is a poem in our eyes; its ample geography dazzles the imagination, and it will not wait long for metres.
> (*Essays & Lectures* 465)

The description matches the poet Whitman became, that is, comprehensive, contemporary, and decidedly American.

When Whitman published the first edition of *Leaves*, he sent Emerson a complimentary copy, and Emerson wrote an enthusiastic and generous letter of reply, which read in part, "I greet you at the beginning of a great career, which yet must have had a long foreground somewhere for such a start" (Whitman, *Selected Letters* 384). Whitman, without asking, published the letter in the *New-York Daily Tribune* and included it in the 1856 edition of *Leaves*, putting on the spine in gold letters "I Greet You at the / Beginning of A / Great Career / R. W. Emerson." He also included a long effusive letter of reply to "dear Friend and Master," along with nine reviews of the first edition, including two laudatory anonymous reviews he had written himself. Emerson was a bit annoyed with Whitman's use of him, but remained a reluctant supporter. He would recommend the book as "wonderful" to several friends and tell Carlyle that "One book, last summer, came out in New York, a nondescript monster which yet has terrible eyes & buffalo strength, & was indisputably American" (*Correspondence* 509). Many of the Transcendentalists recognized a kindred idealist in Whitman, even though they felt he lacked the reserve so many New Englanders practiced.

Out of a sense of curiosity and admiration, Emerson's friends Bronson Alcott and Thoreau visited Whitman in Brooklyn, in 1856, as he was preparing his second edition of *Leaves*. Alcott's account of the visit, as recorded in his journal, is rather comical:

> He receives us kindly, yet awkwardly, and takes us up two narrow flights of stairs to sit or stand as we might in his attic study—also the bedchamber of himself and his feeble brother, the pressure of whose bodies was still apparent in the unmade bed standing in one corner, and the vessel [a chamber pot] scarcely hidden underneath.
> (*Journals* 289–291)

When they go downstairs to the parlor, Thoreau and Whitman study each other, according to Alcott, "like two beasts, each wondering what the other would do, whether to snap or run; and it came to no more than cold compliments between them." Thoreau, in a letter to a friend, admitted being "provoked" by Whitman, yet wrote,

> That Walt Whitman, of whom I wrote to you, is the most interesting fact to me at present. I have just read his 2nd edition (which he gave me) and it has done me more good than any reading for a long time ... He does not celebrate love at all—It is as if the beasts spoke. I think that men have not been ashamed of themselves without reason ... But even on this side, he has spoken more truth than any American or modern that I know. I have found his poem exhilarating—encouraging. As for its sensuality,—& it may turn out to be less sensual than it appears ... Though rude & sometimes ineffectual, it is a great primitive poem—an alarum or trumpet note ringing through the American Camp ... He is a great fellow—
> (*Correspondence* 2: 488–490)

Whitman's independence and love of nature were two ways he and Thoreau resembled one another. Also, they both admired Emerson and Margaret Fuller. Nevertheless, Thoreau's emphasis on chastity in the "Higher Laws" chapter of *Walden* could not be more at odds with Whitman's celebration of sexual relations. Plus, Whitman was convinced that Thoreau lacked sufficient respect for the common man.

The main personal interaction between Emerson and Whitman occurred in 1860, when Whitman was in Boston preparing the third edition of *Leaves*. They took a long walk together on the Boston Common, and Emerson tried to persuade Whitman to tone down the sexual content of his poems, but Whitman resisted. He later told a friend that the worst kind of poem is an expurgated poem. Emerson worried about Whitman's reputation and wanted him to be able to appeal to as large an audience as possible. Whitman with his Quaker background chose not to defer to anyone, in essence repeating what he says in "Song of Myself": "I cock my hat as I please indoors or out" (LoA 45). The two men had dinner together and afterwards Emerson secured Whitman reading privileges at the Boston Athenaeum.

Sexuality

Although the frontispiece of the 1860 edition features Whitman as a respectable dandy of sorts, with curly hair (no hat), dress jacket, and silk scarf, the new series of poems he added, "Enfans d'Adam" (later called "Children of Adam"), are his most sexually explicit. For example, his poem "A Woman Waits for Me" describes the poet's irresistible sexual prowess:

> It is I, you women, I make my way,
> I am stern, acrid, large, undissuadable, but I love you,
> I do not hurt you any more than is necessary for you,

> I pour the stuff to start sons and daughters fit for these
>   States, I press with slow rude muscle,
> I brace myself effectually, I listen to no entreaties,
> I dare not withdraw till I deposit what has so long
>   accumulated within me.
>
> (LoA 259)

Lines such as these caused Whitman to be removed from his job as clerk in the Department of Interior in June of 1865, when James Harlan, Secretary of the Interior, happened to see them in his desk and was scandalized. One beneficial outcome of this action was that a friend of Whitman's William Douglas O'Connor published an influential pamphlet titled *The Good Gray Poet* (1866) that defended and deified Whitman, and compared *Leaves of Grass* to the works of Homer, Dante, and Shakespeare.

For Whitman, sexual prudery had for too long dominated American social life, making men and women ashamed of their bodies. In "Starting from Paumanok," he counters, "Behold, the body includes and is the meaning, the main concern, and includes and is the soul; / Whoever you are, how superb and how divine is your body, or any part of it!" (LoA 184). Even today, of course, many people still have love–hate relationships with their bodies, which Whitman tried to overcome. For him the body was just as natural and beautiful as any other living organism.

Whitman's *Leaves* is very much devoted to the concept of organicism, which was foundational to the Romantic movement in Europe and America at the end of the eighteenth century and the beginning of the nineteenth. In brief, organicism attempts to imagine art as alive, just as all organic nature is alive. Its final form is not mechanically imposed from without, but rather grows from an idea impelling it from within, spontaneously, just as an oak emerges from an acorn, an adult from a child, or grass from a seed in the ground. In his essay "The Poet," Emerson explained,

> it is not metres, but a metre-making argument, that makes a poem,—a thought so passionate and alive, that, like the spirit of a plant or an animal, it has an architecture of its own, and adorns nature with a new thing.
>
> (*Essays & Lectures* 450)

The cover of the 1855 *Leaves* featured embossed vegetation surrounding the title, to suggest the vitality of what was inside; however, it should be added that Whitman's notebooks and revised editions reveal that great care and craft went into the construction of his poems, and the idea that they were living organisms that grew spontaneously on their own is a romantic myth.

In the 1860 edition of *Leaves*, he included a set of poems titled "Calamus," that celebrate the love between men, and Whitman's obvious homoeroticism has led many readers to assume he was experienced in same-sex relations. In the poem "Whoever You Are Holding Me Now in Hand," the speaker imagines being with his "follower," possibly

on a high hill, first watching lest any person for miles around approach
unawares,
Or possibly with you sailing at sea, or on the beach of the sea or some
quiet island,
Here to put your lips upon mine I permit you,
With the comrade's long-dwelling kiss or the new husband's kiss,
For I am the new husband and I am the comrade.

Or if you will, thrusting me beneath your clothing,
Where I may feel the throbs of your heart or rest upon your hip,
Carry me when you go forth over land or sea;
For thus merely touching you is enough, is best,
And thus touching you would I silently sleep and be carried eternally.

(LoA 271)

When asked by an English admirer, the biographer John Addington Symonds, about the implicit homosexuality of the "Calamus" poems, Whitman professed to be shocked at such "morbid inferences" (*Selected Letters* 282), and claimed to have fathered six children, which, of course, is a non sequitur. Late in his career, Whitman became close friends with a young streetcar conductor, Peter Doyle, for whom, his notebook reveals, he had ardent feelings. Whether the two engaged in gay sex remains unknown, and scholars have debated the issue fiercely. As Jimmie Killingsworth ("Whitman and the Gay American Ethos") has helpfully pointed out, homosexuality had no public discourse in mid-nineteenth-century America. Whitman, however, by focusing on male–male love in his "Calamus" poems, laid the groundwork for a new discourse of sexual consciousness that gay men today, living in a predominantly heterosexual society, can now recognize and claim as their own.

Whitman and the Civil War

Both Whitman and Dickinson, scholars have shown, were deeply affected by the Civil War and its massive death toll of more than 620,000. For Whitman, the War seemed to represent a cleansing of sorts, and as David Reynolds has explained, the widespread public celebration of the love between and among male soldiers generated a safe space for him to express his own same-sex attractions, both as a volunteer nurse and a poet. It "gave him the tender 'wound dresser' role that was both patriotic and emotionally satisfying" (414). For Dickinson, the war affected her creative efforts in more philosophical and theological ways, it seems, though she was deeply stirred by it. It stimulated her to interrogate with growing intensity and rigor large questions about the nature of death, pain, immortality, and the ways of God to man. In a number of ways, the war moved both poets to compose some of their most powerful work.

Whereas Whitman's early poetry tends to be sensual and joyful, by 1860, his poetry took on a melancholy and serious tone, in part because of his poverty and family difficulties, but also the country's impending crisis. He would later declare that the War was "the very centre, circumference, unbillicus of my whole career" (Traubel 95). In February 1861, Whitman saw Lincoln in New York City on his way to his inauguration in Washington DC. Feelings were running high at the time, and on April 12, Fort Sumter was fired upon and the Civil War began. Whitman's brother George immediately enlisted, but Walt did not, for he was forty-two years old and the main supporter of his mother and dependent brother Eddie. He did begin writing jingoistic poetry, though, including the recruiting poem "Beat! Beat! Drums!"

Most of those living in the North thought the Civil War would last only a few months, resulting in victory for the Union forces. The disastrous First Battle of Bull Run quickly disabused them of this assumption. Sightseeers and picnickers from Washington had to flee in their carriages as the Confederates routed the Union army in a lopsided victory that left nearly five thousand soldiers dead or wounded. Late in the year of 1862, Whitman's brother George was wounded (not seriously) at the battle of Fredericksburg, Virginia, and Whitman traveled south to visit him and acquired first-hand knowledge of army life and the horrors of battle. In a memorandum book, he recorded,

> December 23 to 31.—The results of the late battle are exhibited everywhere about here in thousands of cases (hundreds die every day), in the camp, brigade, and division hospitals. These are merely tents, and sometimes very poor ones, the wounded lying on the ground, lucky if their blankets are spread on layers of pine or hemlock twigs, or small leaves. No cots; seldom even a mattress. It is pretty cold. The ground is frozen hard, and there is occasional snow. I go around from one case to another. I do not see that I do much good to these wounded and dying, but I cannot leave them.
>
> (*Civil War* 42)

Whitman's visit to the front inspired him to write a series of imagistic poems that have a photographic quality to them, but with sound, color, and motion added. "Calvary Crossing a Ford" and "Bivovac on a Mountan Side" are two fine examples. The first reads:

> A line in long array where they wind betwixt green islands,
> They take a serpentine course, their arms flash in the sun—hark to the musical clank,
> Behold the silvery river, in it the splashing horses loitering stop to drink,
> Behold the brown-faced men, each group, each person a picture, the negligent rest on the saddles,
> Some emerge on the opposite bank, others are just entering the ford— while
> Scarlet and blue and snowy white,
> The guidon flags flutter gayly in the wind.
>
> (LoA 435)

Whitman paired these vignettes with several sentimental narrative poems that dramatize death and dying of young soldiers. "Come up From the Fields Father," and "Vigil Strange I kept," are two of the best.

Whitman's visits to the hospitals in Virginia, and later in Washington DC, where he spent most of the war, convey a compassion and heroism that now staggers the imagination. He made some six-hundred visits during the years 1863 to 1865 and saw between 80,000 to 100,000 soldiers. He later captured the essence of his nursing in a poem titled "The Wound-Dresser," which reads, in part,

> (Arous'd and angry, I'd thought to beat the alarum, and urge relentless war,
> But soon my fingers fail'd me, my face droop'd and I resign'd myself,
> To sit by the wounded and soothe them, or silently watch the dead;) ...
>
> I dress the perforated shoulder, the foot with the bullet-wound,
> Cleanse the one with a gnawing and putrid gangrene, so sickening, so offensive,
> While the attendant stands behind aside me holding the tray and pail. ...
>
> Thus in silence in dreams' projections,
> Returning, resuming, I thread my way through the hospitals,
> The hurt and wounded I pacify with soothing hand,
> I sit by the restless all the dark night, some are so young,
> Some suffer so much, I recall the experience sweet and sad,
> (Many a soldier's loving arms about this neck have cross'd and rested,
> Many a soldier's kiss dwells on these bearded lips.)
> (LoA 442–445)

The poem features a romantic frame that surrounds graphic details, and it anticipates the literary realism that would emerge in the United States after the Civil War.

In 1865, Whitman published his Civil War poems in two books, *Drum-Taps* and *Sequel to Drum-Taps*, both later incorporated into the fourth edition of *Leaves of Grass* (1867). Two of the poems written after the April 14, 1865, assassination of Lincoln, are his best known. The first, "O Captain! My Captain!," has a popular appeal, despite its overwrought refrain:

> But O heart! heart! heart!
> O the bleeding drops of red,
> Where on the deck my Captain lies,
> Fallen cold and dead.
>   (LoA 467)

In contrast, the subtle and well-crafted "Lilacs" is one of the finest elegies in the English language. It draws upon realistic details for its dominant metaphors, as it describes the poet's attempt to mourn the fallen president. As the poem suggests, Lincoln indeed died in the spring, when lilacs were blooming outside Whitman's door in Washington DC. The star in the west, the planet Venus, was indeed there, and the train with Lincoln's body did travel across the land with black smoke forming a cloud overhead, as countless people turned out to pay tribute to the dead president. The hermit thrush Whitman mentions, as a solitary singer, did live in the seclusion of the swamp then around the capitol, and it sang a beautiful song during its spring breeding season. The major symbols in the poem are thus authentic and apt, including the lilac as love of the poet and the star as Lincoln (born in the West, Illinois). Because Venus was actually a planet, it would become a morning star in the east, a fitting symbol of rebirth.

The structure of "Lilacs" is musical with a recitative and then the aria of the bird. At the end, the three items from the beginning—lilac, star, and "thought of him I love," have become lilac, star, and bird. In other words, the bird's consolation has replaced the sad thought of loss. The poet expresses reluctance to join the bird, because he needs to experience his grief before being consoled:

> Sing on there in the swamp,
> O singer bashful and tender, I hear your notes, I hear your call,
> I hear, I come presently, I understand you,
> But a moment I linger, for the lustrous star has detain'd me,
> The star my departing comrade holds and detains me.
> (LoA 461–462)

When the poet finally joins the bird, he walks between the "knowledge of death" and "thought of death" as his companions. Anyone who has lost a loved one knows the difference between the two, with the former being more intellectual and the latter more emotional. Whitman does not conclude the poem with the song of the thrush in section 15, because he most likely wished to universalize, to combine Lincoln's death with the deaths of all the young men whose fates were linked with his. By the end Whitman has offered consolation to the nation, and to all the mothers, fathers, sisters, and brothers, in the North and South, who have lost loved ones. In other words, he has become the thrush, "the solitary singer."

Dickinson and the Civil War

Whereas Whitman's response to the Civil War and its horrors is explicit and prominent, Dickinson's response was more implicit and veiled. It was not until 1984 that the scholar Shira Wolosky showed the nature and extent of Dickinson's engagement with the War. As Wolosky explained, "War dramatically confirmed the anguish and confusion that constituted her world. Death in particular had always seemed the epitome of incomprehensible sorrows and sudden blows. War intensified this image" (41). Dickinson read reports about the progress of the War in a number of periodicals that came to her home, including *The Springfield Republican, Harper's Magazine, Scribner's,* and the *Atlantic Monthly.* She was particularly skeptical of the claims that it was a holy war meant to redeem the nation. A number of Northern writers popularized this belief, including Emerson, whose poem "Voluntaries" (1863) claims that the Union soldiers who died during the doomed attack on Fort Wagner were fighting for Justice:

> And he who battles on her side,
> God, though he were ten times slain,
> Crowns him victor glorified,
> Victor over death and pain.
> (*Collected Poems* 168)

Dickinson's religious skepticism resisted such wishful thinking in any number of her poems, which question the concepts of justice and eternal life in Heaven.

Despite this skepticism, she sympathized with the fallen and used her poetry to express this sympathy. Three of her poems were published anonymously in *Drum Beat*, a newspaper raising funds for Union soldiers, and she wrote several poems memorializing the death of a family friend, twenty-one-year-old Frazar Stearns, son of the president of Amherst College. He died in March of 1862 at the Battle of New Bern, North Carolina. In a letter to her cousins Louise and Francis Norcross, Dickinson reported,

> 'tis the least that I can do, to tell you of brave Frazar—"killed at Newbern," darlings. His big heart shot away by a "minie ball."
>
> I had read of those—I didn't think that Frazar would carry one to Eden with him. Just as he fell, in his soldier's cap, with his sword at his side, Frazar rode through Amherst. Classmates to the right of him, and classmates to the left of him, to guard his narrow face!
> (*Letters* 1: 397–398)

Stearns's mother had died during his childhood, and Dickinson's poem "When I was small, a Woman died—" (FP 518) suggests he has joined his mother in Paradise, or perhaps just in the poet's imagination:

> But, proud in Apparition—
> That Woman and her Boy
> Pass back and forth, before my Brain
> As even in the sky—
>
> I'm confident, that Bravoes—
> Perpetual break abroad
> For Braveries, remote as this
> In Yonder Maryland—

The ambiguity saves the poem from conventionality, and while the confidence in the last stanza may be insincere on Dickinson's part, it would satisfy any member of the public who read it.

The poem "He fought like those Who've nought to lose—" (FP 480) has more of an edge to it. It treats the suicidal urge of a young soldier who boldly invites death but is thwarted by fate, or by his own character:

> His Comrades, shifted like the Flakes
> When Gusts reverse the Snow—
> But He—was left alive Because
> Of Greediness to die

Several of her poems describe the New England landscape with similar irony, by combining the beauties of nature with the blood-drenched battlefield:

> The name—of it—is "Autumn"—
> The hue—of it—is Blood—
> An Artery—opon the Hill
> A Vein—along the Road—
>
> Great Globules—in the Alleys—
> And Oh, the Shower of Stain—
> When Winds—upset the Basin—
> And spill the Scarlet Rain— ...
>   (FP 465)

A similar poem uses natural phenomena to movingly convey the massive number of battlefield deaths left in the wake of horrific battle:

> They dropped like Flakes—
> They dropped like Stars—
> Like Petals from a Rose—
> When suddenly across the June
> A Wind with fingers—goes—
>
> They perished in the seamless Grass—
> No eye could find the place—
> But God can summon every face
> On his Repealless—List
>   (FP 545)

The poem captures, as Whitman's photographic vignettes do not, the thousands of men who died in minutes on the battlefield. At Antietam, for example, within twelve hours some 3,600 men were killed and 23,000 were wounded or missing.

Dickinson's use of images of stars, rose petals, wind, and grass gives the poem a romantic beauty that becomes religious in the final lines. Faith Barrett has suggested that this usage is meant to critique the war and romantic perspectives on it. She writes,

> In these poems, Dickinson points toward the exhaustion of the romantic vision of nature; commenting indirectly on the rise of the weapons technologies that enable armies to inflict massive numbers of casualties in modern combat, Dickinson's work points also toward the inadequacy of first-person expressive lyric stances to bear witness to suffering on this scale.
>
> (109)

It does seem as if the Civil War energized and fulfilled Whitman in ways that it did not for Dickinson. Instead, it disturbed and depressed her. Some six years after the end of the war, Dickinson looked back at the lives lost and expressed deep regret:

> My Triumph lasted till the Drums
> Had left the Dead alone
> And then I dropped my Victory
> And chastened stole along
> To where the finished Faces
> Conclusion turned on me
> And then I hated Glory
> And wished myself were They.
>
> What is to be is best descried
> When it has also been—
> Could Prospect taste of Retrospect
> The tyrannies of Men
> Were Tenderer, diviner
> The Transitive toward—
> A Bayonet's contrition
> Is nothing to the Dead—
>
> (FP 1212)

One could not ask for a more thoughtful anti-war poem. Of course, to imagine the consequences of seeking Victory and Glory through warfare requires men to be more imaginative and tender. It's a large ask, even today.

Conclusion

After Dickinson's death in 1886, her sister Lavinia, who found her fascicles in a bureau drawer, persuaded Austin's mistress Mabel Loomis Todd to edit the poems for publication, and she enlisted the aid of Higginson. Together they published volumes of selected poems in 1890 and 1891, adding titles, punctuation, and, at times, different words to regularize the rhymes. Todd alone edited and published a volume of Dickinson's letters in 1894 and a third volume of poems in 1896. All contributed to Dickinson's reputation, which has continued to soar with the passage of time. In 1955, Thomas H. Johnson presented a new modern edition of Dickinson's poems, removed the titles, and gave them numbers indicating their approximate order of composition. In 1998, R. W. Franklin published a three-volume "variorum" edition and in 1999 a one-volume reading edition. There is an ongoing debate about whether printing the poems alters their meaning as it alters their visual appearance. Many readers find images of the poems in manuscript more meaningful than the printed versions.

Whitman's reputation as America's national poet was established by the time of his death in 1891, based in part on his popularity in England and publicity generated by his English admirers, notably Anne Gilchrist and Edward Carpenter. F. O. Matthiessen's 1941 book *American Renaissance* established Whitman as a major American author, and his reputation was solidified by praise from modernists such as Ezra Pound, and later beat poets of the 1950s and 1960s, especially Allen Ginsberg. As Jimmie Killingsworth has summarized, "With each new interpretation—not only in biography and criticism, but in all the poems, novels, paintings, photographs, and films ... the legacy of his work only grows richer and deeper" (*Introduction* 122).

Suggestions for further reading

Ackmann, Martha. *These Fevered Days: Ten Pivotal Moments in the Making of Emily Dickinson*. New York: Norton, 2020.

Folsom, Ed and Kenneth M. Price, Eds. *Walt Whitman Archive*. https://whitmanarchive.org.

Jackson, Virginia. *Dickinson's Misery: A Theory of Lyric Reading*. Princeton: Princeton University Press, 2005.

Killingsworth, M. Jimmie. *Whitman's Poetry of the Body: Sexuality, Politics, and the Text*. Chapel Hill: University of North Carolina Press, 1989.

Porter, David. *Dickinson: The Modern Idiom*. Cambridge, MA: Harvard University Press, 1981.

Reynolds, David S. *Walt Whitman's America: A Cultural Biography*. New York: Knopf, 1995.

Smith, Martha Nell. *Rowing in Eden: Rereading Emily Dickinson*. Austin: University of Texas Press, 1992.

Smith, Martha Nell, Marta Werner, Julie Enszer, Jessica Beard, and Ellen Louise Hart, Eds. *Dickinson Electronic Archives*. University of Maryland, College Park. http://archive.emilydickinson.org.

References

Alcott, Amos Bronson. *The Journals of Bronson Alcott*. Ed. Odell Shepard. Boston: Little Brown, 1938.

Allen, Gay Wilson. *The Solitary Singer: A Critical Biography of Walt Whitman*. New York: Macmillan, 1955.

Barrett, Faith. "'Drums off the Phantom Battlements': War Poems in Discursive Context." In *A Companion to Emily Dickinson*. Eds. Martha Nell Smith and Mary Loeffelholz. Malden, MA: Blackwell, 2014. 107–132.

Bianchi, Martha Dickinson. *Emily Dickinson Face to Face*. Boston: Houghton Mifflin, 1932.

Bingham, Millicent Todd. *Emily Dickinson's Home*. New York: Harper & Brothers, 1955.

Dickinson, Emily. *The Letters of Emily Dickinson*. Eds. Thomas H. Johnson and Theodora Ward. 3 vols. Cambridge, MA: The Belknap Press of Harvard University Press, 1958.

Dickinson, Emily. *The Poems of Emily Dickinson: Variorum Edition*. 3 vols. Ed. R. W. Franklin. Cambridge, MA: Belknap Press of Harvard University Press, 1998. Abbreviated FP followed by the poem number assigned by Franklin.

Emerson, Ralph Waldo. *Collected Poems & Translations*. New York: Library of America, 1994.

Emerson, Ralph Waldo. *The Correspondence of Emerson and Carlyle*. Ed. Joseph Slater. New York: Columbia University Press, 1964.

Emerson, Ralph Waldo. *Essays & Lectures*. New York: Library of America, 1983.

Erkkila, Betsy. "Emily Dickinson and Class." *American Literary History* 4 (Spring 1992): 1–27.

Folsom, Ed. "Lucifer and Ethiopia: Whitman, Race, and Poetics before the Civil War and After." In *A Historical Guide to Walt Whitman*. Ed. David S. Reynolds. New York: Oxford University Press, 2000. 45–95.

Habegger, Alfred. *My Wars Are Laid Away in Books: The Life of Emily Dickinson*. New York: Modern Library, 2002.

Kaplan, Justin. *Walt Whitman: A Life*. New York: Simon and Schuster, 1980.

Keane, Patrick J. *Emily Dickinson's Approving God: Divine Design and the Problem of Suffering*. Columbia, MO: University of Missouri Press, 2008.

Killingsworth, M. Jimmie. *The Cambridge Introduction to Walt Whitman*. New York: Cambridge University Press, 2007.

Killingsworth, M. Jimmie. "Whitman and the Gay American Ethos." *A Historical Guide to Walt Whitman*. Ed. David S. Reynolds. New York: Oxford University Press, 2000. 121–151.

Leyda, Jay. *The Years and Hours of Emily Dickinson*. 2 vols. New Haven: Yale University Press, 1960.

Matthiessen, F. O. *The American Renaissance: Art and Expression in the Age of Emerson and Whitman*. New York: Oxford University Press, 1941.

Mayhan, William F. "The Idea of Music in 'Out of the Cradle Endlessly Rocking'." *Walt Whitman Quarterly Review* 13 (Winter 1996): 113–128.

Porter, David. *Dickinson: The Modern Idiom*. Cambridge, MA: Harvard University Press, 1981.

Reynolds, David S. *Walt Whitman's America: A Cultural Biography*. New York: Knopf, 1995.

Rich, Adrienne. "Vesuvius at Home: The Power of Emily Dickinson." 1975. Rpt. *On Lies, Secrets, and Silence: Selected Prose 1966–1978*. New York: Norton, 1979. 157–183.

Sewall, Richard B. *The Life of Emily Dickinson*. New one-volume edition. New York: Farrar, Straus and Giroux, 1974.

Sewall, Richard B. *The Lyman Letters*. Amherst: University of Massachusetts Press, 1965.

Thoreau, Henry David. *The Correspondence. Volume 2: 1849–1856*. Ed. Robert N. Hudspeth. Princeton, NJ: Princeton University Press, 2018.

Traubel, Horace. *With Walt Whitman in Camden*. Vol. 3. 1912. Rpt. New York: Rowman and Littlefield, 1961.

Trowbridge, John Townsend. "Reminiscences of Walt Whitman." *The Atlantic Monthly* 89 (February 1902): 163–175.

Turpin, Zachary. "Introduction to Walt Whitman's 'Life and Adventures of Jack Engle.'" *Walt Whitman Quarterly Review* 34 (2017): 225–261.

Wald, Jane. "'Pretty much all real life': The Material World of the Dickinson Family." *A Companion to Emily Dickinson*. Eds. Martha Nell Smith and Mary Loeffelholz. Malden, MA: Blackwell, 2014. 79–103.

Warren, Joyce W. *Fanny Fern: An Independent Woman*. New Brunswick: Rutgers University Press, 1992.

Whitman, Walt. *Civil War Poetry and Prose*. New York: Dover, 1995.

Whitman, Walt. *Complete Poetry and Collected Prose: Leaves of Grass (1855), Leaves of Grass (1891–92), Complete Prose Works (1892), Supplementary Prose*. New York: Library of America, 1982. Abbreviated LoA.

Whitman, Walt. *The Early Poems and the Fiction*. Ed. Thomas L. Brasher. New York: New York University Press, 1963.

Whitman, Walt. *Selected Letters of Walt Whitman*. Ed. Edwin Haviland Miller. Iowa City: University of Iowa Press, 1990.

Wolosky, Shira. *Emily Dickinson: A Voice of War*. New Haven: Yale University Press, 1984.

Zweig, Paul. *Walt Whitman: The Making of the Poet*. New York: Basic Books, 1984.

Index

"Address on the Emancipation of the Negroes in the British West Indies" (Emerson) 58
Adler, George 111
Alboni, Marietta 178
Alcott, Bronson 44–46, 61, 180
Alcott, Louisa May 43, 47
"Alone and in a Circumstance" (Dickinson) 167
American Renaissance (Matthiessen) vii, 190
"American Scholar, The" (Emerson) 38–39
Anti-slavery 9, 58–62, 78, 127–140, 153
Appeal, in Four Articles (Walker) 132
Appleton, Frances "Fanny" 7, 16
"Arsenal at Springfield" (Longfellow) 16
Arvin, Newton 109–110
"Aunt Hetty on Matrimony" (Fern) 67

Baldwin, James 147
Barrett, Faith 188–189
"Bartleby, the Scrivener" (Melville) 120–121
Battle Pieces (Melville) 122
"Because I Could not Stop for Death" (Dickinson) 171
Benito Cereno (Melville) 121
Bentley, Nancy 151
"Berenice" (Poe) 24
"Birth-mark, The" (Hawthorne) 103
"Bogus Intellect" (Fern) 90
Book of Job 97, 113
Braude, Ann 75
Bridge, Horatio 99
Brook Farm 43–44, 102
Brown, John 61–62, 133, 141, 153
Brownson, Orestes 47, 77
Buell, Lawrence 15, 27, 42, 56, 130

"Call to Rebellion" (Garnet) 134
"Calvary Crossing a Ford" (Whitman) 184
Cape Cod (Thoreau) 56–57
Capper, Charles 71
"Celestial Railroad, The" (Hawthorne) 31–32
Channing, Ellery 51–52, 56–57, 68
Channing, William Henry 76
Child, Lydia Maria 152, 153
"Children's Hour, The" (Longfellow) 7
"City in the Sea, The" (Poe) 4
"Civil Disobedience" (Thoreau) 59
Cole, Phyllis 34, 75, 78, 83
Colonization 130–131
Confessions (Turner) 129
Confidence Man, The (Melville) 121–122
"Conqueror Worm, The" (Poe) 170
Cooper, James Fenimore 1
Cranch, Christopher 31, 35
"Cross of Snow, The" (Longfellow) 16
"Crossing Brooklyn Ferry" (Whitman) 172–173
Crumley, Paul 76

"Day is Done, The" (Longfellow) 5
Delbanco, Andrew 122
Dial 42
Dickinson, Emily 157–171, 186–189; on "Circumference" 169–171; and the Civil War 186–189; defining poetry 157–158, 162; and family relations 160–161; and Higginson 165–167; love interests of 161, 163–164; and natural phenomena 168–169; seclusion of 164–165
"Divinity School Address, The" (Emerson) 40–41

Douglass, Frederick 58, 131, 133–141, 153; as abolitionist 133–141; beating in Indiana 134–135; and John Brown 141; and literacy 137; *Narrative of the Life* 135–139; separation from Garrison 139–140; and Stanton 139; and Stowe 146; and violence 135–136
Dred (Stowe) 130
Duyckinck, Evert 95, 120

Emancipation in British West Indies 9, 58, 131, 135
Emerson, Mary Moody 34
Emerson, Ralph Waldo 32–42, 58–62, 117, 135, 142, 187; "The American Scholar" 38–39; "Divinity School Address" 40–41; and Fuller 69–70; literary nationalism of 39; Melville on 36, 37, 121; *Nature* 33–35; and slavery 131–132; subjectivism of 35–37
Erkkila, Betsy 165
"Essential Oils—are wrung—" (Dickinson) 158
"Ethan Brand" (Hawthorne) 104
Evangeline (Longfellow) 12–13
"Experience" (Emerson) 41

Fable for Critics, A (Lowell) 27
"Fall of the House of Usher, The" (Poe) 23
Fern Leaves from Fanny's Portfolio (Fern) 86
Fern, Fanny (Sarah Payson Willis) 65–67, 83–91, 177; and feminism 89–91; financial struggles of 85–86; Hawthorne's opinion of 88; *Ruth Hall* 87–88; and sentimentalism 86; subject of slander 89; on Whitman 89–90
Folson, Ed 176
Foner, Philip 134
Franklin, R.W. 190
Fruitlands 43
Fugitive Slave Act 60, 134, 141–143, 175
Fuller, Margaret 10, 32, 42, 65–83, 176; and anti-slavery 82, 91; "Conversations" 66, 71; and Emerson 69–70; and Hawthorne 102–103; Italian dispatches of 81–83; on marriage 72–73; and spiritualism 74–75; *Woman in the Nineteenth Century* 71–74

Garibaldi, Giuseppe 80
Garnet, Henry Highland 134
Garrison, William Lloyd 129, 132
Gilbert, Susan Huntington 161

Goethe, Johann Wolfgang 36, 37–38, 68, 73
Good Gray Poet, The (O'Connor) 182
"Great Lawsuit, The" (Fuller) 71–72
Greeley, Horace 75–76
Grimké, Angelina 133

Harker, Jaime 86
Hartman, Saidiya V. 136
"Haunted Palace, The" (Poe) 4
Hawthorne, Nathaniel 88, 95–109; early tales 100–102; literary development 98–100; and pacifism 100, 109; prose style 106; *The Scarlet Letter* 104–108; theory of romance 105; and the Transcendentalists 102–103; on treatment of women 103–104; and witchcraft 101
Hawthorne, Sophia Peabody 111
"He fought like those Who've nought to lose—" (Dickinson) 188
Hendrick, Joan D. 144
"Her face was in a bed of hair" (Dickinson) 161
Higginson, Thomas Wentworth 159, 165–167, 189
"Hints to Young Wives" (Fern) 67
Holmes, Oliver Wendell 95
House of the Seven Gables, The (Hawthorne) 108–109
"How to write a Blackwood's article" (Poe) 24
Hyperion (Longfellow) 7

"I cannot dance upon my Toes—" (Dickinson) 166
"I felt a Funeral, in my Brain" (Dickinson) 169
"I know that He exists" (Dickinson) 170
"I like a look of Agony" (Dickinson) 162
"I shall keep singing!" (Dickinson) 167
Incidents in the Life of a Slave Girl (Jacobs) 147–153
"Independence" (Fern) 90
international copyright law 1–2
Irving, Washington 1–2
"Israfel" (Poe) 18

Jacobs, Harriet 129–130, 147–154; as author 147–148; as activist for people of color 153–154; *Incidents in the Life of a Slave Girl* 147–153; and L. Maria Child 147–148, 152; and N. P. Willis 151; on sexual harassment 148, 151;

and Stowe 147, 154, and women readers 150–151
James, C.L.R. 128
"Jewish Cemetery at Newport, The" (Longfellow) 14
Johnson, Thomas H. 189–190

Karcher, Caroline L. 122
Kennedy, J. Gerald 21
Killingsworth, Jimmie 183, 190

"Lady Doctors" (Fern) 90
Lapore, Jill 15
Leaves of Grass (Whitman) 177–183
"Leila" (Fuller) 69
Levine, Robert S. vii, 135, 138
"Life among the Contrabands" (Jacobs) 154
Life and Times of Frederick Douglass, The (Douglass) 141
"Ligeia" (Poe) 22
"Little Bunker Hill, A" (Fern) 89
"Little Mary's Story" (Fern) 85
Longfellow, Henry Wadsworth 2–4, 5–16, 27, 99; and anti-slavery 9; attacked by Poe 10; criticism of 10–12; *Evangeline* 12–13; and literary nationalism 5–6; personal losses 7, 16; racialism of 13–14; reputation 27; support of African-Americans 21
Longfellow, Mary Storer Potter 7
Louverture, Toussaint 122–123
Lovejoy, Elijah 133
Lowell, James Russell 3, 9, 23, 27, 56

Macpherson, James 80
"Main-Street" (Hawthorne) 96
Maine Woods, The (Thoreau) 54–56
Martin, Robert K. 123
Matthiessen, F. O. 113
McDowell, Deborah E. 136
McFeely, William S. 140
McGettigan, Katie 2
McGill, Meredith L. 2
McMullen, Kevin 90
Melville, Herman 96–98, 109–124; *Billy Budd* 122–123; and the Book of Job 97, 114; difficult youth 109–111; and Hawthorne 95–98, 109, 120, 122, 123–124; and homoeroticism 123–124; *Moby-Dick* 112–119; and race conflict 118; early novels 111–112
"Midnight Ride of Paul Revere, The" (Longfellow) 3, 15

Mills, Bruce 75
"Minister's Black Veil, The" (Hawthorne) 101
Moby-Dick (Melville) 112–120
"Model Husband, The" (Fern) 86
"Modern Old Maid, The" (Fern) 91
Mosses from an Old Manse (Hawthorne) 96–97
My Bondage and My Freedom (Douglass) 138, 139
"My Kinsman, Major Molineux" (Hawthorne) 100–101
"My Lost Youth" (Longfellow) 4
"My Triumph lasted till the Drums" (Dickinson) 189

"name—of it—is 'Autumn'—, The" (Dickinson) 188
Narrative of Arthur Gordon Pym, The (Poe) 19–21
Narrative of the Life of Frederick Douglass (Douglass) 135–39
"narrow Fellow in the Grass, A" (Dickinson) 169
national literature 2, 5–6
Nature (Emerson) 31, 33–37
Newton, Benjamin Franklin 161

"O Captain! My Captain!" (Whitman) 185
O'Connor, William Douglas 182
"Ode, Inscribed to W. H. Channing" (Emerson) 13–14
Otter, Samuel vii, 88
"Our Native Writers" (Longfellow) 5
"Out of the Cradle Endlessly Rocking" (Whitman) 172, 179

Packer, Barbara 81
"Paradise of Bachelors and Tartarus of Maids, The" (Melville) 121
Paul, Sherman 50
Petrulionis, Sandra Harbert 61
"Philosophy of Composition" (Poe) 12
Pierce, Franklin 99
"Plea for Captain John Brown, A" (Thoreau) 61
Poe, Edgar Allan 2–4, 10–12, 17–28, 74; early struggles of 17–19; and John Allan 18–19; major tales 21–24; *Narrative of Artur Gordon Pym* 19–21; as poet 18, 26; and race 21; reputation of 28; sensation and satire of 24–25; tales of ratiocination 25

Poems of Ossian (MacPherson) 80, 157
Poems on Slavery (Longfellow) 9
"Poet, The" (Emerson) 180, 182
"Poetic Principle, The" (Poe) 11
Polis, Joe 55
"Predicament, A" (Poe) 24
"Psalm of Life, A" (Longfellow) 8

racialism 13–15
racism 58–59, 118, 138–140, 146–147, 176
"Rappacinni's Daughter" (Hawthorne) 103
"Rat is the concisest Tenant, The" (Dickinson) 169
"Raven, The" (Poe) 3, 12, 26–27
Representative Men (Emerson) 37–38
"Resurgemus" (Whitman) 175–76
Revolution, Haitian 127–28
Revolutions, European of 1848 80
Reynolds, David 183
Rich, Adrienne 165
"Ropewalk, The" (Longfellow) 9
"Route of Evanescence, A" (Dickinson) 168
Ruth Hall (Fern) 87–88

Scarlet Letter, The (Hawthorne) 99, 104–108
Sewall, Richard B. 163
"Shall I take thee, the Poet said" (Dickinson) 163
Shanley, Lynden J. 52
Sims, Thomas 60
"Skeleton in Armor, The" (Longfellow) 8
"Slavery in Massachusetts" (Thoreau) 61
Smith, Susan Belasco 74
Smith-Rosenberg, Carroll 65
"Song of Myself" (Whitman) 172, 173–174
"Soul selects her own Society—, The" (Dickinson) 165
Specimen Days (Whitman) 172
Stanton, Elizabeth Cady 78
"Starting from Paumanok" (Whitman) 182
Steele, Jeffrey 73, 76–77
Stowe, Harriet Beecher 131, 133, 142–147, 153; on Colonization 131; and Douglass 146; and Jacobs 152, 154; racism of 146–147; reputation of 147; and sentimentalism 147; *Uncle Tom's Cabin* 142–147
Summer on the Lakes (Fuller) 74–75

Sundquist, Eric 130
Swedenborg, Emanuel 174

"Tell all the truth but tell it slant—" (Dickinson) 168
Theory of Colours (Goethe) 36
"There was a Child Went Forth" (Whitman) 171
"They dropped like Flakes—" (Dickinson) 188
"Thoreau" (Emerson) 46
Thoreau, Henry David 2, 32, 46–62, 122, 142, 180–181; and *Bhagavad Gita* 53, 54; "Civil Disobedience" 59; and Emerson 46; and John Brown 61–62; and Native Americans 55–56; search for Fuller's remains 57; on sounds and revelation 50–51, 53; *Walden* 52–54
Thoreau, John (brother) 47–48
"Threnody" (Emerson) 41
"Title divine—is mine!" (Dickinson) 164
"To a Certain Cantatrice" (Whitman) 178
"To Helen" (Poe) 18
Todd, Mabel Loomis 189
Tompkins, Jane 144
Transcendental Club 42
Transcendental Wild Oats (L. Alcott) 45
"Transcendentalist, The" (Emerson) 30, 35
Traubel, Horace 174
Tucker, Ellen Louisa 32
Turner, Nat 127, 128–130
Turpin, Zachary 174
Typee (Melville) 111

Uncle Tom's Cabin (Stowe) 142–147
Unitarianism 34

"Village Blacksmith, The" (Longfellow) 8–9
"Voluntaries" (Emerson) 187
Von Frank, Albert 75

Wadsworth, Reverend Charles 163–164
"Wakefield" (Hawthorne) 104
Wald, Jane 162
Walden (Thoreau) 52–54
Walker, David 132
"Warning, The" (Longfellow) 9
Warren, Joyce 91
Week on the Concord and Merrimack Rivers, A (Thoreau) 50–51
Weinstein, Cindy 146
"What Soft—Cherubic Creatures—" (Dickinson) 164

"What to the Slave Is the Fourth of July" (Douglass) 140
"When I was small, a Woman died—" (Dickinson) 187
"When Lilacs Last in the Dooryard Bloom'd" (Whitman) 159, 178, 185–186
Whitman, Walt 26, 89–90, 157–159, 171–186, 190; and the Civil War 183–186; and Emerson 179–181; family 171–172; and homoeroticism 182–183; and idealism 173; *Leaves of Grass* 177–183; and Lincoln 177; and politics 175–176; racism of 176; and Thoreau 173
"Whoever You Are Holding Me Now in Hand" (Whitman) 182–183
"William Wilson" (Poe) 23–24

Willis, N. P. 85, 151
Willis, Sarah Payson *see* Fern, Fanny
Wolosky, Shira 186
Woman in the Nineteenth Century (Fuller) 68, 71–74,
"Woman Waits for Me, A" (Whitman) 181
Women's Rights Convention of 1848 77–78
"Working-Girls of New York, The" (Fern) 66
"Wound-Dresser, The" (Whitman) 185
"Wreck of the Hesperus, The" (Longfellow) 8

Yeats, William Butler 26

Zweig, Paul 175

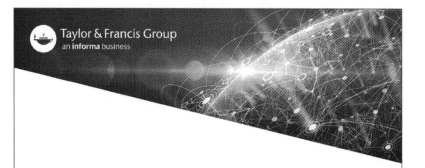

Printed in the United States
by Baker & Taylor Publisher Services